EPHESIANS

BELIEF

*A Theological Commentary
on the Bible*

GENERAL EDITORS

Amy Plantinga Pauw
William C. Placher†

EPHESIANS

ALLEN VERHEY and JOSEPH S. HARVARD

WESTMINSTER
JOHN KNOX PRESS
LOUISVILLE · KENTUCKY

© 2011 Allen Verhey and Joseph S. Harvard

First edition
Published by Westminster John Knox Press
Louisville, Kentucky

11 12 13 14 15 16 17 18 19 20—10 9 8 7 6 5 4 3 2 1

Book design by Drew Stevens
Interior photo by Gisele Wulfsohn; image courtesy David Krut
Publishing and the Constitutional Court of South Africa
Cover design by Lisa Buckley
Cover illustration © David Chapman/Design Pics/Corbis

Library of Congress Cataloging-in-Publication Data

Verhey, Allen.
  Ephesians : a theological commentary on the Bible / Allen Verhey and
Joseph S. Harvard — 1st ed.
    p. cm. — (Belief: a theological commentary on the Bible)
  Includes bibliographical references and index.
  ISBN 978-0-664-23266-5 (alk. paper)
  1. Bible. N. T. Ephesians—Commentaries. I. Harvard, Joseph S. II. Title.
  BS2695.53.V47 2011
  227'.507—dc22

                                                              2010036830

PRINTED IN THE UNITED STATES OF AMERICA

♾ The paper used in this publication meets the minimum requirements of
the American National Standard for Information Sciences—
Permanence of Paper for Printed Library Materials, ANSI Z39.48-1992

Westminster John Knox Press advocates the responsible use of our natural resources.
The text paper of this book is made from 30% post-consumer waste.

Contents

Publisher's Note

William C. Placher worked with Amy Plantinga Pauw as a general editor for this series until his untimely death in November 2008. Bill brought great energy and vision to the series, and was instrumental in defining and articulating its distinctive approach and in securing theologians to write for it. Bill's own commentary for the series was the last thing he wrote, and Westminster John Knox Press dedicates the entire series to his memory with affection and gratitude.

William C. Placher, LaFollette Distinguished Professor in Humanities at Wabash College, spent thirty-four years as one of Wabash College's most popular teachers. A summa cum laude graduate of Wabash in 1970, he earned his master's degree in philosophy in 1974 and his Ph.D. in 1975, both from Yale University. In 2002 the American Academy of Religion honored him with the Excellence in Teaching Award. Placher was also the author of thirteen books, including *A History of Christian Theology, The Triune God, The Domestication of Transcendence, Jesus the Savior, Narratives of a Vulnerable God,* and *Unapologetic Theology.* He also edited the volume *Essentials of Christian Theology,* which was named as one of 2004's most outstanding books by both *The Christian Century* and *Christianity Today* magazines.

Series Introduction

Belief: A Theological Commentary on the Bible is a series from Westminster John Knox Press, featuring biblical commentaries written by theologians. The writers of this series share Karl Barth's concern that, insofar as their usefulness to pastors goes, most modern commentaries are "no commentary at all, but merely the first step toward a commentary." Historical-critical approaches to Scripture rule out some readings and commend others, but such methods only begin to help theological reflection and the preaching of the Word. By themselves, they do not convey the powerful sense of God's merciful presence that calls Christians to repentance and praise; they do not bring the church fully forward in the life of discipleship. It is to such tasks that theologians are called.

For several generations, however, professional theologians in North America and Europe have not been writing commentaries on the Christian Scriptures. The specialization of professional disciplines and the expectations of theological academies about the kind of writing that theologians should do, as well as many of the directions in which contemporary theology itself has gone, have contributed to this dearth of theological commentaries. This is a relatively new phenomenon; until the last century or two, the church's great theologians also routinely saw themselves as biblical interpreters. The gap between the fields is a loss for both the church and the discipline of theology itself. By inviting forty-two contemporary theologians to wrestle deeply with particular texts of Scripture, the editors of this series hope not only to provide new theological resources for the church, but also to encourage all theologians to pay more attention to Scripture and the life of the church in their writings.

We are grateful to the Louisville Institute, which provided funding for a consultation in June 2007. We invited theologians, pastors, and biblical scholars to join us in a conversation about what this series could contribute to the life of the church. The time was provocative and the results were rich. Much of the series' shape owes to the insights of these skilled and faithful interpreters, who sought to describe a way to write a commentary that served the theological needs of the church and its pastors with relevance, historical accuracy, and theological depth. The passion of these participants guided us in creating this series and lives on in the volumes.

As theologians, the authors will be interested much less in the matters of form, authorship, historical setting, social context, and philology—the very issues that are often of primary concern to critical biblical scholars. Instead, this series' authors will seek to explain the theological importance of the texts for the church today, using biblical scholarship as needed for such explication but without any attempt to cover all of the topics of the usual modern biblical commentary. This thirty-six-volume series will provide passage-by-passage commentary on all the books of the Protestant biblical canon, with more extensive attention given to passages of particular theological significance. The authors' chief dialogue will be with the church's creeds, practices, and hymns; with the history of faithful interpretation and use of the Scriptures; with the categories and concepts of theology; and with contemporary culture in both "high" and popular forms. Each volume will begin with a discussion of *why* the church needs this book and why we need it *now*, in order to ground all of the commentary in contemporary relevance. Throughout each volume, textboxes will highlight the voices of ancient and modern interpreters from the global communities of faith, and occasional essays will allow deeper reflection on the key theological concepts of these biblical books.

The authors of this commentary series are theologians of the church who embrace a variety of confessional and theological perspectives. The group of authors assembled for this series represents more diversity of race, ethnicity, and gender than any other commentary series. They approach the larger Christian tradition with a critical respect, seeking to reclaim its riches and at the same time to acknowledge its shortcomings. The authors also aim to make available to readers a wide range of contemporary theological voices from many parts of the world. While it does recover an older genre of writing, this series is not an attempt to retrieve some idealized past. These commentaries have learned from tradition, but they are most importantly commentaries for today. The authors share the conviction that their work will be more contemporary, more faithful, and more radical, to the extent that it is more biblical, honestly wrestling with the texts of the Scriptures.

William C. Placher
Amy Plantinga Pauw

Preface

O Lord our God,
your Word is a lamp to our feet
and a light to our path.
Give us grace to receive your truth in faith and love,
that we may be obedient to your will
and live always for your glory;
through Jesus Christ our Savior.
Amen.[1]

The *Book of Common Worship* of the Presbyterian Church (U.S.A.) calls for a prayer for illumination before the reading of Scripture in The Service for the Lord's Day. This particular prayer for illumination has been our prayer for the work of this commentary. Prayer is, as we will see, critical to Ephesians, and it is appropriate to seek the illumination of the Spirit in reading it. This particular prayer, moreover, expresses an assumption at work in this commentary: God's Word in Scripture serves as "a lamp to our feet and a light to our path." The text is not only to be read and understood, but it is also to be performed. Indeed, it is only truly understood when it forms our individual lives and our life together, when it guides our steps.

As we read Ephesians, we were often struck by its poetic language and its liturgical cadence and often reminded of the prayers, hymns, and affirmations used by the church in worship. Liturgical materials shape the life and witness of a Christian community; they evidently

---

1. *Book of Common Worship* (Louisville: Westminster John Knox Press, 1993), 60.

shaped the theology at work in Ephesians, and they have also shaped our effort to understand Ephesians in this commentary.

Writing this commentary has been a collaborative effort between two ordained ministers of Word and Sacrament in the Reformed tradition. One of us is a professor of Christian ethics at Duke University and the other is a pastor of a downtown church in Durham, North Carolina. The different contexts in which we have practiced our vocations have enriched our conversations about Ephesians. Nevertheless, we have tried to write with a common voice. It is our prayer that our voice may help the churches to receive God's truth "in faith and love," to be obedient to God's will, and to "live for the praise of [God's] glory" (Eph. 1:12).

Working together has been a reminder that we are not "Lone Rangers" in the church—and that the two of us are not a Lone Ranger and his faithful academic companion. We are bound together with others in community. The collaboration on this book goes way beyond the two of us. We have sought to listen to the ancient words of Ephesians with an openness to what those who have engaged this text before us have to teach us. We have tried to listen to a variety of voices from different perspectives. Ephesians, with its account of an inclusive church, a church where walls of separation and hostility are broken down and everyone has a voice, would seem to require it.

Our work has also been enriched by conversations in an adult Sunday school class we taught at the First Presbyterian Church of Durham. For three months in the fall of 2008, a group of forty to fifty adults read and studied Ephesians. They listened together to this letter, to our initial reflections, and to one another. We learned much from these sisters and brothers in Christ. Among them was David Knauert, then a graduate student in Old Testament at Duke. He gave us good counsel, meeting with us separately as well as attending the class. We lament his sudden death in November 2009, just as he was about to begin a promising career as teacher, scholar, and servant of the church.

Karl Barth reminded us with his *Church Dogmatics* that theology is the work of the church for the church. Barth encouraged us to listen to Scripture with our attention also directed to what is going on in the world God loves so much and for which Christ died. Listening to Ephesians with an ear to what is happening in the beginning of the twenty-first century has led us to the conviction that Ephesians challenges the church to claim its identity as the community God has established as a witness to a new humanity. This identity and that witness are critical to a world threatened by the enmity that attends differences among nations, cultures, and faiths. Ephesians is a clarion call for us to live in peace, to love and respect those whom it is too much our impulse to despise, to live into God's good future.

It is easy to consider your latest project or sermon the most important thing going. We ask only that you join us in listening to Ephesians and to the cloud of witnesses that accompany it. In no way do we feel this theological commentary is the last word on Ephesians. It is, at best, our limited, provisional attempt to listen to a word from the Lord contained in Ephesians with the hope and prayer that we will be "obedient to God's will" in our time, and to God be the glory!

We are grateful to Don McKim for his valuable contributions as our editor and to Maria E. Francisco for her helpful assistance. We acknowledge, finally, how much we benefit from the patience, insights, and support of Carlisle Harvard and Phyllis Verhey. For them and for all the ways they enrich our work and our lives we are deeply grateful.

Abbreviations

LCC   Library of Christian Classics
LXX   Septuagint
NRSV   New Revised Standard Version
RSV   Revised Standard Version
TDNT   *Theological Dictionary of the
        New Testament*

Introduction:
Why Ephesians? Why Now?

Why a Theological Commentary on Ephesians?

The Letter of Paul to the Ephesians is, like all of Christian Scripture, both scripted and script. It is scripted—that is, it was written. Ephesians was written once upon a particular time by an author who did certain things with the words available to him and to the initial readers. But, as a part of the whole of Christian Scripture, it is also script—that is, it is to be somehow performed.[1] It is to be performed in the worship and practices of the churches, in their theology and in their rhetoric, in their ethics and in their politics. Scripture as scripted is an object to us, a given, the product of the activity of others. Scripture as script is an instrument for us[2] as we struggle to give a worthy performance of it.

Because Ephesians is both scripted and script, it is open to at least two different kinds of interpretation. ("At least two different kinds of interpretation"—that may win the prize as the most understated remark of this volume.) We mean, of course, simply to distinguish the interpretation of Scripture *as scripted* from the interpretation of Scripture *as script*.

---

1. We owe this notion to Nicholas Lash, "Performing the Scriptures," *Theology on the Way to Emmaus* (London: SCM Press, 1968), 37–46. See also Allen Verhey, "Scripture as Script and as Scripted: The Beatitudes," in *Character Ethics and the New Testament: Moral Dimensions of Scripture*, ed. Robert L. Brawley (Louisville: Westminster John Knox Press, 2007), 19–34.
2. Nicholas Wolterstorff makes this distinction between "object" and "instrument" in *Art in Action: Toward a Christian Aesthetic* (Grand Rapids: Eerdmans, 1980), 80.

Most commentaries on Ephesians (and on other parts of Scripture) focus on the interpretation of it as *scripted*. Such commentaries make an effort to answer the vexed scholarly questions about authorship and audience and about the book's date and genre. They bring to the interpretation of the text as *scripted* considerable erudition in the vocabulary and grammar of the Greek language, a scholarly expertise concerning the sources and genres that the author of Ephesians had available to him, and much research into the history of the first century. We have learned much from such commentaries, but at the end of such commentaries Ephesians frequently remains an artifact, an object, and sometimes a foreign object at that, however carefully examined and explained.

This is not such a commentary. This commentary will focus on Ephesians as *script*, as script to be performed by the church today, as somehow normative for the theology and practices of the church today, for its ethics and politics today. The text we read is not simply an artifact, not simply an object. It must somehow form and reform both our talk of God and our common life that we might join in "the praise of [God's] glory" (Eph. 1:12). To attend to Scripture as *script* is what we understand the task of a *theological* commentary to be.

Scripture and Church as Correlative Concepts

To consider Ephesians as *script* is not only legitimate but required by Christian convictions and practices. It is required by the decision of the church to include Ephesians in the canon of Scripture and by the commonplace affirmation of the creeds and confessions of the churches that this canon of Scripture is somehow normative for the churches' faith and life. It is required by the practice of Christian communities who continue to read the biblical materials not simply as an interesting little collection of ancient Near Eastern religious literature but as Christian Scripture, not only as curious literary artifacts but as canon, not only as scripted but as script. That practice is not an optional one in Christian community; it is essential to Christian community.

It is essential because, as David Kelsey has shown, "Scripture" and "church" are correlative concepts. Part of what we mean when we call a community "church" is that this community reads Scripture as *somehow* normative for its identity and its common life. To say "church" is to name a community that gathers around Scripture and uses it *somehow* to form and to reform its talk and its walk. And part of what we mean when we call certain writings "Scripture" is that these writings ought *somehow* to shape the language and the common life of the church. To say "Scripture" is not simply to name a little collection of ancient Near Eastern religious texts; it is to name the writings that Christian churches take as "canon," as the rule *somehow* for its thought and life.[3] Simply reading Scripture as *scripted* while ignoring Scripture as *script* is not an option for the church, not at least if it is to continue to be the church. That is why a *theological* commentary is an important task.

Without the church the writings called "Scripture" would not exist. It was the church that gathered these documents into a collection, a whole, a canon, because in them the church found the story of its life. Without the church these writings are at best simply a little library of ancient Near Eastern religious literature. Moreover, apart from the synagogue or the church the canon of the synagogue or the church falls into fragments, and we find ourselves back at that place where we are only interested in an artifact of the history of Israel or of Christians, bracketing consideration of the contemporary significance of the text. But if there is no "Scripture" without church,

> **"Church" and "Scripture"**
>
> Part of what it means to call a community of persons "church" . . . is that use of "scriptures" is essential to the preservation and shaping of their self-identity [and] part of what it means to call certain writings "scripture" is that . . . they ought to be used in the common life of the church to nourish and reform it.
> —David Kelsey
>
> *The Uses of Scripture in Recent Theology* (Philadelphia: Fortress Press, 1975), 98.

---

3. David Kelsey, *The Uses of Scripture in Recent Theology* (Philadelphia: Fortress Press, 1975), 89–119. As Kelsey also made plain, to say that Scripture ought to be used "somehow" does not say precisely how Scripture should be used to shape the church's faith and life. The agreement *that* Scripture has authority does not entail agreement about *how* Scripture should function as authoritative.

neither is there any church without Scripture,[4] for without Scripture the church loses its identity and its way, its character in the drama of the script.

This commentary on Ephesians, a theological commentary, attempts to read it within the Christian community and to read it as part of that whole called "canon."

Reading Ephesians in Christian Community: *"Needful of the Minds of Others"*

A very pious but slightly senile old pastor, who was given to the use of clichés in his prayers, frequently included the familiar petition that God would "make us ever mindful of the needs of others." One morning, however, that cliché came out a little differently. He asked instead that God would "make us ever needful of the minds of others."[5] However accidental that petition, it was surely answered in our work on this commentary.

We have been reminded that we are "needful of the minds of others" again and again. Among those minds are surely many who belong to the guild of NT scholars and who have focused on Scripture as scripted, as written. We are "needful of" and grateful for the textual critics who have worked to figure out what words were in fact written. We are "needful of" and grateful for the philologists who have worked on what those particular words or expressions or figures meant in their own cultural and social and literary contexts. And we are "needful of" and grateful for those other biblical scholars who have worked to figure out who wrote Ephesians and to whom, at what particular time and in response to what specific conditions,

---

4. Scripture is the book of the church. It was, after all, the church that canonized certain writings and not others. The churches that made the decision to canonize these writings had already received these writings, had made a habit of reading them, and had discovered in them the authority they acknowledged in the decision to canonize them. It is fair to say, then, that the church did not so much create Scripture as acknowledge it; these were the texts within which the Spirit moved to give life and to guide. Even so, that decision was obviously of critical importance to the construction of Scripture. And it was of no less importance to the identity of the church! And it is important also to our interpretation of Ephesians as part of the "canon."

5. This story was told to one of us by a friend, Dr. Robert Visscher. He also traced the source of the story: Patrick Henry, *The Ironic Christian's Companion* (New York: Penguin Press, 1999), 153. In Patrick Henry's telling, however, it was his mother-in-law who, while repeating the familiar table grace, asked God to make us "ever needful of the minds of others."

what sources and traditions the author had available, and how he used and modified those sources and traditions. We owe a great debt to these scholars, and we have been reminded that we are "needful of the minds of others" each time we have pulled down, for example, Aland's Greek text of the New Testament or one of the great lexicons or commentaries.[6]

Nevertheless, we owe a still greater debt to the church. It is in the church, after all, that Scripture is regarded not only as scripted but also as script. Scripture is finally the church's book, not the property of a guild of distinguished biblical scholars. We are grateful for those theologians of the church who have read Ephesians as script to be performed in the theology, worship, and common life of the church. And we are grateful for "the saints." Among that number we, like Ephesians itself (1:1), count not only a few exemplary individuals but also all of those who are gifted and called by the Spirit, all of those "sanctified" by Christ as they struggle to live the story they love to tell. Among that number we count "the saints" who are at First Presbyterian Church of Durham and who joined us in a Sunday school class reading Ephesians as script to be performed.

The church is our community of interpretation. Within this community, as Ephesians reminds us (4:7–13), there is a diversity of gifts. In that Sunday school class some were gifted with exegetical learning and skills. They brought their knowledge of Greek and their training in the tools of historical, literary, or social investigation not just to the texts but to the community. We are glad for their contribution to the communal task of interpretation. Others were gifted with an awareness of the traditions of interpretation and performance within the church, both within the larger church and within a particular community. Some were gifted with a vivid imagination, capable of envisioning a lively performance of Ephesians. Some were gifted with a passion for righteousness, a hunger for justice, and others were gifted with a sweet reasonableness, peacemakers among us. Some were gifted with intellectual clarity, and some with simple piety. We were and are "needful of" and grateful for those diverse gifts, glad for each of their contributions to the communal task of interpretive performance.

6. See the list of works that we found most helpful in the Selected Bibliography.

Such gifted people, including those gifted with exegetical learning, may not boast of their gifts, or claim to have no need of the other members of the interpretive community. The task of interpretive performance is a communal one. We read Ephesians in Christian community, glad for the diversity of gifts we find there.

Within the Christian community—and in that Sunday school class—there is not only a diversity of gifts but also a diversity of interpretations. There were diverse ways of reading and envisioning the performance of Ephesians. Reading Scripture in Christian community does not mean that we will always agree. There have been diverse ways of interpreting and performing Scripture for as long as there have been Christian communities. Jewish Christians did not all read the Hebrew Scripture one way, but they read it differently than many Gentile Christians did. To read Scripture in Christian community is not to insist upon unanimity in reading and performing it. It is rather to insist that, together with those with whom we differ, we continue to read Scripture together, handing down and assessing existing traditions of the interpretation and performance of Scripture.

We look to the Christian community and its past performances of the canon, including the little part of it called Ephesians, to equip us as interpreters. We are equipped by the church, but we are also *answerable* to the church, to the community that owns these texts as canon. We read Scripture—and perform it—as "members of one another" (Eph. 4:25). The Bible is the book of the church, and while the church puts the book in the hands of individuals (as every good Protestant says it must), it does not recognize any "right to private interpretation." It does not surrender the task of interpretation to either "private" individuals or to some magisterium, whether ecclesiastical or academic. It does not license the substitution of any interpretation, including its own at any particular moment of its history, for Scripture itself. In the communal conversation and interpretation, gifted individuals and ecclesiastical leaders and academic scholars have important roles to play and contributions to make, but the church does not gather around them. It gathers around Scripture.

The church, moreover, also refuses to substitute its too frequently inept performances for the script it still loves to read and longs to perform. And in its longing to perform this script, it will silence neither Scripture nor the gifted members of the community who bring their skills for interpretation and performance to the community. That community, as Ephesians will underscore, must be an inclusive community. It includes many biblical scholars, to be sure; but it also includes saints and strangers. It includes people who are different from us in gender, race, class, nationality, and sexual orientation. It includes those on the margins who are still too often beaten down and humiliated—and sometimes beaten down and humiliated by the ways we have read and performed Scripture in the past. We are answerable to them for the way we read Ephesians.

There is a feedback loop here, sometimes called a "hermeneutical circle," between the community and the text. The interpretation and performance of the text is equipped by and responsible to the community, but the interpretation and performance of a text may also challenge the reading community, requiring of it a revision of its past reading, a reform of its past performance. While we look to the church to equip us as readers, we also look to Scripture, including Ephesians, to renew and reform the church, including our reading and our performance of Scripture. So the church—and each of its members—is called to be ever reforming as it reads Scripture and remembers its story. This is one reason why the church keeps reading Scripture, including Ephesians.

Reading Ephesians as Part of the Canon

In Christian community, as we have said, the Bible is "canon," not just a miscellaneous collection of ancient religious texts, and Ephesians must be read as part of *that* whole. "Canon" serves both to identify the whole within which any part must be understood and to characterize the whole as somehow normative for the church's thought and conduct. The Christian canon may be further characterized as an extended narrative. The wholeness of this canon is a narrative wholeness.[7]

---

7. There are other ways to characterize the wholeness of Scripture, of course. See further Kelsey, *Uses of Scripture.*

The story begins with creation, with God making all things and making all things good. The story continues—and the plot thickens—with human pride and sloth, with the human refusal to honor God as God or to give thanks to God. Human sin might have smashed the cosmos back to chaos, but God would not let sin or death or the flood be the end of the story. God comes again to covenant and to bless. God calls Abraham and begins a project that promises blessing not only to Abraham's children but to all the nations. Ephesians remembers and celebrates that project, giving thanks for the election and calling of Israel, and it claims that in Christ, in Israel's Messiah, God's project has been, is being, and will be accomplished.

The stories of Jesus stand at the center of the Christian story—and at the center of the Christian canon. He came announcing the good future of God, and he made that future present; he made its power felt in his works of healing and in his words of blessing. He was put to death on a Roman cross, but God raised him up from the dead and vindicated him as Lord and Christ. Because Jesus was raised, the Spirit was poured out, and because the Spirit was poured out, a community was formed in memory of Jesus and in hope for God's good future. This Jesus, the Christ, the crucified and risen Lord, stands at the center of Ephesians as well. And the community that is formed by Christ and the Spirit, Ephesians insists, is the project of God coming to fruition. Ephesians names that project "peace," "one new humanity in place of two" (Eph. 2:15). God is keeping his promise to bless Israel and all the nations, to bless both Jews and Gentiles. They will find that blessing together. The community that knows God's power and grace is blessed and called to be an inclusive community and to make God's project known, even to the principalities and powers that would divide humanity and sponsor not peace but enmity.

At the end of the story and at the end of the canon there is a vision of this crucified and risen Lord, "seated on the throne" in the heavenly places, announcing, "See, I am making all things new" (Rev. 21:5). The story has not yet ended, but Christians claim to have a vision of where it will end. The author of Ephesians certainly does, and he prays that his readers may share it, that "you may know what is the hope to which [Christ] has called you" (Eph. 1:18). If by God's grace and by "the gospel of peace" (6:15) we come to know that hope and that calling, then we must lead a life worthy of it (4:1), performing peace and one new humanity in the church and displaying it to the world.

Ephesians is part of the canon, part of that story. The community reads with discernment when it reads any part (and every part, including Ephesians) in the light of that story. It is the story we love to tell—and long to live. That is the key. It is *our* story, the church's story. The Christian community reads Ephesians not simply to serve the task of historical recollection but to serve the task of memory. Ephesians called—and calls—its readers to remember the story, to fashion an identity and a community that is worthy of the story.

There is a feedback loop here too, another hermeneutical circle, between the parts and the whole. The parts can finally only be understood in the light of a whole, but the whole can only be understood in the light of the parts. The understanding of each is always provisional, always challenged and corrected as the parts are illumined by the whole and the whole by the parts. This is another reason we keep reading Scripture—and Ephesians—in the church.

The story is, as both the beginning and the ending witness, and as Ephesians insists, a universal story, the story of all things (Eph. 1:10). It is the story that gathers up and transforms all our other stories into the light of God's work and cause. It is not the case—or at least it ought not be the case—that our identity is provided by some other story so that we salvage something from Scripture and leave the rest for recycling or the dump. No, it is this story in which we find ourselves, this story that gives us an identity and makes us a community, this story that is determinative for what we salvage and redeem from all the other stories of our lives, taking every thought captive, discerning together what is fitting to the story, what is worthy of the gospel.

A Story We Can Trust

The novelist Reynolds Price once noted that the world is full of stories, but we crave the one, true story we can trust. "While we chatter or listen all our lives in a din of craving—jokes, anecdotes, novels, dreams, films, plays, songs, half the words of our days—we are satisfied only by the one short tale we feel to be true: *History is the will of a just God who knows us.*"
　　　　　　—Reynolds Price

A Palpable God (New York: Atheneum, 1978), 14.

Moreover, it is a continuing story. We claim to know something about the end of the story by the resurrection of this Jesus from the dead, but we do not claim that the story has ended. Scripture is script, but the curtain has not yet fallen. We are not only readers but performers, and as performers we find ourselves part of the drama, not just spectators. Scripture as script does not invite us to pretend we live in David's Jerusalem or in Jeremiah's—or in first-century Ephesus. It does, however, demand that we live here today in a way that is worthy of the story that includes Abraham and David and Jeremiah and the churches of the Lycus Valley and that makes no sense without Jesus of Nazareth. We are actors, agents in a continuing story. Performance will require both fidelity and creativity.[8] The community performs the script with moral discernment when it tests its own actions by the story of which it too is a part. We test our character and conduct by whether they fit the story, by whether they are worthy of the gospel.

Why Ephesians? Why Now?

The first and fundamental answer to these questions is simply that Ephesians is part of the Christian canon, part of the Scripture that still forms and reforms identity and community in the churches and still calls the churches to a faithful performance of the story. As part of the whole Ephesians provides a compelling retelling of the story of God's grace and power and calls its readers to lives and a common life "worthy" of it.

But another answer may also be given. For Christian churches in America today Ephesians is one part of the whole that is in many ways particularly apt and particularly challenging. In the midst of cultures that sponsored enmity and violence, Ephesians announced

---

8. Fidelity to the narrative requires a process of continual change, of creativity. Without it performance of the script is rendered anachronistic eccentricity. Nicholas Lash makes the point quite nicely with respect to the traditions of ecclesiastical dress among the Franciscans: "If, in thirteenth-century Italy, you wandered around in a coarse brown gown . . . your dress said you were one of the poor. If, in twentieth-century Cambridge, you wander around in a coarse brown gown, . . . your dress now says, not that you are one of the poor, but that you are some kind of oddity in the business of 'religion'" ("Performing the Scriptures," 54).

the gospel of peace and called the churches to embody it. Now the churches find themselves again—or still—in the midst of cultures that nurture enmity and violence. Now, again, such cultures are in the air we breathe, and the enmity they sponsor infects the life of the churches. If the focus of Ephesians was a Roman culture that sponsored enmity against the Jews and a Jewish culture that nurtured condemnation of the Gentiles, perhaps the focus has shifted. But the problem remains, not only because anti-Semitism remains but also because in a great variety of ways the cultures around us nurture hostility toward those who are not like us, who are different from us because of race or nationality or sexual orientation or some other marker of their difference. Now, again, Ephesians' announcement of a gospel of peace is a good—and challenging—word, a reminder that the problem is not difference but enmity, that the solution is not violence but the work of the Messiah, and that the plan of God is not uniformity but peaceable difference.

Ephesians is a particularly apt and challenging part of the whole because in the midst of churches threatened by division, Ephesians announced the good news of the unity of Christ's body. Now, again, the churches find themselves threatened by division. There is a long history of churches accommodating themselves to the divisions found within society, divisions by race, class, and ethnic origin. H. Richard Niebuhr in his *Social Sources of Denominationalism* recounted that

---

The Church's Story

The church's story with God did not end with the latest events recorded in Scripture. Across the centuries the company of believers has continued its pilgrimage with the Lord of history. It is a record of faith and faithlessness, glory and shame. . . . We confess we are heirs of this whole story. We are charged to remember our past, to be warned and encouraged by it, but not to live it again. Now is the time of our testing as God's story with the church moves forward through us. We are called to live now as God's servants in the service of people everywhere.

—*A Declaration of Faith (1976),* Presbyterian Church (U.S.A.)

In *Reformed Witness Today: A Collection of Confessions and Statements of Faith Issued by Reformed Churches,* ed. Lucas Vischer (Bern: Evangelische Arbeitsstelle Oekumene Schweiz, 1982), 255.

history in the United States as well as anyone. Now, however, many denominations and congregations are themselves split into "conservative" and "liberal" camps by their passion about issues like the ordination of homosexual persons. The issues may have changed, but the issues that threatened to divide the churches addressed by Ephesians were no less momentous to Jewish Christians and to Gentile Christians in the first century than any contemporary issues are to Christians today. Now, again, Ephesians' insistence that there is "one body and one Spirit" (4:4) comes to us as a good—if challenging—word.

Ephesians is an apt and challenging part of the whole also because in the midst of an empire that made pretentious claims to ultimacy and enforced its will by violence, Ephesians announced that by raising Jesus from the dead God had won a victory over "the powers" and had put them in their place. Now, again, the churches find themselves in the midst of an empire that makes pretentious claims to ultimacy and enforces its will by violence. If the context for Ephesians was the Roman Empire and the Pax Romana that it secured by violence, the context now is the claims of the United States to hegemonic power in the world and its efforts to secure a Pax Americana by violence. Now, again, the announcement that God's power is greater than "the powers" is a gracious—and challenging—word.

For first-century Christians uncertain of their identity, Ephesians reminded them of their baptism and assured them that by God's grace they had been given a new identity in Christ, made part of a new community and a "new humanity" (2:15). Today, again, there are Christians unsure of their identity. The cultures that surround us are no less skilled at "identity theft" than the cultures that surrounded the Christians of the first century. Ephesians can remind us, too, of our baptism, remind us of the grace of God in Jesus Christ that has established a new social reality, "one new humanity," and remind us that God graciously makes us part of it. It can remind us that our identity as Christians is a gift, a gracious—and challenging—gift.

To Christians uncertain of their future and the world's, Ephesians reminded them of the plan of God revealed in Christ, "a plan for the fullness of time, to gather up all things in [Christ]" (1:10), and assured them of the triumph of God and of their own inheritance and hope. Today, again, Christians are uncertain of the future, and Ephesians still is a message of hope. When Ephesians points us toward the risen and exalted Christ, we catch a glimpse of God's good future, a future assured by God's great power and faithfulness, a future that is already present and making its power felt in the common life of the churches, a future that by God's grace is sure to be. That too is today a good—and challenging—word. To be sure, this good word probably seemed to many in the first century, as it surely seems to many in our own century, as just too good to be true. But Ephesians reminded them—and can remind us—that "truth is in Jesus" (4:21). If we think this word of hope is just too good to be true, Ephesians points us to Jesus as the Christ. In Christ the truth is on display: the truth about God, the truth about humanity, the truth about the cosmos.

The truth about God is God's grace and power. God's grace was there at the very beginning, "before the foundation of the world" (1:4). God's grace was there when Abraham was called to be a blessing to the nations, when a people was formed by "covenants of promise" (2:12). God's grace was there in Jesus and in the works of that Jewish Messiah by which the Gentiles are made to share in those promises (2:13–17). God's grace is present in the church, that new social reality that is itself a work of God's grace. And "the immeasurable riches of [God's] grace" (2:7) will be there at the end. This gracious God is powerful to save. That is the truth. The "immeasurable greatness of [God's] power" (1:19) was at work when God raised that Jewish Messiah from the dead and exalted him to sovereignty over "the powers" (1:20–22). There God vindicated Jesus as the Christ, and there God vindicated God's own faithfulness, God's own truthfulness. God can be trusted. That is the truth. God's power is not like the power of empire. It is gracious, not violent; it does not coerce but invites. But it is God's power, not the power of empire, that creates the world, sustains the world, and will bring it to its own blessed destiny. God is God. God's grace and power can be trusted. That is the truth, and it puts to rest the suspicion that the message of hope in Ephesians is just too good to be true.

The truth about humanity and about our lives is also "in Jesus."

When God raised him from the dead, God also vindicated the work of this Jewish Messiah. He fulfilled the ancient covenant promise of a blessing on all the families of the earth (Gen. 12:3) by "making peace" (Eph. 2:15), by creating "one new humanity" (2:15), by putting hostility to death (2:16), by liberating us from the power of death and from our captivity to "the powers" (2:5–6). That truth is not yet fully on display, but it is already established in Christ, and it is sure to be.

Meanwhile Christ stands over, and over against, a false reality. And meanwhile the church is called to live the truth and to speak it (4:15), to reject the deceptions and the lies of the cultures that nurture enmity, to put the truth on display and to make it known, even to "the powers" (3:10).

By its emphasis on the truth that is "in Jesus," Ephesians can help us to meet our own worry that the Christian hope is just too good to be true. But hard on the heels of that worry comes a second, namely, that this good—and challenging—word is just too challenging to be practical. Surely some Christians in the first century found it so, and surely for some Christians today the Christian hope and the exhortation "to lead a life worthy of the calling to which you have been called" (4:1) seem to present an impossible ideal. By its emphasis on the truth that is "in Jesus" Ephesians can help us meet that worry too. The good future of God is not some ideal that stands outside history. It is a reality already within history, established in the work of Jesus and by his resurrection in our world and in our history, a reality from which our world and our history have, happily, no escape. It is not an ideal that we, exercising our own strength, must attempt to achieve. It is a reality to which we respond, and to which by God's grace we are able to respond faithfully. To be sure, there is a lot of growing to do before we conform to Christ (4:15). To be sure, it is demanding and challenging, and if we had to rely on our own strength, "our striving would be losing." But it is not our own power on which we must depend but God's power. God strengthens us through the Spirit (3:16), "the power at work within us [that] is able to accomplish abundantly far more than all we can ask or imagine" (3:20).

Ephesians, moreover, identifies some important and practical ways in which that reality makes its power felt among us, enabling us to grow (4:16), empowering us to "live for the praise of [God's] glory" (1:12), and to bless God. This is another reason to read Ephesians and to read Ephesians now. It displays and models a practical Christian moral discernment, a challenging but practical ethic, a way of forming community, character, and conduct that is still instructive for the churches today.

It displays, for example, a *pastoral* ethic. Paul (or a gifted Paulinist) is pastorally concerned to help the Christian community respond to its situation and its challenges faithfully. It displays an *ecclesial* ethic. The readers are invited to understand themselves, their blessing and their calling, as members of one body, Christ's body, the church. Moreover, the practices of the church, including the greeting in worship, prayer, doxology, and baptism, play an important role in moral formation and discernment. It nurtures community and calls the community to be faithful to the identity God has given it, to live a common life that demonstrates the triumph of God and puts it on display for the world. It displays an *evangelical* ethic. The gospel is announced whether the indicative mood or the imperative mood is used. It is the gospel that is pastorally related to the challenges faced by the community. It is to the gospel that the church is invited to respond with faith, hope, and love. It displays an *eschatological* ethic. The readers are invited to respond now, already, to God's good future, established and revealed in Christ. It displays a *christological* ethic. The Christian community is to be decisively formed by its participation in Christ, the Jewish Messiah, the crucified one who has been raised from the dead and now sits at God's right hand, above the "principalities and powers."

Most stunning of all, perhaps, Ephesians displays a *prayerful* ethic. The first three chapters are largely in the form of an extended prayer. Both author and readers are attentive to God, and as they attend to God, they learn to relate to all else as all else is related to God. Prayer is a practice that recognizes that God is ultimate—and that the powers are not. Prayer is a practice that attends to God and to the cause of God; it forms both our words and our works to doxology, to the praise of God's glory, and allows God's cause to govern both our petitions and our deeds. It displays also, therefore, a *doxological* ethic.

In many ways Ephesians displays a *boundary-breaking* ethic. The walls that separate and alienate people from one another have been broken down by the work of the Messiah, and they are broken down in the common life of the church. Ephesians displays an ethic of *peaceable difference*. Ephesians also displays, however, an ethic *that affirms existing moral traditions*. That may seem odd, given the claim that it is a boundary-breaking ethic, but both are true. In its last three chapters it makes considerable use of existing moral traditions in the church, including the household code (5:21–6:9), affirming those traditions while also modifying and qualifying them in the light of Christ's work.

These are all reasons to read Ephesians together—and to read it together *now*. In the midst of the hostilities and the enmities of our world its message of Pax Christi still comes to us as good news and as a demanding script. It calls us no less than its original readers still to believe in God's good future and still to live into it. It is a good word—and a challenging one—and it displays an ethic that can help us to meet the challenge today.

Performing Ephesians

As we have said, attention to Scripture—and to Ephesians—as script invites and requires performance, and we do not interpret Ephesians well without hearing and heeding that invitation. But what do we mean by "performance"? Let us give some brief attention to a few of the ways Ephesians is performed in Christian community.

One performance of Ephesians is the sermon, the proclamation of the gospel on a Sunday morning. We hope this commentary is useful to those who are charged to preach. A sermon on Ephesians is a performance of Scripture that must be tested for its creative fidelity to Scripture as scripted, but it must also be tested by whether it is apt to enter the hearts of those who hear it and pass into our lives and our life together.

Another performance of Scripture—and of Ephesians—is prayer. Much of Ephesians is prayer, and we hope this commentary does not just report that the author prays but nurtures and sustains the practice of prayer. Ephesians does not just contain prayer; it invites prayer (6:18), and it prompts prayer.

It contains and evokes the sort of attention to God that is adoration, for example, and we perform Ephesians when we "bless . . . the God and Father of our Lord Jesus Christ" (1:3) for God's work and way with Jesus, for God's great power in raising him from the dead and establishing God's own good future. Then "the praise of his glory" may spill over into our lives and our common life.

Ephesians invites and prompts prayers of thanksgiving, and we perform Ephesians when we give thanks for the ways God has blessed us and God's creation, "giving thanks to God the Father . . . in the name of our Lord Jesus Christ" (5:20). Such gratitude may then form our lives as well as our prayers.

Ephesians prompts prayers of confession. In prayers of confession we perform Ephesians by hearing the announcement of the good future of God in it as "over against ourselves," by mourning that the evidence among us of God's great power and of God's great mystery is so insipid. Prayers of confession may delight in the assurance that we have by the grace God has "lavished on us," "the forgiveness of our trespasses" (1:7), but we may and should regret that we are stingy with the forgiveness of others.

And Ephesians prompts our petitions, petitions for the good future of God, for "one new humanity," for "peace," and for the church's ministry in making that good future known and present. The practice of prayer is corrupted when we use it as a kind of magic to get what we want, whether a fortune, or four more healthy years, or a resolution to an interpretive or moral dispute. When petition is a form of attention to God, when it performs Scripture, however, then we pray—and pray boldly—that God's cause will be displayed, that God's good future will be present. We pray and pray boldly for a taste of that future, not so much in some ecstatic spiritual experience but in such ordinary things as everyday bread and everyday mercy, in such mundane realities as tonight's rest and tomorrow's peace, in such earthly stuff as comfort for the grieving, justice for our communities, and reconciliation of the races. We form and govern our petitions by this vision of God's good and peaceable future and by the aching acknowledgment that it is not yet, still sadly not yet. Then we may form and govern also our lives by that vision.

Order My Steps

Order my steps in Your word, dear Lord.

Lead me, guide me, everyday.

The world is ever changing, but You are still the same.

If You order my steps, I'll praise Your name.

Order my steps, in Your word.

Order my tongue, in Your word.

Guide my feet, in Your word.

Wash my heart, in Your word.

Show me how to walk, in Your word

Show me how to talk, in Your word.

[refrain] I want to walk worthy, my calling to fulfill.

Please order my steps, Lord, and I'll do Your blessed will.

—Glenn Burleigh

"Order My Steps," Performed by United Voices of Praise, *One in the Spirit* (United Church of Chapel Hill, 1999).

Worship spills over into life, as we have said. We perform Ephesians when our lives and our communities are shaped by this vision of God's future and by aching acknowledgment that it is not yet. We perform Ephesians when we interpret not only this text but our worlds in the context of the memory and the hope of the Christian community. We perform Ephesians when we form and reform our communities and their politics into something fitting "one new humanity" (2:15). We perform Ephesians when we confidently confront "the principalities and powers."

We perform Ephesians when we "lead a life worthy of the calling to which [we] have been called" (4:1), when we learn and practice the skills of peaceable difference, when we break down walls that divide, when we "speak the truth to our neighbors, for we are members of one another" (4:25), when we "live in love" (5:2). Because this commentary focuses on Scripture as script, we will need to return again and again to the question of how we can perform it with fidelity and creativity in our own historical context.

Against Abandoning Attention to Ephesians as Scripted

Our attention to Ephesians as *script* to be performed is not a license for poor exegesis. We need not—and should not—dispense with attention to Ephesians as *scripted*, as written at a particular time by an author who did certain things with the words available.

The call to perform this script itself invites attention to the script as scripted. As Nicholas Lash has observed, the life of the believing community is "the fundamental form of the *Christian* interpretation of scripture."[9] The common life of the church, its practices and politics, its conduct and character, is a performance of Scripture, and such performance is an interpretation of Scripture. If that is so, then we may—and must—assess the truthfulness or the integrity of our performance (in part, at least) by attending to Scripture as *scripted*.

A performance of any script is an interpretation. A performance can be improved if the acting troupe attends carefully to what the author did once with the words at his or her disposal. To be sure, such study is hardly a guarantee of a good performance. Lacking other gifts, a troupe will give a wooden and spiritless performance of a carefully studied text. Moreover, careful study of the script is not even strictly necessary for an excellent performance. A troupe may have seen (or heard) enough fine performances in the past to perform not just adequately but splendidly. Even so, even though careful study of the original script as scripted is neither sufficient nor strictly necessary, it remains important. It is important both for those who would check the "integrity" of a performance (or review and reform a tradition of performance) and for the troupe, for those who have the responsibility to perform. Moreover, because there are different performances (and traditions of performance), and because no performance definitively captures the meaning of the script, study of the script as scripted, as written, remains critical as a test for and guide to performance.[10]

---

9. Lash, "Performing the Scriptures," 40.
10. Lash observed not only that "the fundamental form of the *Christian* interpretation of scripture is the life, activity and organization of the believing community" but also that biblical scholarship and critical reflection make an "indispensable contribution"

This is true of any performance of any script, of a performance of Shakespeare's *Romeo and Juliet*, for example, but it is surely true of the performance of Scripture as script. Let us admit that Scripture is not simply an "object" waiting to be used, that it is always already used and "performed" in the life of particular churches. But Scripture may also not be reduced simply to the set of performative interpretations of any particular church. We may not substitute any church's performative interpretation of Scripture for Scripture itself. Such a substitution would vitiate the possibilities of reform and renewal of a church and its common life by reading Scripture together, for such a reading would simply be to look at an image of ourselves and to authorize it as biblical. Scripture is not *simply* "object," but it is "object," independent of the churches' interpretation.

In making this case for careful exegesis, we acknowledge once again that we are "needful of the minds of others" and grateful to those from whom we have learned to attend to what the author of Ephesians did with the words at his disposal. To read Scripture as *script* to be performed, some in the community must read it carefully as *scripted*. To read Scripture in Christian community requires that the community nurture and sustain biblical scholarship as an important contribution to the communal effort to understand and perform Scripture, and it requires our own best efforts to be careful interpreters of Scripture as *scripted*.

Moreover, even if we wanted to neglect attention to Ephesians as *scripted*, Ephesians itself would not let us, for it begins with an address. It reminds us that that it was written once upon a time by a particular author for a particular audience. That address has been a source of much dispute concerning Ephesians. We conclude this introduction, therefore, with some brief attention to that address and to the questions that conventionally preoccupy introductions to Ephesians.

---

to the "performative interpretation of scripture" (ibid., 42–43). For Lash there is no "performative interpretation," no set of practices in particular communities, in which the "meaning" of Scripture is definitively captured; and, because this is so, "the range of appropriate interpretations . . . is constrained by what the text 'originally meant'" (p. 44). The performative interpretation that "*is* the life of the church" must also always, therefore, be open to reform and renewal by the effort to understand Scripture as scripted and by reflection about the relation of such interpretation to performative interpretation.

Authorship, Audience, and Genre

The address, the conventional opening of a letter, is found in the opening verse: "Paul, an apostle of Christ Jesus by the will of God, To the saints who are in Ephesus and are faithful in Christ Jesus." In spite of this opening verse, however, some have claimed that the text we call Ephesians is not really from Paul, is not really to the Ephesian church, and is not really a letter. The scholarly arguments concerning these matters are long, frequently tedious, sometimes fanciful, but not without importance for reading Ephesians as scripted—and as script. To provide a definitive solution for these issues is beyond both our competence and our ambition. Without hoping to resolve the critical questions, however, we would at least note our conclusions and assumptions. We may begin with the question whether it was scripted by Paul.

From Paul?

That Paul was the author of Ephesians was unanimously accepted until the sixteenth century. Erasmus, noting the stylistic differences between Ephesians and other Pauline epistles, may have been the first to suggest that Paul might not have written Ephesians. Subsequent centuries witnessed what looked like an irreversible tide against the traditional assumption that Paul was the author.[11] While it may be too much to claim that the tide has turned, it is fair to say that it no longer looks quite so irreversible.[12]

Those who deny that Paul is the author typically call attention to three arguments: (1) The language and style of Ephesians are

---

11. For the history of criticism to the mid-twentieth century see Ernst Percy, *Die Probleme der Kolosser- und Epheserbriefe* (Lund: Gleerup, 1946), 1–18.

12. See, for example, the impressive list of scholars in Markus Barth, *Ephesians 1–3* (Anchor Bible 34; Garden City, NY: Doubleday, 1974), 37–38, who represent what Barth calls "four schools of thought" concerning the authorship of Ephesians: (1) those who have affirmed Pauline authorship; (2) those who regard Ephesians as Pauline but as scripted by a secretary or a member of the "school of Paul" deputized by Paul; (3) those who deny that Ephesians was written by Paul; and (4) those who claim that the evidence is inconclusive and refuse to make a judgment about authenticity. Barth calls this fourth group "the smallest, but it may well be the most prudent" (p. 38). His own judgment seems to be that the evidence is not conclusive enough to "invalidate the judgment of tradition" that ascribes Ephesians to Paul (p. 41).

quite different from the undisputed Pauline epistles but shared with later NT writings and the Apostolic Fathers. (2) Ephesians has an extensive relationship with Colossians; almost half of the verses in Ephesians have some parallel to Colossians; yet there are also differences between Ephesians and Colossians. (3) The theology of Ephesians is said to differ significantly from the theology of Paul. Each of these arguments has some merit, but none of them seems to us to be strong enough to require the conclusion that Paul could not have written Ephesians.

The language and style are different, to be sure, but not so different as to require a different author from the acknowledged Pauline epistles,[13] especially if the indebtedness of Ephesians to traditional liturgical and catechetical materials is allowed and if Colossians is acknowledged as Pauline. Moreover, arguments from style and vocabulary do not warrant a lot of confidence. The style and vocabulary of Plato's *Republic* is quite different from his *Laws*, but the differences do not seem to require the conclusion that Plato is not the author of both.

The relationship with Colossians is striking. Ephesians is closest to Colossians in style, and some phrases are almost exactly the same (notably, Eph. 1:4 and Col. 1:22, Eph. 1:15 and Col. 1:4, Eph. 2:13 and Col. 1:20, Eph. 4:2–3 and Col. 3:12–13, Eph. 6:21–22 and Col. 4:7–8). Nevertheless, there are differences. For example, both use "mystery," but in Colossians the "mystery" is christological, referring to God's eschatological act of salvation in Christ (Col. 1:26–27; 2:2; 4:3), and in Ephesians the "mystery" is ecclesiological, referring to the unity of Jew and Gentile as the firstfruits of that salvation (Eph. 1:9; 3:3–4; and 5:32, where "mystery" refers to marriage as analogous to the relation of Christ and the church). But what do we conclude from this? It does not seem implausible to us that, having written Colossians and preparing to send it off with Tychicus, Paul would write another letter for the churches on the way to Colossae, a letter that echoes some of the phrases of the other letter just completed. Those phrases, however, are put in the service of his vision for

---

13. Percy laboriously displayed that many of the differences have parallels in the undisputed letters (*Probleme*, 19–35).

those other young churches along the way. One would then expect both similarities and differences (and the different use of "mystery" would represent a development of Paul's thought, drawing the implications for the church from the eschatological act of God in Jesus Christ). Such an account of the relationship of these letters seems to us to be as plausible as the suggestion that someone copied phrases from Colossians in order to sound like Paul. How, then, does one explain the differences? And if Colossians is also regarded as written by someone other than Paul, why copy phrases from it if the purpose is to sound like Paul?

Finally, the theology of Ephesians is frequently contrasted with Pauline theology. This last is the decisive argument for many. Kümmel says, for example, that "the theology of Ephesians makes the Pauline composition of the Epistle completely impossible."[14] That judgment seems to us, however, to be completely implausible. As Markus Barth has said, "It does not take much trouble to discover exactly the same message and exhortations in the major part of Ephesians as in the other letters that carry Paul's name."[15] He goes on to call attention to "grace alone," to the centrality of the death and resurrection of Christ to God's revelation, to human liberation, to the message with which Paul is entrusted (the inclusion of Jews and Gentiles in Christ and in the church), and to the call to live in ways that are "worthy" of such a message.[16] To be sure, he also calls attention to certain "doctrinal distinctions" that may be found in Ephesians,[17] but he (and we) find nothing in the theology of Ephesians that makes Pauline authorship "completely impossible." The differences are plausibly explained as developments of Pauline theology; they need not be regarded as contradictory to it.

One point here is of special importance to us. The argument that there is a radical difference between the theology of Paul and Ephesians sometimes starts with the assumption that Paul had a

---

14. Paul Feine, Johannes Behm, and Werner Georg Kümmel, *Introduction to the New Testament*, trans. A. J. Mattill Jr., 14th ed. (Nashville: Abingdon, 1966), 254.
15. Barth, *Ephesians 1–3*, 31.
16. Ibid., 32.
17. Ibid. He lists them and describes them in pp. 33–36, and a slightly different list of "unique elements" is given on pp. 41–44.

"Lutheran" theology of "justification by grace through faith," that he announced the gospel as the answer to the individual's question, "How can I get right with God?" Then, to be sure, Ephesians with its focus on the church and on the social character of reconciliation sounds quite different indeed. But if that understanding of Paul is challenged and corrected (as it is and should be[18]), if justification by grace is recognized as a social reality already in Galatians and Romans (where the context is also always the relation of Jew and Gentile) and not just as relief for a troubled conscience (an aspirin of sorts to provide peace of mind), then Ephesians is properly understood not as a departure from Paul but as a development of Pauline theology.

The arguments are not decisive enough to force the conclusion that Ephesians was not written by Paul, but they are weighty enough to keep the question of authorship open. It might have been scripted by Paul late in his life, possibly during his Roman imprisonment, but if not by Paul, then surely by a faithful and brilliant Paulinist. With that acknowledgment of uncertainty, we will in the commentary usually follow the tradition of the churches and simply refer to the author as Paul.

To the Ephesians?

There are very good reasons to suppose that this epistle was not intended for the Ephesians, at least not as the primary recipients. First, the address in the earliest and best manuscripts does not include any reference to Ephesus. To be sure, later manuscripts include reference to Ephesus, and they are followed by many translations (including the NRSV). And to be sure, the title or superscription "To the Ephesians" was present from the second century, added to the text when the letters came to be collected. That Marcion, the

---

18. The initial challenge to such an account of Paul may have been Johannes Munck, *Paul and the Salvation of Mankind*, trans. Frank Clarke (Richmond: John Knox Press, 1959), followed by many others, notably Krister Stendahl, *Paul among Jews and Gentiles and Other Essays* (Philadelphia: Fortress Press, 1976). Today there continues to be considerable work done that challenges such an account and provides an alternative, the "new Paul." See most recently and comprehensively Douglas A. Campbell, *The Deliverance of God: An Apocalyptic Rereading of Justification in Paul* (Grand Rapids: Eerdmans, 2009).

second-century heretic who proposed a canon composed of Pauline epistles and an abridged Gospel of Luke, had given the epistle the title "To the Laodiceans," however, also suggests that very early manuscripts of the letter did not include "in Ephesus" within the address.

Perhaps there was more than one copy of Ephesians in early circulation containing different names for different destinations of the same letter, and perhaps a careful early scribe, noting the differences, left a blank in the manuscript hoping a later scholar would be able to provide the proper information.[19] Or perhaps the original letter did not name a particular destination, leaving it to the courier (Tychicus? see 6:21) to supply the name of the church to whom he was reading the letter.[20] Either explanation would fit the suggestion that the letter was a circular letter, intended for several congregations, not just Ephesians. That does not solve all the problems. One may wonder, for example, if it was intended as a circular letter, why the author did not follow Paul's pattern in Galatians of identifying the area rather than a particular city. Nevertheless, the suggestion that the letter was a circular letter, probably intended for the churches of the Lycus Valley, perhaps carried by Tychicus on his way to Colossae, seems the best explanation of the lack of "in Ephesus" in the address.

Besides the manuscript evidence, it seems unlikely that Ephesians was written to the Ephesians because it has almost no references to either the author or the recipients. We learn of Paul only that he is in prison (3:1; 4:1) and almost nothing about the recipients. The author does not greet others by name or send greetings from his associates. Only Tychicus is mentioned by name, identified as the one who brings news to them of Paul's situation and well-being (Eph. 6:21, as in Col. 4:7–9). This is surprising, given Paul's usual practice,

---

19. So G. Zuntz, *The Text of the Epistles: A Disquisition upon the Corpus Paulinum* (Oxford: Oxford University Press, 1953), cited by C. F. D. Moule, *The Birth of the New Testament* (New York: Harper & Row, 1962), 205.

20. James Ussher, who was the first to argue that Ephesians was a circular letter destined for several churches in Asia Minor, suggested in the seventeenth century that the name would be supplied by the courier. There are, however, no parallels to such a procedure in ancient literature. See Paul J. Kobelski, "The Letter to the Ephesians," in *The New Jerome Biblical Commentary*, ed. Raymond E. Brown et al. (Englewood Cliffs, NJ: Prentice Hall, 1990), 883.

and all the more surprising because, according to Acts 19:10, Paul had spent over two years in Ephesus. He knew Ephesus well, and it seems unlikely that Paul would send a letter to Ephesus so unusually lacking personal references and concrete details about the life of the church. Again, the suggestion of a circular letter commends itself. The young churches of the Lycus Valley may have "heard of" (3:2) Paul's commission to preach to the Gentiles, but they have evidently not experienced it. "Surely" the recipients had been taught the gospel (4:21), but they seem not to have been taught it by Paul. We could expect a circular letter to these churches to lack personal and concrete references.

If Tychicus ended up in Ephesus (2 Tim. 4:12), it is also possible that a copy of the letter ended up there too. When Paul's letters were gathered into a collection, it may have been Ephesus that supplied this letter and by supplying it became associated with it.

A Letter?

Those who deny that Ephesians is a letter usually start from the observation just made that Ephesians has almost no references to the particular circumstances of either the author or the recipients. One may admit that Ephesians is not as occasional a letter as Paul typically wrote. And one may also admit that there were—and are—literary works that pretend to be letters, that adopt certain conventions of a letter, but that are really more like an essay. (One thinks, for example, of Seneca's *Letters on Conduct*, ostensibly addressed to Lusilius, his young friend, or more recently Gil Meilaender's wonderful collection of essays in *Letters to Ellen*.)

But if it is not a letter, what is it? A number of interesting suggestions have been made, suggestions that have sometimes helpfully called attention to certain features of this text. Francis W. Beare, for example, characterized Ephesians as "an attempt to formulate a philosophy of religion, which is at the same time a philosophy of history, out of Pauline materials."[21] Such a characterization does call attention to the conviction in Ephesians that Christ is the key to

21. Francis W. Beare, "The Epistle to the Ephesians," in *Interpreter's Bible*, ed. G. A. Buttrick (Nashville: Abingdon, 1953), 10:604.

God's purpose in history, but it nevertheless seems an inept characterization of Ephesians. John C. Kirby, to cite one other example, characterized Ephesians as a "liturgy."[22] Kirby's characterization follows a helpful account of liturgical traditions in the synagogue and the church and attention to echoes of those traditions in Ephesians, but it does not seem quite right to call it a "liturgy."

It remains the case that Ephesians has adopted the conventions of a letter—and that it does so, it seems to us, without philosophical or literary or liturgical pretensions. It seems best to regard it as a circular letter or encyclical.[23] Such letters, carried by envoys, had been used by Jewish authorities in Palestine to communicate with communities of the Diaspora (note Acts 9:1–2 and 28:21) and were evidently adopted by the Jerusalem Christian community to report the results of the Jerusalem Council (Acts 15:22b–29). Galatians, James, the letters of Peter, and Jude may be taken as other illustrations of this letter type within the New Testament. Such letters do, as those examples make clear enough, have a specific occasion. But so does Ephesians! It should be regarded as a letter not just because it adopts the conventions of a letter but decisively because, like Paul's other letters, it does address a particular problem. The problem may not be as local as the quarrel of Euodia and Syntyche (Phil. 4:1–3), but it is a specific problem, and moreover, a problem that put the success of Paul's mission in jeopardy. The problem was the hostility, the enmity, between Jew and Gentile.

The Occasion for the Circular Letter

The mission of Paul to the Gentiles had prompted more than one controversy about the relations of Jews and Gentiles in the church. Paul consistently insisted on the full inclusion of the Gentiles and on the unity and equality of Jew and Gentile in the church. For the Galatians and the Romans the relation of Jew and Gentile had

22. John C. Kirby, *Ephesians: Baptism and Pentecost* (London: SPCK, 1968), 165; earlier, p. 126: "Strictly speaking, Ephesians is not a letter at all, but a prayer and a discourse thrown into the form of a letter."

23. See David E. Aune, *The New Testament in Its Literary Environment* (Philadelphia: Westminster Press, 1987), 180.

been, in different ways, the occasion for Paul's letters. In Galatia some were insisting that Gentile converts needed to become Jews, that they needed to be circumcised and observe the law of Moses in order to become fully Christians. In Rome some Jewish Christians condemned the Gentiles for their lawlessness, and some Gentile Christians scorned and despised the Jews for their scruples.[24] The unity and equality of Jew and Gentile were for Paul closely related to "the truth of the gospel" (Gal. 2:5, 14) and to the "obedience of faith" (Rom. 1:5; 16:26). And little wonder: the act of God in Christ had established a social reality in which "there is no distinction" between Jew and Gentile (Rom. 3:22; 10:12). In baptism they had been made "one in Christ Jesus," so "there is neither Jew nor Greek" (Gal. 3:28; cf. 1 Cor. 12:13). In Christ's cross Gentiles have died to sin (Rom. 6:1–11) and Jews have died to the law (Rom. 7:1–6). Jew and Gentile are equally "justified by his grace as a gift . . . to be received by faith" (Rom. 3:24–30; see also Gal. 3:6–14). Paul's talk of justification by faith is set in both epistles within the context of the relations of Jews and Gentiles in the churches.

This unity and equality of Jew and Gentile was an eschatological reality, to be sure, and Paul never denied that the Jewish Christians were Jews or that the Gentile Christians were Gentiles. He never demanded that the Jews stop observing the law or that the Gentiles start living like Jews; in fact, he repudiated such demands (Gal. 2:14). Paul insisted, nevertheless, that the eschatological reality shape the social reality of the church in the present. It must be performed, not just contemplated. Jews need not live like Gentiles, but they may not condemn and repudiate them either; Gentiles need not be circumcised or live like Jews, but they may not despise and scorn them either (Rom. 14–15). The gospel was performed in communities of peaceable pluralism, marked by freedom and love for those who were and remained different. Paul enjoined them to "welcome one another, therefore, just as Christ has welcomed you, for the glory of God" (Rom. 15:7; cf. also 14:1).

That gospel had been performed and the eschatological reality made present in the collection. At the Council of Jerusalem Paul and

---

24. Paul Minear, *The Obedience of Faith* (London: SCM Press, 1971), 7–17.

Barnabus had promised "to remember the poor" in Jerusalem (Gal. 2:10). The fulfillment of that promise, the collection among the Gentile churches accepted by the Jerusalem church, expressed the unity of Gentile and Jewish Christians. In giving the gifts the Gentile Christians acknowledged their indebtedness to the Jews (Rom. 15:27; 2 Cor. 9:12); and in receiving them the Jewish Christians acknowledged the "surpassing grace of God" among the Gentiles (2 Cor. 9:13–14). It was a sign that the enmity between Jew and Gentile had been and was being overcome. It sealed the formation of one community—although still composed of Jews and Gentiles—that could give thanks "to God for his indescribable gift" (2 Cor. 9:15).

The collection was a great "performance" of the gospel, but Paul's visit to Jerusalem ended up with Paul in prison, first at Caesarea and then arriving in Rome around the year 60. From there it was clear that the relations of Jew and Gentile in the empire were deteriorating. The animosity between Jews and Gentiles in the empire periodically prompted efforts at appeasement on both sides but usually simply "smoldered,"[25] breaking out from time to time in repression or rebellion, as it did in the Jewish rebellion of 66–73.

The enmity was "a holy enmity" on both sides. To the Jew the Roman or the Greek was an idolater; to the Roman the Jew was an atheist, refusing to acknowledge the gods or the divine authority of Caesar. When the Jewish rebellion broke out in 66, the war that followed was no polite reassertion of Roman authority. It was a bloodbath. Moreover, the enmity of war spilled over in anti-Jewish riots in Alexandria, Caesarea, and Antioch.

This political situation must not be underestimated, for it threatened a central accomplishment of Paul's mission; the unity of Jew and Gentile was in jeopardy. It was this political crisis, we think, that prompted the encyclical we call Ephesians.[26] Whether written

---

25. Philonis Alexandrini, *Legatio ad Gaium*, ed. and trans. E. Mary Smallwood (repr. Leiden: Brill, 1970), 119, referring to the anti-Jewish riot in Alexandria during the reign of Gaius: "When the promiscuous and unruly Alexandrian mob discovered this [i.e., that they had no punishment to fear from Gaius] it supposed that a most opportune moment had come its way and attacked us. It unmasked the hatred which had long been smoldering." A description of the atrocity follows.

26. See especially the brief remarks of C. H. Dodd concerning Ephesians in "Christianity and the Reconciliation of the Nations," *Christ and the New Humanity: Two Essays*, Facet Books, Social Ethics Series 6 (Philadelphia: Fortress Press, 1965), 10–16.

by Paul as he observed the progress toward war or by a faithful and creative interpreter of Paul during the war, the letter reminds Jewish Christians of their unity with Gentiles and Gentile Christians that they have made the Jewish heritage their own. Both Jew and Gentile are to discover their identity and community in Christ, as formed by their baptism, not in the racial and political animosities of their time.

> For he is our peace; in his flesh he has made both groups into one and has broken down the dividing wall, that is, the hostility between us. He has abolished the law with its commandments and ordinances, that he might create in himself one new humanity in place of the two, thus making peace, and might reconcile both groups to God in one body through the cross, thus putting to death that hostility through it. (Eph. 2:14–16)

Out of Jew and Gentile a new humanity had been created in Christ. The first effect, the firstfruits, of Christ's reconciling work was the church. But this identity—with its gift and its demand of reconciliation between Jew and Gentile—was at risk because of the political situation and the culture of hostility between Jew and Gentile. That culture attempted identity theft. But while the Pax Romana crumbled, the Letter of Paul to the Ephesians announced the good news—and demanded a performance—of the Pax Christi.

1:1–2

A Letter to Us:
Address and Greeting

A Letter

"Paul, an apostle of Christ Jesus by the will of God, To the saints who are in Ephesus and are faithful in Christ Jesus: Grace to you and peace from God our Father and the Lord Jesus Christ." It is obvious enough. We are reading a letter. It begins the way first-century letters usually begin. There would be an address identifying the sender and the recipient, and then a greeting.[1] The letters of Paul all follow that conventional pattern. It is a letter we read.

It is obvious enough, but no less important for being obvious. Letters are typically not written to be read by others. Anyone who has written or received a letter knows that. As someone has said, to read any of Paul's letters, including Ephesians, is like opening someone else's mail. That alone might caution us against reading this letter as if it were written "for us."

The canon, however, invites us not only to read this letter to the Ephesians but to read it as, in some sense, written for us. So we take it up again to read it, confident that we will discover again, as so many before us have, that it is not only Paul (or some Paulinist) speaking

---

1. Consider one typical example: "Sempronius to Maximus his brother many greetings. Before all things may you fare well I pray." See Howard Clark Kee, *The Origins of Christianity: Sources and Documents* (Englewood Cliffs, NJ: Prentice-Hall, 1973), 263. A third typical feature of the opening of a letter in addition to the address and greeting is also on display here, a prayer for well-being. Sempronius continues in the body of the letter to report that he has heard that Maximus has been slothful in caring for their mother and to request that he "not grieve her in any way."

but God, and speaking not only to some first-century Christians in Ephesus (or the Lycus Valley) but to us.

As we take it up to read again and to read it as for us, the title and the address immediately remind us that it is a letter to the Ephesians. The canon itself reminds us that this *is* a letter. It does not eliminate the conventions of a letter in an effort to suggest that this is a timeless document that simply fell from heaven. It does not hide that this document has an historical setting by giving it a canonical setting. So, when we take it up again to read it, we will do well to acknowledge with the canon that this letter to us was first a timely and pastoral letter to some Christian churches of the first century.

That it is a letter is the first clue that we have a *pastoral ethic* here. It is not simply a theological treatise, not simply a moral treatise of the sort the Stoics might write "concerning the fitting." There is plenty of talk of God, and plenty of talk of morality, but it is not given as a general and timeless treatise. It is a letter, a concrete address to particular congregations dealing with a specific problem. The category of "the fitting" still fits. The author invites these communities to a life and a common life "fitting to" or "worthy of" (Eph. 4:1) the calling to which they have been called. When one of the saints at First Presbyterian who attended our Sunday school class on Ephesians said that she thought Ephesians was beautiful but impossibly abstract, we knew we had some work to do. In Ephesians the author proclaims the gospel as good news, to be sure, but he never lets these churches forget that the gospel is demanding. As these churches respond to the particular circumstances in which they found themselves in the first century, the author demands that they respond also to God and to what the gospel tells us that God is doing in God's world. That is all we mean by calling it "a pastoral ethic."

The particular circumstances to which they must respond—and within which they must respond to God—are not described with the specificity of the report of a quarrel between Euodia and Syntyche (as in Phil. 4:2–3), but the circumstances were concrete and real. And they challenged the truth of "the gospel of peace" (Eph. 6:15). As we argued in the introduction (pp. 27–30), the occasion for the letter was the enmity between Jew and Gentile in the Roman Empire in the time surrounding the Jewish revolutionary war of 66–73. It was "a holy enmity" on both sides. To the Jew the Gentile was an idolater. And to anyone loyal to the empire the Jew was an atheist, refusing to acknowledge the gods of Rome and of the emperor. That enmity put Paul's great accomplishment of the unity of Jew and Gentile in the church at risk. That unity was addressed in the letters recognized as from Paul and demonstrated by the collection among the Gentiles for the poor in Judea. It was a great accomplishment, but it was threatened now by the political situation and by the cultures of enmity among both Jews and Gentiles.

It was a timely letter, a pastoral ethic, reminding the Christians of the Lycus Valley of their Christian identity, their community "in Christ," the identity and community to which the gospel had called them and that they had been given in their baptism. That identity and community had been put at risk by the enmity of Jew and Gentile in the Roman Empire in the last half of the first century. The "principalities and powers" sponsored and fanned that enmity, nurturing cultures of enmity, but this timely letter reminded the churches that they had a different story to tell and to perform, a different hope. It was the story of Jesus, the Christ, who sits enthroned "in the heavenly places," "far above all rule and authority and power and dominion" (Eph. 1:20, 21). It was the hope for "peace," for "one new humanity" (2:15).

That is the gospel here, the story Paul proclaimed and the story the church owned as its own. That gospel, that story, is still proclaimed and received in the churches, and it still calls the church to a faithful response. The Jewish revolutionary war (66–73 CE) may have been long ago, but a "War on Terror" still evokes suspicion and enmity and threatens Christian identity. The language of "principalities and powers" may seem antiquated and alien, but the realities named by that language are as contemporary as today's news. The animosity of Jew and Gentile persists, and is joined by other enmities between other ethnic and economic groups. Reports of enmity both globally and locally are enough to make even Christians wonder if the story they love to tell is true, enough to silence any attentive pastor.

But the story *is* true. This Jewish Messiah has been raised from the dead. He sits at God's right hand. And any pastor attentive to that story can hardly remain silent. In the midst of—and in spite of—the hold that enmity seems to have on the world, if the story is true, then there is hope. This is indeed a letter "to us," proclaiming a "gospel of peace" (Eph. 6:15) and calling the church to announce it and to perform it.

From Paul the Apostle

The address of this letter—and of all Paul's letters—is, as we have said, conventional for a first-century letter. But Paul did some artful things with these conventions, and by those artful things he put his letters in the service of his mission to the churches. So here, as is almost always the case, Paul identified himself as "an apostle" (or perhaps a faithful Paulinist identified the letter as an effort to be faithful to Paul, the "apostle," still urging the churches to a common life worthy of Paul's proclamation of the gospel). The only places where Paul fails to identify himself in this way are Philippians, 1 and 2 Thessalonians, and Philemon. Moreover, he always addressed his letters to the church (or churches).[2] Sometimes, as is the case here, the word "church" is not used, but there is never any doubt that the recipients are the church (or churches). For example, when Paul had addressed the letter to the Romans, "To all God's beloved in Rome, who are called to be saints" (Rom. 1:7), there is no doubt that the churches in Rome are addressed. Here, similarly, the letter is addressed: "To the saints who are faithful in the Messiah Jesus."[3]

Such artful modifications mark the letters (including Ephesians) as instruments in Paul's service to the churches; they are not merely a friendly correspondence with some acquaintances. His letters (including this letter) are his way of being present as an apostle when he is absent (cf. 2 Cor. 13:10). As noted in the introduction, many question whether the letter is actually from Paul's hand. There

---

2. Even the letter we call Philemon was addressed: "To Philemon our dear friend and coworker, to Apphia our sister, to Archippus our fellow soldier, and to the church in your house" (Phlm. 1).

3. We have already observed in the introduction above that "in Ephesus" is not in the earliest and best manuscripts of Ephesians. The difficulty is in making sense of the Greek text of the address without "in Ephesus." Barth (*Ephesians 1–3*, 67–69) acknowledges the difficulty of translation but makes a good case for "to the saints who are faithful to the Messiah Jesus."

we found the arguments concerning authorship inconclusive. Perhaps Paul did write it. Or perhaps an associate wrote it according to Paul's instruction while he was imprisoned in Rome. But if not, then at least this much must be said: it was written after his death by a faithful and creative Paulinist who, by means of this letter, still makes Paul present to the churches despite his absence.

Paul always wrote as an *apostle*, as "one sent," as an envoy. Here (and two other times, 2 Cor. 1:1 and Col. 1:1) "an apostle" is expanded to "an apostle of Christ Jesus by the will of God." That expansion clarifies the meaning of Paul's apostleship. Paul could sometimes use "apostle" to refer to a person appointed by a church for some mission. For example, he called Epaphroditus the "apostle" of the Philippians (Phil. 2:25; NRSV "messenger") because he was sent as their representative to minister to Paul's needs. Again, Paul called those who were appointed by the churches to assist Paul in gathering (and probably "auditing") the collection "apostles of the churches" (2 Cor. 8:23; NRSV "messengers"; see 8:16–22). But Paul identifies himself as "an apostle of Christ Jesus by the will of God." He is not simply authorized by the churches; he is authorized by the Christ and by God's calling.

He is authorized by Jesus, the Christ, the Messiah. His mission to the Gentiles was authorized by the Jewish Messiah. To be sure, early in the church's history "Christ" had almost become part of Jesus' proper name. And it may have that meaning in the address; at least nothing in the address itself would require the translation "by Jesus, the Christ." Other occurrences in Ephesians, however, are reminders that the significance of "Christ" as the anointed agent of God to fulfill God's promises to the Jews and to bring God's good future has not been forgotten (e.g., 1:12; 3:6). There is no salvation for the Gentiles apart from their participation in the promises to Israel fulfilled in the Messiah and announced in the gospel. Ephesians will underscore that point.

He is authorized by Jesus, the Christ. He has authority, then, but it is a peculiar authority, an authority fitting to the ways Jesus acted as Messiah. It is an authority exercised in weakness, in suffering, in patience, in humility. In Corinth, for example, Paul had contrasted his authority and his behavior with the so-called super-apostles (2

Cor. 11:5; 12:11). Without attempting to identify these "super-apostles," we know that they "boast according to human standards" (11:18). Paul too could "boast" about his credentials, his revelations and ecstatic experiences, but he recognizes that he would be "speaking as a fool" (11:21). He ends up "boasting" about his weakness (11:30). He has authority, but the authority Christ gave is for "building up," not "tearing down" (10:8; 13:10). It is an authority that is exercised in serving, in bearing the burdens of God's mission to the world, of participation in the death of Christ that others may live (4:12). The same paradoxical combination of self-conscious authority and self-forgetful humility is found in Ephesians 3:1–13, a passage that links God's grace, Paul's apostleship, Paul's imprisonment, and God's plan for the nations. We will come to that passage in due course. Here it is enough to observe that although Paul writes as an apostle, he does not write like a tyrant, lording it over others. To be sure, he can utter apostolic commands (e.g., 1 Cor. 5:1–5), but he prefers to commend and to ask, here even to "beg" (Eph. 4:1). He acts and writes as a servant, as a servant of Christ and, because he is a servant of Christ, as a servant of the churches. Paul's apostolic authority is the authority of a servant, a pastoral authority.

Perhaps Ephesians is written by a later Paulinist, but if so, then the author performs Pauline "apostolicity." He not only makes Paul present in his absence; he performs a servant leadership in the tradition of Pauline performances of his role as apostle. Moreover, he calls the church to its own apostolicity, to a mission that participates in God's mission, to a mission that is performed in ways that are worthy of Jesus, the Christ, the one who still calls and sends. The church's apostolicity is performed in its receiving and proclaiming the gospel, in its gathering for worship and its dispersing to serve God's cause in the world, and in its life as an inclusive community, its hospitality to those a culture of enmity tells us to despise.

A Greeting and an Envelope

Paul does artful things also with the conventional greeting. The commonplace greeting was *chairein* ("greetings"), but by an inspired play on words *chairein* is wonderfully transformed to *charis* ("grace"). *Charis*, "grace," occurs in all the Pauline greetings, and in all of them it is accompanied, as here, by "peace."[4] The typical Pauline greeting, moreover, is supplemented (except in 1 Thessalonians) by identifying the giver of grace and peace, usually as here, "from God our Father and the Lord Jesus Christ." Paul's greeting has surely become a conventional part of many Christian worship services. Judging from the presence of this combination not only in Paul but also in 1 Peter 1:2, 2 Peter 1:2, and Revelation 1:4, it may already have been (or quickly became) a commonplace greeting in the context of Christian worship.

It is likely that Paul's letters, including the Letter to the Ephesians, would first have been read in the context of the community's gathering for worship, and it is certain that the canon presumes that it will continue to be read in the context of the gathered community. This is our first clue that we have an *ecclesial ethic*. The letter and the ones who read and hear it thus have a context—the worship and faith of the gathered community. And the greeting has the same context. But one may ask how such a greeting would have been read and heard in the churches of the Lycus Valley, given their other context, the culture of racial enmity.

It can only be read and heard as God's greeting, as Paul performing God's greeting. That sets not only worship but also community in response to God. God's greeting announces that this gathering is not based on anything other than God's grace, not on the basis of status in society or wealth or race but simply on the basis of God's grace and calling. The ecclesiology of Ephesians is already performed in the greeting. It is not so much that Christians gather as that they *are gathered*, gathered by God's grace. They are the recipients of God's greeting. They are "gifted."

The greeting, like any greeting, calls for a response, an answering. God's greeting alone makes us able to respond, but it also makes us responsible. The answering includes the praise of God, to be sure, and Paul's praise follows hard on the heels of the greeting, but

---

4. This addition to the greeting Paul may have adopted from the conventional greeting in Hebrew and Aramaic letters, *shalom*.

worship and prayer must spill over into lives and into a common life "to the praise of [God's] glory" (1:12, 14). The answering, the response, includes learning to see other members of this gathering as "gifted" by God's grace and Spirit, learning to greet one another, to be hospitable to those whom cultures of enmity teach us to despise. The greeting is, after all, "grace and peace." In response to God's greeting, members of the gathered community, rich and poor, mighty and marginalized, Jew and Gentile, "pass the peace," greeting one another in the name of the one who greeted them.

The greeting in this letter may not be considered trivial or merely conventional, especially given the cultural context of racial enmity. It was not simply a necessary and conventional prelude to the really important matters to follow, to the theological insights and moral guidelines that are relevant to the problem of racial enmity. The greeting, this practice of ecclesial community, already formed and informed community and identity. It initiated members of the community into both community and worship, initiated them into an alternative culture, a culture not of enmity but of hospitality, of greeting, of grace and peace. Theological insight and moral guidelines are important, to be sure, but they are set in the context of worship and of this greeting. They are set in the context of a performance of the very reality to which they feebly point. It is an ecclesial ethic.

Greetings

Emmanuel Katongole, to whose reflections on the greeting in Christian worship these paragraphs are indebted, tells the story of a mass in Malaysia in an ethnically diverse congregation.

> Mass began outside the church, with the priest greeting the congregation, and everyone in the congregation greeting everyone else. . . . We had to extend greeting not only to those next to us but to each person in the congregation. For what happened was that the greeting was part of the procession into the church whereby the congregation formed two lines, with the person at the end of each line passing through the formed lines and greeting everybody in the line. Although it was quite a while before the last person got into the church, by that time we had all had a chance to touch, kiss, shake the hands, and look into the eyes of everyone else in the congregation.
>
> —Emmanuel Katongole

"Greeting: Beyond Racial Reconciliation," in *The Blackwell Companion to Christian Ethics*, ed. Stanley Hauerwas and Samuel Wells (Oxford: Blackwell, 2004), 74–75.

What might it mean to perform God's greeting in the worship of First Presbyterian Church in Durham? Or in the worship of your church? One answer, and by no means an insignificant one, is to say that it is performed when the pastor performs God's greeting in worship. But how might the congregation perform a fitting response to it in worship and in life to the praise of Christ's glory? How might we respond to God's grace? How might we perform peace? Besides the response of praise and thanksgiving, must our response not now include the sad recognition that Sunday morning worship in our culture is typically among the most segregated times and the sanctuary among the most segregated spaces? Must it not now include the churches' repentance that Christian communities seem sometimes simply to confirm the dominant cultural assumptions and to sustain contemporary cultures of enmity? Do we really believe that we are gathered by God's grace, that we are not simply a voluntary association? Have we really heard (and believed) the greeting of God? "Grace to you and peace from God our Father and the Lord Jesus Christ."

It is worth observing that the close of the Letter to the Ephesians echoes this greeting: "Peace be to the whole community, and love with faith, from God the Father and the Lord Jesus Christ. Grace be with all who have an undying love for our Lord Jesus Christ" (6:23–24). "Grace and peace. . . . Peace and grace." They create an artful envelope for this letter to some first-century churches and to us.

1:3–14

Beginning with Prayer

After the address and a greeting, a first-century letter typically included a prayer for the well-being of the recipient. Conventionally it was simply, "May you fare well I pray." Paul does artful things also with this third part of the opening of a letter, transforming it into a prayer of thanksgiving for the churches. (In the Letter to the Galatians there is no such prayer of thanksgiving; Paul is too angry with them.) In Ephesians, however, the prayer after the greeting does not simply extend for a verse or two. Here the prayer dominates the opening chapters, beginning with praise and thanksgiving (1:3–14), continuing with petitions for the church (1:17–22; 3:14–19), and ending with doxology (3:20–21).

Hard on the heels of the greeting comes an explosion of praise. "Blessed be the God and Father of our Lord Jesus Christ," it begins— and it continues in one long sentence to the end of verse 14, blessing God for God's blessings upon the people of God. This prayer and praise is the response to the greeting of God. The ones to whom this letter is read are prompted to bless God, to praise God, to give thanks to God for God's blessings. They are prompted to count those blessings, to name them, and to see what God has done and is doing and will do. The blessings stretch from a time "before the foundation of the world" (1:4) to the Sunday on

> **A Chorus for Ephesians 1:3–14**
>
> Count your blessings, name them one by one,
> count your blessings, see what God has done.
>
> —Johnson Oatman Jr.

which the letter was read, and from there to any Sunday on which the letter is read and into God's good future.

On Blessing God

Paul here adopts the formula of blessing God rather than his more typical "I give thanks to my God always for you . . ." (1 Cor. 1:4). On one other occasion, 2 Corinthians 1:3–4, the prayer of thanksgiving takes the form of blessing God for God's great gifts. Such a blessing also occurs in 1 Peter 1:3–5.

The act of blessing God was familiar as a form of thanksgiving in the Jewish community, familiar in the Hebrew Scriptures, in the liturgies of the synagogue, and in the prayers of the home. In the Hebrew Scriptures, for example, when Jethro, the priest of Midian and the father-in-law of Moses, was told of God's deliverance from Egypt, he exclaimed, "Blessed be the LORD, who has delivered you from the Egyptians and from Pharaoh. Now I know that the LORD is greater than all gods, because he delivered the people from the Egyptians, when they dealt arrogantly with them" (Exod. 18:10–11). At the dedication of the temple, when "the glory of the LORD filled the house of the LORD," Solomon's prayer began and ended with such a blessing (1 Kgs. 8:11, 15, 56). Ezra's great prayer of remembrance, confession, and petition in Nehemiah 9:6–37 was prefaced by the invitation by the Levites: "Stand up and bless the LORD your God from everlasting to everlasting. Blessed be your glorious name, which is exalted above all blessing and praise" (Neh. 9:5). And, of course, "Blessed be the LORD" is a familiar refrain in the Psalms (e.g., Ps. 106:48).

The blessing also found its way into Jewish liturgical prayers. The prayers of Solomon and of Ezra have a liturgical setting, but there are numerous examples of such a blessing also in the prayers of the synagogue. To give just one ancient example of many, the *yotzer* was a blessing, a *berakot*, before the Shema,

> Blessed art thou, O Lord our God, King of the Universe, who formest light and createst darkness; who makest peace and

> createst all things; who givest light in mercy to the earth and
> to those who live thereon, and in goodness renewest every
> day continually the work of creation. Be thou blessed, O Lord
> our God, for the excellency of the work of thy hands, and for
> the bright luminaries which thou hast made; let them glorify
> thee.[1]

To such prayers the Jewish assembly was expected to reply, "Amen."

The formula with which the *yotzer* and many other prayers of the synagogue began, *Baruk attah Adonai elohenu melek ha-olam asher . . .* , "Blessed art thou, O Lord our God, King of the Universe, who . . . ," also found its way into the homes of pious Jews, in, for example, the prayers over wine and food. Indeed, this formula of praise could accompany every action of the pious Jew from awakening to sleeping. There is a prayer for washing hands, "Blessed art thou, O Lord our God, King of the Universe, who has sanctified us with His commandments, and commanded us concerning the washing of hands." There is even a prayer for the cleansing of the colon.

The Jewish Christians in the Lycus Valley would have found this form familiar. They would have known they were to say "Amen" at the end of it. And by the use of this Jewish formula the Gentiles in these churches would be reminded that they had been grafted into Israel and into its worship of God. The medium fit the message.

As familiar as the *berakot* was (and is) to the Jews, it has fallen out of use in Christian liturgy. We are familiar, of course, with thanksgiving and with praise, but we seldom use the form, "Blessed be God. . . ." And when we encounter the form in Scripture, we tend to think of it simply as an expression of thanksgiving or praise. It is that, of course, but when we reduce it to that we neglect an important nuance. Just what that nuance is may be uncovered by considering why it has fallen out of use. We suggest that the reason is that we are a little uncomfortable blessing God. God, after all, is the source of all blessing. Who are we, recipients of God's blessings, to be blessing God? We retain the notion of God blessing us and the memory of

---

1. Cited in Kirby, *Ephesians*, 87, who gives other examples as well. His account of "The Form of the Jewish Berakoth," 84–89, was helpful for this section.

Christ's announcement of a blessing upon the poor and the hungry and the suffering and the persecuted (Luke 6:20–23). And we retain the practice of blessing one another and our homes and our food and much else. But blessing God seems, well, like chutzpah, presuming that God needs our blessing. It seems to make God the recipient of blessing rather than the source of all blessing. It seems to render God passive.

But this mysterious "passivity" of God is precisely the nuance we should not neglect. By a powerful and creative word God created the universe and all that is in it, by God's constant care God sustains it, and by God's grace God redeems it. God is agent, active. But God creates, sustains, and redeems the creation into a fertile and free otherness from God. God gives God's creatures their own distinctive powers and upholds those powers, concurring in their own works, not rendering the creation passive but active in God's own project. By God's creative power, care, and grace, God is not the only agent in the universe. God summons the light and the lights into existence (Gen. 1) and then summons them to glorify God.[2] And they do (Ps. 19:1), yielding their sinless obedience. So also God summons human beings into existence and then summons them to be active in God's own cause, to be God's agents, to bless God. When human pride and sloth prevent our obedience, God continues to summon us, comes again to covenant and to bless, but never reduces either the creation or the human creature to a thing simply to be manipulated or coerced. We are agents, free in our otherness from God, summoned to a share in God's cause and in God's glory.

We are agents, then, but not independent agents. We depend upon God. And God remains the source of all blessing (Num. 6:22–27; 23:20). Without God's blessing the cosmos descends into chaos, and our efforts to bless descend to futility. Our dependence upon God, even for the agency with which we may bless God, is perhaps signaled in the passive voice of the *berakot*, "Blessed be. . . ." The active voice—to say, "I bless God"—might indeed tempt us to chutzpah, to forget our dependence upon God. Nevertheless, God

---

2. See, for example, the *yotzer* above, Ps. 148, and the *Benedicte* from The Prayer of Azariah and the Song of the Three Jews in the Apocrypha.

summons us to take an active role in God's own project of blessing. The mysterious "passivity" of God is not powerlessness but an invitation to free and active friendship with God, sharing in the cause of God.

It is not enough simply to mouth some words of blessing. As the *berakot* itself expresses "the praise of his glory" (Eph. 1:6, 12, 14), so must our lives and our common life. We must live doxologically. *Soli Deo gloria.* Such is the performance of the *berakot.*

Blessings "in Christ"

There is an important innovation in this use of the traditional *berakot* in Ephesians (and in 2 Corinthians and 1 Peter). God is here identified as "the God and Father of our Lord Jesus Christ" (v. 3). Remembrance of what God has done is a standard feature of the traditional form, but here there is remembrance of what God has done "in Christ" (1:3, 4, etc., eleven times in 1:3–14). The list of blessings counted is not itself particularly innovative. God chose us (1:4). God made us God's own children (1:5). God redeemed us, forgave our sins, lavished grace upon us (1:7–8). And God made known God's will to us (1:9). All of these blessings might have found their way into a prayer of the synagogue. They are God's blessing upon the Jews. But here these blessings are counted as the blessing of God "in Christ."

That is the startling innovation, repeated often enough that we cannot miss it, although we can hardly yet make sense of it. In these verses God is consistently the agent, and "in Christ" seems simply to identify the instrument of God's action. Still, the rich significance of the Pauline phrase "in Christ" as our union with Christ, our participation in Christ, our being joined to Christ, our being initiated into Christ, should not be neglected here, and will not be neglected in the remainder of Ephesians (see, e.g., 2:4–7, 15, 22).

Consider, for example, the first in the list of blessings, the one that epitomizes all the rest. God has "blessed us in Christ with every spiritual blessing in the heavenly places" (1:3). "In the heavenly places" is a phrase that appears only in Ephesians (here and in 1:20; 2:6;

3:10; 6:12). It is the mysterious and unseen realm above and behind this world. It is not another world, a different world, unconnected with this one. It is the realm at once of God, who creates and sustains this world, and of the "spiritual forces of evil" (6:12), who are at work in this world to destroy it. It is the realm of a cosmic conflict. On the one side are God and his Christ; on the other are the principalities and powers who would usurp God's rule. That cosmic conflict is a battle for sovereignty in this world, not some other one. It is the very cosmic conflict in which Christians find themselves enlisted (6:12). The decisive battle has been fought and won in this conflict, fought and won in this world, when God raised Jesus from the dead. The powers of death and doom had done their damnedest, but God raised Jesus up and set him at his right hand "in the heavenly places" (1:20). Christ is already enthroned, but the powers continue to assert their doomed rule upon the earth. Even so, in that great triumph we are blessed already—however mysteriously—to have a share by our being united "with Christ," by our participation "in Christ" (2:5–6).

The Secret

There is another innovation in this *berakot*. It would not be surprising to the Jewish Christians of the Lycus Valley that in remembrance of God's blessings the *berakot* should count God's election of a people "to be holy and blameless" (1:4) or God's making a people "his children" (1:5) or God's acts of redemption, forgiveness, and grace (1:6–8a), or God's making known God's will (1:9). Each of these blessings is traditional, even if here they are set in the context of what God has done "in Christ." The last of them, however, the blessing of the revelation of God's will, contains an innovation that may have shocked some of them, for it is not at Sinai that God has "with all wisdom and insight" made known God's will, but in Christ. This little shock may have prepared them for the greater shock to come in 2:15, that Christ "has abolished the law with its commandments and ordinances, that he might create in himself one new humanity in place of the two, thus making peace." That comes later, and we will return to it in due course. But here already God's will is not simply identical with the revelation at Sinai. The law could permit—indeed, require—a division between those who knew and kept the law and those who did not, between "us" and "them," between "the righteous" and "the sinners." If the law was the principal marker of identity for these Jewish Christians, they were already being challenged to reform their identity "in Christ," and that would mean, as we will see, to reform their community by hospitality to Gentiles.

Then comes what we take to be the climax of this *berakot*, blessing God for making known "the mystery of [God's] will" (1:9), blessing God for letting us in on the secret, the "mystery," of God's will.[3] This is the first mention of "the mystery," but it will not be the last. Here already, though, it is clear that that "mystery," that secret, is God's good future, "a plan for the fullness of time, to gather up all things in [Christ]" (1:10).

"To gather up" is a translation of *anakephalaioō*. One can find in that Greek verb the noun for "head," *kephalē*. The sense seems to be that in God's good future God will bring all things together under one head, namely Christ. In the translation from Greek to Latin (and to the Latin Vulgate) *ana-kephalaioō* became quite naturally *re-capitulare*, and it carried the additional sense of "renew."[4] Perhaps we can hear an echo of this climactic verse in Revelation 21:5, "See, I am making all things new." But it is enough simply to say that the plan of God is that all things would be united and renewed with Christ as "the head over all things" (Eph. 1:22). It is clear in both Ephesians 1:10 and 1:22 that "all things" includes not just humanity but the whole created cosmos and not just human beings but the angelic powers as well.

3. Like Barth, *Ephesians 1–3*, 123–27, we much prefer "secret" to "mystery." First, it has nothing to do with the "mystery religions." Second, "mystery" makes it sound like a puzzle to be solved. Hence we will use "secret" unless directly quoting from the NRSV.

4. That was the translation and the sense preferred by Irenaeus, who took the renewal to require recapitulation in the sense of "repetition." It was Irenaeus's view that Jesus, fully God and fully man, retraced the steps of Adam and brought humanity to its proper destination. Because Jesus passed through the different stages of life, all humanity can share in his work. His quite elaborate account of the "recapitulation" can be appreciated for its effort to refute the gnostic claims that drove a wedge between the creator and the redeemer. The work of the creator is not destroyed but renewed by the work of God in Christ. But his account may be a little too elaborate—and because Jesus died young, one may wonder about the recapitulation of those who, like us, are no longer young.

Remembrance has brought us to this point. It is because this community remembers Christ that it also hopes. It hopes for the good future of God, which is the good future for God's creation, for "all things." This good future is our "inheritance" in Christ (1:11), and the Spirit is the "pledge," the earnest, of that inheritance (1:14), the firstfruits of God's good future.

Jew and Gentile and the Praise of God's Glory

"In Christ" there is one more striking implication, one additional startling innovation in this *berakot.* "In Christ" the Gentiles share this inheritance; they are "fellow heirs" (3:6). It is simply the fulfillment of the promise to Abraham, "and in you all the families of the earth shall be blessed" (Gen. 12:3). But in Christ that promise comes to fulfillment, comes to fruition, in an identity and a community in which Jew and Gentile are "gathered up" under Christ as head. There is no more "us" and "them."

To be sure, in the final verses of this *berakot,* there is a distinction between "we, who were the first to set our hope on [the] Christ [that is, Jewish Christians]" and "you [who later] heard the word of truth, the gospel of your salvation, and had believed in him [that is, Gentile Christians]" (1:12, 13). There remain Jew and Gentile, but "in Christ" they have a common identity. "In Christ" they are made one community. It is not that the Jew must act like a Gentile or the Gentile like a Jew, but they must both act like Christians, blessing God for letting them in on the secret. They must both live "for the praise of his glory" (1:12, 14). That living praise will require the formation of character and community fitting to the gospel and resistant to the cultures of enmity in the first century. So let the Jews be hospitable to the Gentiles, not condemning them as "sinners," and let the Gentiles delight in and be grateful for their share in the promises to the Jews.

The triune God is at work in the world and in the church, and Paul calls the churches to respond by lives that praise his glory. In this magnificent *berakot* Paul counted all these blessings as blessings of God the Father, as blessings that are ours "in Christ," and as blessings that culminate in the gift of the Spirit, "the pledge of our inheritance" (1:14), the firstfruits of God's good future. It is the triune God who blesses the church and calls it to agency, to serve God's cause.

The emphasis falls on service, not on status. The blessings of God, after all, do not provide a status for the church about which it may boast but a calling for the church to which it must respond. God chose us, not that we might boast about our election, but that we might be "holy and blameless before him in love" (1:4). God adopted us, redeemed us, forgave us, let us in on the secret, gave us an inheritance that surpasses our imagination, and poured out the Spirit as a pledge of that inheritance "so that" (1:12) in the church both "we" and "you," both Jewish Christians and Gentile Christians, "might live for the praise of his glory." Or, to translate that phrase from 1:12 more literally, so that we "might *be* a praise of God's glory." The blessing of God that finds voice in Paul's *berakot* must find flesh in the conduct and character and community of the churches. We do not fulfill the vocation to *be* a praise of God's glory simply by joining our voice to a hymn on a Sunday morning or simply saying "Amen" to a prayer. The vocation to *be* a praise of God's glory is much more demanding than that. The church is a community called to lives and a common life of *doxology*, a community called to lives and a common life that display already something of the good future of God. *Soli Deo gloria.*

Chosen to Serve

According to Scripture, it is true that God loves, protects, blesses, and saves those who are chosen to be God's people. But that is not the main thing the Bible says about them. It says that they are chosen not to be God's pets or privileged elite but to be God's *servants*, chosen not to receive and enjoy for themselves all the benefits of God's saving grace others do not have but to be instruments of God's grace so that others may receive and enjoy these benefits also.

—Shirley C. Guthrie Jr.

Christian Doctrine, rev. ed. (Louisville: Westminster John Knox Press, 1994), 139.

FURTHER REFLECTIONS
Toward a Prayerful Ethic

Ephesians invites us to pray. Much of the first three chapters is prayer. It opens with the *berakot* (1:3–14). It reports prayers of thanksgiving (1:15–16). It continues with prayers for the churches (1:17–22; 3:14–21). Those whom God had gathered and greeted in the churches of the Lycus Valley were invited to pray. At the close of the instructions to the churches, they are reminded once again to pray (6:18–20). And nearly two millennia later those who hear Ephesians read on a Sunday morning are still invited and instructed to pray. In response to God's gathering us and greeting us we are still to attend to God.

Ephesians sets its talk of God and its instructions concerning the common life in the context of prayer. The prayers for the churches provide the context for the rich theological reflections of 2:1–3:13. And the first three chapters provide the context for the moral exhortations that begin at 4:1. Ephesians invites the contemporary church, too, not just to pray but to set our theology and ethics in the context of such prayerful attention to God. Theology then would not talk of God as though God were merely another object in the world for objective and scientific investigation, some object to be talked about dispassionately. Rather theology would talk of God as the one we face in adoration and praise, the one who prompts expressions of gratitude and repentance, as the one upon whom we depend and to whom we bring our petitions. It would talk of God in response to God's grace in making us agents of God's cause, in response to the blessings of God, including that great blessing by which we are enabled and called to bless God. Theology would find its character and its context in prayer.

And as in Ephesians, our own talk about the common life, about our character and conduct and community, about ethics, would also be set in the context of prayerful attention to God. Prayer is certainly part of the Christian life. Indeed, it is, as John Calvin said, the most important part, "the chief exercise of faith."[5] But more than that, it is

---

5. John Calvin, *Institutes of the Christian Religion*, title of 3.20; ed. John T. McNeill, trans. Ford Lewis Battles, LCC 20–21 (Philadelphia: Westminster Press, 1960), 2:850.

the part of the whole Christian life that cannot be left out without the whole ceasing to be the Christian life. As Karl Barth has said, the Christian life is a life of prayer, a life of "humble and resolute, frightened and joyful invocation of the gracious God in gratitude, praise, and above all petition."[6]

We can begin to see some of the connections between prayer and the Christian life if we consider Alasdair MacIntyre's definition of a practice. A practice, he said, is

> a form of socially established cooperative human activity through which goods internal to that form of activity are realized in the course of trying to achieve those standards of excellence which are appropriate to, and partially definitive of, that form of activity with the result that human powers to achieve excellence and human conceptions of the ends and goods involved are systematically extended.[7]

It is not, we grant, a particularly easy passage. It rivals Ephesians for the length of the sentence. But it is an illuminating passage.

Prayer is a practice, a "socially established cooperative human activity." Christians learn to pray in community—by praying. The *berakot*, for example, was learned in Jewish community, adopted and adapted by Jewish Christians, and Gentile Christians initiated into the church are also here (if not before) initiated into this particular practice of prayer.

In learning to pray, Christians learn as well the good that is "internal to that form of activity." In learning to pray they do not learn a technology to achieve certain extrinsic goods. In learning to pray they learn a practice—and the good intrinsic to that practice. They learn, that is, to attend to God, to look to God. And they learn that not just intellectually, not just as an idea. In learning to pray, they learn a human activity that engages their bodies as well as their minds, their affections and passions and loyalties as well as their rationality, and that focuses their lives and their common life upon God. To

---

6. Karl Barth, *Church Dogmatics* IV/4, *Lecture Fragments: The Christian Life*, trans. Geoffrey Bromiley (Grand Rapids: Eerdmans, 1981), 43.

7. Alasdair MacIntyre, *After Virtue: A Study of Moral Theory* (Notre Dame: University of Notre Dame Press, 1981), 175.

attend to God is not easy to learn—or painless. And given our invet-
erate attention to ourselves and to our own needs and wants, we
frequently corrupt it. We corrupt prayer whenever we turn it into a
technology, into a means to accomplish some other good than the
good of prayer, whenever we make of it an instrument to achieve
wealth or happiness or life or health or moral improvement. In learning to pray, Christians learn to look to God and, after the blinding
vision, to begin to look at all else in a new light. In prayer they do not
attend to something beyond God that God—or prayer—might be
used in order to reach; they attend to God. That is the good intrinsic
to prayer, the good "internal to that form of activity," simple attention to God.[8]

In learning to pray, they learn as well certain "standards of excellence" that belong to prayer and its attention to God, that are "appropriate to" prayer and "partially definitive" of prayer. Calvin identified
some of these when he listed his "rules" of prayer: reverence, sincer-
ity, humility, and hopeful confidence.[9] Our own list is (unsurprisingly)
similar. In learning to pray, Christians learn *reverence*, the readiness
to attend to God as God and to attend to all else in their lives as
related to God. They learn *humility*, the readiness to acknowledge
that we are not gods but the creatures of God, cherished by God but
finite and mortal and, yes, sinful creatures in need finally of God's
grace and God's future. They learn *gratitude*, a disposition of thankfulness for the opportunities to delight in God and in the gifts of
God. Attentive to God, they grow attentive also to the neighbor as
related to God; in learning to pray, they learn to *care*, to care even
for those the culture would teach us to shun and to despise. Looking to God they learn *hope*, a disposition of confidence and courage that comes not from trusting ourselves and the little truth we
think we know well or the little good we think we do well, but from
trusting the grace and power and cause of God. These standards
of excellence form virtues not only for prayer but also for daily life.
The prayer-formed person—in the whole of her being and in all of

8. On prayer as attention see especially Iris Murdoch, "On 'God' and 'Good,'" in *Revisions:
Changing Perspectives in Moral Philosophy*, ed. Stanley Hauerwas and Alasdair MacIntyre
(Notre Dame: University of Notre Dame Press, 1983), 68–91.
9. *Institutes* 3.20.4–16.

her doing—will be reverent, humble, grateful, caring, and hopeful.[10] The prayer-formed community will be marked by the same standards of excellence; it too will be reverent, humble, grateful, caring, and hopeful. Christians do not pray in order to achieve these virtues; they are not formed when we use prayer as a technique. Nevertheless, they are formed in the practice of prayer with its standards of excellence; they are formed in simple attentiveness to God; and they spill over into new virtues for daily life—and for the common life.

No wonder then that Calvin could call prayer the "chief exercise of faith." No wonder then that Barth could call the Christian life a life of prayer, a life of "invocation." No wonder then that Ephesians sets the Christian life in the context of prayer. Perhaps we can begin to see the links between our performance of this practice and our performance of our calling, the connection between these standards of excellence and the virtues that belong to common life in the church. At least we may be able to envision what MacIntyre suggested in the last clause of his definition, that "the result [of such a practice with its 'internal good' and its 'standards of excellence' is] that human powers to achieve excellence and human conceptions of the ends and goods involved are systematically extended."

Consider also the forms that prayer may take, the forms of attention to God. We have noted that Ephesians begins with a *berakot*, a form of prayer that was and is commonplace in Jewish communities but that has been largely lost among Christians. This blessing God for God's blessings reminded us that we are agents by God's grace, dependent upon God but called to participate freely in God's cause of blessing. We do not need here to say more about this form of attention to God. But while earlier we distinguished the *berakot* from other acts of praise and thanksgiving, it shares with virtually every form of prayer this feature, that it calls upon God as the one who is worthy of our praise, our adoration, and our lives in "praise of God's glory." Prayer is invocation; it is to call upon God.

To call upon God is to recall who God is and what God has done. It requires remembrance, for we invoke not just any old god, not

---

10. See Donald Saliers, "Liturgy and Ethics: Some New Beginnings," *Journal of Religious Ethics* 7 (Fall 1979): 173–89. Because prayer is a "characterizing activity," the standards of excellence that belong to prayer are formed in those who practice prayer.

some nameless god of philosophical theism, not some idolatrous object of someone's "ultimate concern," but the God remembered in religious community and in its Scripture. We invoke a particular God. But this God is invoked as Lord of all things. This particular God is the God of the universe. This God is not some tribal deity. He is God of both Jew and Gentile, God of all races, and Lord of all nations. If we invoke some God who shares and sponsors our particular cultures of enmity, then our invocations—and our lives—need correction, and Ephesians can provide it.

Invocation is remembrance, and remembrance is not just recollection but the way identity and community are constituted. So we invoke the God made known in mighty works and great promises, and as we do we are oriented to that God and to all things in relation to that God. Ephesians invokes God—and blesses God—as the fountain of every blessing. When we invoke God as creator, we learn to regard all that God has made as good and to regard nothing God made as God. When we invoke God as redeemer, we learn not to deny the fault that runs through our world and through our lives but to look to God to correct the fault, to rescue us from the power of sin and death, and to straighten out the world God made good. We call upon God in remembrance that God has heard the cries of those who hurt, that God has cared. We call upon God in remembrance of a crucified Messiah, one who suffered and died. On that cross the truth about our world was nailed. The truth about our world is dripping with blood and hanging on a Roman cross, the symbol of an empire's power. The truth about our world is the power of sin and death, at once terrifying and banal. But that same cross reveals also another truth about our world. It reminds us not only of the reality and power of evil but also of the real presence of God in the midst of our suffering and of the constant care of God. And when we call upon God as the one who raised this Jesus from the dead, we know again that God has vindicated both God's own faithfulness and this Jesus as the one who makes known and real God's cause in the world.

In invocation and remembrance all the other forms of attention to God are given birth. Having called upon God, we move quite naturally to prayers of thanksgiving. Attention to God prompts us to give thanks for gifts both great and small. And among those gifts are opportunities to fulfill some tasks both great and small. Attentive to God and to the cause of God, we give thanks for the good gifts of the creation and for the grace by which we are given a share in redemption. We give thanks for opportunities to delight in our friends and families and for opportunities to be reconciled with an enemy. Thanksgiving is a form of attention to God, a form prayer often takes—and it is a fundamental feature of the Christian life!

Thanksgiving is the joyful response to the goodness and grace of God. That grace always goes before us, and it always calls us to gratitude. According to Romans 1:21 the root sin of humanity was the failure to honor God as God and to "give thanks" to God. And the root virtue for the Christian life is gratitude.

Gratitude

Q. We have been delivered from our misery by God's grace alone through Christ and not because we have earned it: why then must we still do good?

A. To be sure, Christ has redeemed us by his blood. But we do good because Christ by his Spirit is also renewing us to be like himself, so that in all our living we may show that we are thankful to God for what he has done for us, and so that he may be praised by us.

　　　—Heidelberg Catechism,
　　　　Lord's Day 32, Q & A 86

Little wonder then that Ephesians calls for thankfulness (5:4, 20). Indeed, its call for thankfulness seems a little extravagant when it instructs its hearers to give thanks "to God the Father at all times and for everything in the name of our Lord Jesus Christ" (5:20). We will have to return to that verse later in the commentary. For now it is enough to say that it need not be read as a numbing requirement to give thanks when, for example, a child is killed by a drunk driver or when a soldier is killed in an unjust war. To be sure, even then one may give thanks that God is present, that God cares for us in the midst of suffering, and that we may be sure God's cause will triumph over sin and death. And even then one may give thanks that one may learn compassion in suffering endured, that one may find the courage in faith simply to get out of bed after such a loss. But as long as the lament psalms are part of the canon, we need not always be thankful, not for everything. To put it differently, we may give thanks to God that we do not always have to give thanks. We may be grateful that we do not always have to be grateful. We may lament.

Surely lament is another form of attention to God, another form prayer takes.[11] There is no explicit prayer of lament in Ephesians, but it knows that the good future that God has made known in Christ is not yet, still sadly not yet. It knows that the power of evil is still at work (2:2) in spite of the resurrection of Jesus. It aches for the final triumph of God when there will be peace. It is not hard to imagine that someone among those who heard Ephesians read on that Sunday morning would attend to God in the form of a lament. Following the pattern of lament she might invoke God, give voice to a complaint about some injustice or about the hold that enmity has on the world or about the suffering endured in an effort to be faithful. She might pray to God finally to set the world straight, and she might close her prayer with the certainty of a hearing, an expression of confidence that God's good future is sure to be. Until that day, however, lament remains an appropriate form of attention to God and to the cause of God. Until that day when all will be thankfulness and praise, Christians will share the groaning of the creation and the suffering of humanity, and they will give it voice. To look to God is not to look away. The grace of God does not call us to Stoic indifference. It calls us sometimes to mourn, to be those "aching visionaries"[12] who long for God's good future and who weep because it is not yet, still sadly not yet.

Moreover, prayers of confession belong to the category of lament. And although there is no explicit prayer of confession in Ephesians, either, the letter surely would evoke confession from those Jews and Gentiles who had found it difficult to embrace the

11. Much excellent work has been done recently on lament. On lament in Scripture see, for example, the collection of Walter Brueggemann's writings on the Psalms in Patrick D. Miller, ed., *The Psalms and the Life of Faith: Walter Brueggemann* (Minneapolis: Fortress Press, 1995). On reclaiming lament as a practice of the church see, for example, Kathleen D. Billman and Daniel L. Migliore, *Rachel's Cry: Prayers of Lament and Rebirth of Hope* (Cleveland: United Church Press, 1999); and Sally A. Brown and Patrick D. Miller, eds., *Lament: Reclaiming Practices in Pulpit, Pew, and Public Square* (Louisville: Westminster John Knox Press, 2005).
12. Nicholas Wolterstorff, *Lament for a Son* (Grand Rapids: Eerdmans, 1987), 86.

other. Ephesians knows that the church has not always lived in ways that are worthy of its calling, in ways that are fitting to the gospel of peace. It is not hard to imagine that someone else among those who heard Ephesians read on that day would attend to God in the form of a confession. Following the pattern of lament he might invoke God, give voice to his sorrow about an injustice he committed or about the hold that enmity has on him or about his unwillingness to suffer for the sake of God's cause in the world. Here again there could be at the end the certainty of a hearing, an expression of confidence in God's grace. Those who would be attentive to God, who invoke God, move quite naturally to prayers of confession, for those oriented to God and to the cause of God are reoriented to all else. It is called *metanoia*, a turning, repentance. Confession is good for the soul, but it is also good for community. The honest recognition of our own fallibility can make us more patient with the failings of others. It can help us to be critical without condescension and helpful without conceit.

There is yet another form of attention to God. We move quite naturally also from the invocation of God to petition. Perhaps we move too quickly to petition, too carelessly. It is tempting to regard prayer as a kind of magic to get what we want, a way to put God at our disposal. But real and simple attention to God will be attentive first to what God wants, to God's cause, and will put ourselves finally at God's disposal. Then we will form our petitions on the model of the one who taught us to pray. We will pray that God's name and power will be hallowed, that God's kingdom may come, that God's future will be established "speedily and soon."[13] Because that good future is already established in the resurrection of Jesus from the dead, we may pray—and pray boldly—as the Lord taught us, for a taste of that future, for a taste of it in such ordinary things as everyday bread and everyday forgiveness, in such ordinary things as tonight's rest and tomorrow's life, in such mundane stuff as a little justice. Attentive to God and to God's cause, we will pray for—and work for—the healing of bodies and communities and, indeed, the

---

13. A phrase from the Kaddish, the Jewish prayer that was surely used by those who taught Jesus to pray.

whole creation. But because that good future is not yet, we may continue to lament and to pray no less boldly for the presence of the one who suffers with us, the one who made the human cry of lament his own cry. Our petitions—and our lives—will be governed by the cause of God, by the revelation of God's will and way.

In all of these forms of attention to God the Christian life is shaped.

Prayer as the Chief Exercise of Faith

Calvin describes prayer as "the chief exercise of faith." . . . The language of "exercise" suggests that there is an active dimension of prayer, that it is an endeavor that requires our attention and discipline in our daily lives. Indeed, Calvin himself says, "It is, therefore, by the benefit of prayer that we reach those riches which are laid up for us. . . . We dig up by prayer the treasures that were pointed out by the Lord's gospel, and which our faith has gazed upon." It is not enough to sit back and acknowledge God from a distance. God is around, beneath, before, and beside us all the time, but if we never actively stop to notice this, to call out a breath of thanksgiving or petition, lament or praise, then we live falsely, pretending that we live as independent beings. Prayer requires our attention so that we might have our eyes opened to the way things really are.

—Martha L. Moore-Keish

Christian Prayer for Today (Louisville: Westminster John Knox Press, 2009), 83.

1:15–23

The Prayer for the Church, Part One

That They May Know Their Hope

Paul moves from blessing God to his petitions for the church almost seamlessly. He pauses at the end of his praise to commend the Christians of the Lycus Valley. He has heard, he says, of their faith and love (1:15), and those reports have prompted prayers of thanksgiving. Given the familiar triad of faith, hope, and love, one might ask why he does not also give thanks for their hope. The reason, we think, is that there was a crisis of hope in the churches of the Lycus Valley. They may not have recognized it as a crisis of hope, but they seem to have forgotten or neglected the "secret" that God had made known to them, the "plan for the fullness of time," to "gather up all things" in Christ (1:10). At any rate, Paul turns immediately from his report of prayers of thanksgiving to pray for them, and the burden of his prayer is that they "may know what is the hope to which [God] has called [them]" (1:18).

The prayer echoes the opening *berakot*. God is invoked as "the God of our Lord Jesus Christ, the Father of glory" (1:17; cf. 1:3). The petitions themselves echo the remembrance of God's blessings, particularly the blessing of having been let in on the secret. Paul had blessed God because God "has made known to us the mystery of his will" (1:9), and now he prays to God that "you may know what is the hope to which he has called you" (1:18). One might ask, we suppose, whether God had made it known. The problem is only apparent, resolved by the eschatological reservation that attends our knowledge. Now we "know only in part," but in God's good future we "will know fully," even as we are "fully known" (1 Cor. 13:12). And there is another echo; the climax of the *berakot*, the secret, the "plan for the fullness [*plērōmatos*] of time, to gather up [*anakephalaiōsesthai ta panta*] all things in him" (Eph. 1:9–10), is surely echoed in the climactic conclusion of this prayer, that God has "made him the head over all things [*kephalēn hyper panta*] for the church, which is his body, the fullness of him who fills all in all [*to plērōma tou ta panta en pasin plēroumenou*]" (1:22–23).

Paul's prayer is an example of pleonasm, seldom satisfied with one word or phrase where two or three (usually three) will do better. Pleonasm may be regarded by the prosaic as redundancy, but the prayer is anything but prosaic, and the pleonasm is fitting to the surpassing significance of his petition. It is as though the language is impoverished, unable to contain either "the praise of [God's] glory" or the riches of their "inheritance." So he piles phrase upon phrase, all pointing to the same good future of God: "the hope to which he has called you, . . . the riches of his glorious inheritance, . . . the immeasurable greatness of his power for us who believe" (1:18–19).

This hope is immeasurable—and almost unspeakable. But Paul speaks it anyway. It is what he does. He proclaims the risen Lord. And there, in the resurrection of Jesus the Messiah from the dead, he finds the basis and the measure of the "hope" and the "inheritance" and the "greatness of his power." Their hope, our hope, is in accord with ("according to") the great power that God displayed when God "raised [Jesus] from the dead" (1:19–20).

But once more words fail. The measure of their hope is the resurrection; the riches of their inheritance is in accord with the resurrection; but the power displayed in raising Jesus from the dead has no human measure either. So again Paul piles up phrase upon phrase in 1:20–23 to attempt to take the measure of the resurrection. It is pleonasm, but there is not a wasted word. There is no redundancy. God raised Jesus *from* the dead, to be sure, but that is not yet the full measure of God's power or of their hope. So he adds another phrase. God raised Jesus *to* God's right hand. There "in the heavenly places" the risen Christ sits enthroned "far above all rule and authority and power and dominion" (1:21).

At this point Paul might have pointed the church to Psalm 82, a psalm envisioning God's judgment "in the midst of the gods." The "gods" of the nations are judged for their injustice, for their failure to "give justice to the weak and the orphan" and to "maintain the right of the lowly and the destitute" (82:3). And the judgment is in God's word, "You are gods, children of the Most High, all of you; nevertheless, you shall die like mortals, and fall like any prince" (82:6–7). After that vision, the psalm concludes, "Rise up, O God, judge the earth; for all the nations belong to you" (82:8). God has indeed risen up in raising Jesus from the dead, and all the principalities and powers, all the gods of the nations, sponsoring injustice and enmity, are judged.

Paul turns instead, however, to another psalm, to Psalm 8, and adds another phrase in his effort to measure the power of the resurrection and their hope. God raised Jesus *from* the dead and *to* sovereignty over the powers . . . and "put all things under his feet." The phrase repeats the claim of the risen Christ's sovereignty over the powers, but by the citation of Psalm 8:6 it links the victory over the powers both to the renewal of humanity and to the Christian hope.

Psalm 8 is a song of praise, beginning and ending with "O LORD, our Sovereign, how majestic is your name in all the earth" (Ps. 8:1, 9). It expresses the "praise of his glory" that the *berakot* had expressed and that "we [Jewish Christians]" and "you [Gentile Christians]" were called to express (and be) in their lives. In Psalm 8 God "set [God's] glory above the heavens" (8:1); nevertheless, little children can know of it and sing of it. The same heavens that reminded the psalmist of God's glory also prompted, however, a sense of the insignificance of humanity and the question, "What are human beings that you are mindful of them?" (8:4). The psalmist then answers his own question by remembering the creation: "Yet you have made them a little lower than God" (8:5), and he continues, "You have given them dominion over the works of your hands; you have put all things under their feet" (8:6). What a magnificent creature a human being is! And how majestic the Creator!

But the psalmist's response to his own question may prompt a question of our own. Is it true? It may have been true at the creation (Gen. 1:26), but is it still true? Human beings seem to have forfeited the magnificence of their creation. A dash of realism seems to be called for. As the author of Hebrews says in quoting this same psalm, "As it is, we do not yet see everything in subjection to them" (Heb. 2:8). Then he says, "But we do see Jesus, who for a little while was made lower than the angels, now crowned with glory and honor" (Heb. 2:9; following the Septuagint [LXX], Hebrews had translated Ps. 8:5 as "You have made them for a little while lower than the angels," the divine beings, the angelic powers; see Heb. 2:7). We do not yet see humanity in the splendor of its creation or the angelic powers in service to humanity, "but we do see Jesus"!

Paul makes the same move here. He reads Psalm 8:6 as a reference to the risen Christ without leaving behind its reference to humanity. We may still ask whether it is true of humanity, but when we are let in on the secret, the mystery, we have an answer to that question. It is true of Jesus, the Son of Man, and because it is true of Jesus, we may know it is God's plan that it will be true of humanity as well. Humanity may have forfeited its magnificence, but in Jesus the Messiah it is restored, renewed. The angelic beings, the principalities and the powers, may for a time lord it over humanity, pressing human beings into their service and nurturing their alienation from God, from each other, and from the good creation. "But we do see Jesus," the one who reveals both God and our own true humanity, the glorious destiny that fits our good creation. We do see Jesus, the new humanity!

Paul goes on then, adding one more phrase in the effort to measure the power of the resurrection and our hope. The phrase emphasizes the solidarity of the risen Christ with the church. (It is the first time Paul explicitly mentions the church, even if it is not the first hint that Ephesians displays an ecclesial ethic.) This concluding phrase is clearly climactic, but it is notoriously difficult to translate. Without pausing to defend our translation of 1:22b–23 over against others, let us simply provide it: "[God] has given him [that is, Christ], the head of all things, to the church, which is his body, filled by the one who fills all things completely."[1]

---

1. "[God] has given [*edōken*] him [that is, Christ], the head of all things [an 'accusative used predicatively' (C. F. D. Moule, *An Idiom Book of New Testament Greek*, 2nd ed. [Cambridge: Cambridge University Press, 1960], 35)] to the church [not 'a dative of advantage' but a more natural dative], which is his body, filled [taking *plērōma* in a passive rather than active sense]

It is the secret made known, the "plan for the fullness of time, to gather up all things in [Christ]" (1:10), in action. In the *berakot* the plan of God had been put in this way, that all things would be brought together and renewed, with Christ "the head of all things." The God we are called to praise is no particularistic cult deity. This God is no tribal deity. This is not the sort of God who can be enticed to do us a favor now and then by the right sort of ritual observance. This God is the God of "all things," the God of the universe, the God of the whole creation, the one by whom all things were made and the one who will bring all things to their completion, to their perfection, the one who unites all things in peaceable difference.

In this climactic clause (1:22b–23) the same thought is reiterated. Leave the church out of this verse and it becomes an account of God making Christ the head of all things and in that way bringing all things to fulfillment. But Paul does not leave the church out of it! The church is not just a spectator in God's action, it is blessed to be part of God's project, an agent. God gave Christ, who is made the head of all things in the resurrection, to the church, not as our possession but as our Lord too, as our head too. And the church is his "body."

That the church is the "body" of Christ is a familiar Pauline theme. The Corinthians, for example, had been reminded, "Now you are the body of Christ and individually members of it" (1 Cor. 12:28). There has been much debate about where Paul got this idea. Arguments can be made that he got it from Stoicism or from Gnosticism or from OT notions of "corporate personality" or from rabbinic speculation about the body of Adam or from the Eucharist of the church. We will not attempt to resolve that scholarly dispute. But whatever the original source of this image of the body, it would surely have been shaped in Pauline communities by the language of the Eucharist.

---

by the one who fills [taking *plēroumenou* as a 'dynamic middle' participle, which serves the purpose of emphasizing the subject in the verb's action (James Hope Moulton, *A Grammar of New Testament Greek*, vol. 1, *Prolegomena*, 3rd ed. [Edinburgh: T. & T. Clark, 1908], 152)] all things completely [*en pasin*]." Besides the grammatical possibility of this translation we would point to the parallel in the temple imagery at the end of chap. 2. The temple was filled with the glory of the Lord (1 Kgs. 8:11), the very glory that would finally fill the whole earth (Ps. 72:18–19). See the commentary below on 2:20–22.

Ephesians does not mention the Eucharist, but the churches it addressed surely observed it, and they had been formed by the Eucharist to think of Christ's "body" in distinctive ways. In the Eucharist the bread is called the "body" of Christ, and that bread, that "body," is shared in Communion. "The bread that we break, is it not a sharing in the body of Christ? Because there is one bread, we who are many are one body, for we all partake of the one bread" (1 Cor. 10:16b–17). Little wonder, then, that Paul admonished the Corinthians for not "discerning the body" when they observed the Supper in ways that humiliated the poor (1 Cor. 11:17–29). And one need not wonder whether the churches at Ephesus were reminded of the unity that they were given in Christ and to which they were called by Christ when they heard this reference to "the church, which is his body."

But there were other associations too, associations also formed by the Eucharist. That bread, that "body," is given "for you" (1 Cor. 11:24). The bread—and the body—is a means by which the risen Lord is present and made manifest. It is a token of the eschatological banquet and of God's good future. What the bread is to the church, the church is to the world. It is the body given for others, called to mission. It is the body that makes—or should make—Christ and the cause of God manifest in the world. It is the body that provides—or should provide—a little foretaste of God's good future.

To call the bread the "body of Christ" does not, we think, require a doctrine of transubstantiation, but it is more than mere metaphor. And to call the church the "body of Christ" does not, we think, require some doctrine of an "extension of incarnation." The church is not Christ; the church is not the Messiah; but to call the church the "body of Christ" is again more than mere metaphor. The church is not Christ, but it is intimately related to Christ. It exists in solidarity with Christ, "in Christ." It does not substitute for the absent Christ; it is dependent upon the risen Christ. And it is made an agent of God's cause. The church is Christ's "body" by being a means by which Christ is present in the world, by being a way Christ—and the secret—are made manifest in the world. It can only fulfill that calling by being the one "body" of Christ, by the oneness of the many members. It serves the cause of God in the world as an agent in "gathering up all things" and as a foretaste of that good future.

There is one other point apropos this image. The body is but a corpse without the life-giving Spirit. In the Genesis story the mud becomes a living being when God breathes into it. The life of the body depends on "the breath" of God, the Spirit of God (see Eph. 1:13). It is absolutely dependent upon the breath and the blessing of God. It is Christ who "fills" the body, who gives it life. We are made alive together in him (2:5). And it is Christ finally who "fills all things completely." The church is not the Christ, but the risen Christ gives life to the church, making it an agent, empowering it to serve God's cause.

This is blessing, but it is also demanding. The church is blessed and called to make Christ manifest, to be filled with Christ and to serve the Christ who brings all things to their completion and perfection in the good future of God. In that way it also serves both God and the world, an agent itself in God's project of blessing and renewing the cosmos.

This prayer for the church was a prayer that they "may know what is the hope to which [God] has called [them]" (1:18). This knowledge is hardly a matter of tongue and head alone; this knowledge must, as Calvin said, "enter our heart and pass into our daily living, and so transform us into itself that it may not be unfruitful for us."[2] It must be lived, performed. We do not know whether it was "fruitful" in the lives and the common life of the churches of the Lycus Valley. But it must somehow be "fruitful" in our lives and in the common life of our churches. How can this knowledge be "fruitful" for us? How shall we perform this hope?

The Blemished Body of Christ

I see the church as the body of Christ. But, oh! How we have blemished and scarred that body through social neglect and fear of being nonconformist.

—Martin Luther King Jr.

Letter from Birmingham Jail (Philadelphia: American Friends Service Committee, 1963), 12.

---

2. Calvin, *Institutes of the Christian Religion* 3.6.4; ed. John T. McNeill, trans. Ford Lewis Battles, LCC 20–21 (Philadelphia: Westminster Press, 1960), 1:688.

Clearly, the church has not always performed it well. But how could we perform it better? How can we participate in God's project, making manifest the power of God and our inheritance? How can we make manifest that it is Christ who is supreme over the principalities and powers? How can we show that Christ has shown our true humanity? Those questions must be put off for now, but Ephesians may well help us with them.

FURTHER REFLECTIONS
The Powers

In giving some account of Christ's sovereignty over the powers, Ephesians 1:21 says that Christ is seated "far above all rule and authority and power and dominion, and above every name that is named, not only in this age but also in the age to come." This is the first mention of the "powers" in Ephesians, but it will not be the last. They will be mentioned again in 2:2, 3:10, and 6:12, and they are always there in the background of this letter, a kind of leitmotif to the claim of Christ's sovereignty.

The author is not inventing a concept here. The concept was familiar to first-century Jews and Gentiles, among whom it was widely agreed that there were unseen forces at work in the world, heavenly beings who exercised power on the earth.[3] These "powers" were real, and they influenced life on earth.

Among the Jews the concept of the "powers" may be traced both to the angels who served as "messengers" of God, carrying out various assigned tasks, and to the many "gods" who claimed

3. This has been widely recognized since Martin Dibelius published his pioneering study, *Die Geisterwelt im Glauben des Paulus* (Göttingen: Vandenhoeck & Ruprecht, 1909). A number of excellent studies have examined the concept of the "powers." A select bibliography would include Hendrikus Berkhof, *Christ and the Powers* (Scottdale, PA: Herald Press, 1962); G. B. Caird, *Principalities and Powers* (Oxford: Clarendon Press, 1956); Clinton D. Morrison, *The Powers That Be* (Naperville, IL: Allenson, 1960); and a series of books by Walter Wink, *Naming the Powers: The Language of Power in the New Testament* (Philadelphia: Fortress, 1984); *Unmasking the Powers: The Invisible Forces that Determine Human Existence* (Philadelphia: Fortress Press, 1986); and *Engaging the Powers: Discernment and Resistance in a World of Domination* (Philadelphia: Fortress Press, 1992). We also recommend a book on preaching by Charles L. Campbell, *The Word before the Powers: An Ethic of Preaching* (Louisville: Westminster John Knox Press, 2002).

sovereignty, whether over fertility, like the nature deities, or over nations, like various national deities. Israel's monotheism, after all, was not so much theoretical as practical. Israel rejected the worship of other gods, but it did not always deny their existence. To be sure, the prophets sometimes did, mocking the idols and those who worshiped them. But there was in the Old Testament frequently a lively struggle between God and the gods, between God and Baal, for example, and between God and the gods of the nations that held the people captive. Still, as those struggles made manifest, there is only one God who is truly sovereign. And there is only one God to whom loyalty is due. That one God is the God of both creation and covenant. That one God, the psalmist proclaims, is "a great King above all gods" (Ps. 95:3). According to Deuteronomy 32:8, when God had "apportioned the nations," God assigned one each to these minor deities;[4] and in the vision of another psalmist, when God took "his place in the divine council," he condemned "the gods" for their injustice and oppression (Ps. 82).

These "gods" get demoted to angelic powers in Jewish apocalyptic literature, but there they become much more frequently the topic of reflection and speculation. They still influence life on earth, both by upholding the structures of the cosmos (see, e.g., *2 Enoch* 19) and by leading nations. Sometimes these angelic powers function as directed by God, but sometimes they usurp God's authority (e.g., *1 Enoch* 89:59–64) and act in opposition to God (e.g., Dan. 10:13, 20). There is, in a good deal of apocalyptic literature, a cosmic conflict between God and the rebellious powers who try to assert their own sovereignty (hopelessly) against the sovereignty of God.

Among the Gentiles the concept of the "powers" would not be difficult to understand. They had their own ideas about the "powers" and "world rulers." In general, as Clinton Morrison concludes, among the Gentiles in the Greco-Roman period "the world was considered subject to the guardianship and authority of gods, spirits, and *daimones*."[5] The place and power of a plurality of divine beings

---

4. Following the text found at Qumran (4QDeut) and the LXX. The Masoretic Text is different. See the marginal note in NRSV.

5. Morrison, *Powers That Be*, 76.

was manifest in astrology, in magic, and not least in the cult of the emperor.

Nowhere in Paul or in the rest of the New Testament are the "principalities and powers" made a discrete topic of instruction. But their existence is assumed by both author and audience, whether Jew or Gentile, and they are frequently mentioned (as in Eph. 1:21) when the complete sovereignty of Christ is affirmed (see also, e.g., Rom. 8:38–39; 1 Cor. 15:24–26; Col. 1:16).

When they are mentioned, they are given a bewildering assortment of titles. In Ephesians 1:21 alone we find *archai* (usually "rulers"; Eph. 3:10; 6:12; Rom. 8:38; 1 Cor. 15:24) and *exousia* ("authorities"; Eph. 3:10; 6:12; 1 Cor. 15:24; Col. 1:16; 2:10, 15) and *dynameis* ("powers"; Rom. 8:38; 1 Cor. 15:24) and *kyriotetos* ("dominions"; Col. 1:16). And the list is not exhaustive. Ephesians 1:21 adds a reference to "every name [*onamatos*] that is named." And elsewhere additional titles are given: *pneumatika* ("spiritual forces"; Eph. 6:12) and *kosmokratoras* ("world rulers"; Eph. 6:12) and *archonta* ("rulers"; Eph. 2:2; 1 Cor. 2:6, 8), *thronoi* ("thrones"; Col. 1:16) and *theoi kai kyrioi* ("gods and lords"; 1 Cor. 8:5), and *stoicheia* ("elemental spirits"; Gal. 4:3, 9; Col. 2:8, 29).[6] Clearly these are terms for "spiritual beings," but they are no less clearly social and political terms, and they can be used quite straightforwardly to refer to human agents, social structures, and cosmic elements. They refer to realities at once "spiritual" and "secular," at once visible and invisible. Or to make the same point differently, the modern distinction between the "spiritual" and the "secular" powers was not made in the first century. These terms refer to the realities of our cultural, social, and political existence, realities that were no less crucial for them than they are for us, realities that are no less mysterious for us than they were for them, powers that were and remain complex, ambiguous, and problematical.

According to Paul these "powers" were (and are) part of the creation (Rom. 8:38–39; Col. 1:15–17), part of that which God made and called "good." They were not independent of God or antithetical to God in the beginning. The cosmic dualism of apocalyptic does

6. See further Wink, *Naming the Powers*, 1–35.

not go all the way down. They were (and are) the underpinnings of creation and of a common life, perhaps roughly equivalent to the "orders of creation." God set them in place to hold the world together, to preserve it in God's love. That is obvious enough in the case of the angelic powers related to the ordering of natural processes, day and night, seed and harvest. But it is also true for those powers related to social and political life. The proximate contexts of human life were created good. Political authority, for example, and the spiritual power associated with it are good gifts of the Creator. Political authority was not initiated with the fall of humanity. Even without the fall somebody would have to decide what time lunch would be served and what schedule the trains can keep without colliding with each other. Without government there would be chaos. Even after the fall, governments are necessary. Indeed, they are more necessary; they are servants of God to keep chaos from overwhelming our common life (see Rom. 13:1–5). They are still part of the good creation of God, intended for the good of creation and of humanity. But they have been corrupted.

We do not know them now or experience them now simply as God intended them to function, as ministers of God's cause in the world. We know them now as corrupted and co-opted by the mysterious power of sin in the world. Because of human sin these angelic powers have been transformed into demonic powers, and the political and economic and cultural structures that shape our social life have been transformed into demonic structures. They still hold the world together, but humanity regards them now not as part of God's creation but as the gods of creation. In this demonic reversal, they become no longer the servants of God but our lords. They are the "rulers of this age" (1 Cor. 2:6). They, rather than God, are made the basis of our confidence and hope; they, rather than God, receive our loyalty and provide our identity and community; they enslave us (Gal. 4:8). In humanity's revolt from God, the powers were ascribed an ultimacy that is not their own. The powers thus usurped God's ultimacy.

The "powers" are part of the good creation of God, but they have been co-opted and corrupted by the power of sin. Given this corruption, governments are tempted to tyranny. They are tempted to surround themselves with sacred authority, to pretend to possess an absolute power that is not their own. The fallen nature of the powers may be discerned (1) in claims to divine authority, (2) in confusing a nation's self-interest with God's cause, (3) in tyrannical oppression of the poor, (4) in a rhetoric that nurtures enmity and denies to the enemy their identity as the cherished children of God, and (5) in the confidence that the national interest (and God's cause) can be secured by violence. The Roman Empire may serve as an example. Rome had its cult of the emperor. And it boasted about the Pax Romana, and made Pax a goddess. But the Pax Romana was built on the backs of slaves and secured by violence and Mars, the god of war. Rome displayed the bestiality of empire, depicted by the beasts of Daniel and Revelation.

The "powers" are part of the good creation of God, but they have been co-opted and corrupted by the power of sin. They may continue to preserve the world from chaos, but they do it now not simply as servants of God but as gods that enslave us. The most important word, however, is yet to be said. Let Ephesians say it: God has raised Jesus Christ to sovereignty over the powers (1:20–21). Let Colossians say it: Christ "disarmed the rulers and authorities and made a public example of them, triumphing over them" (Col. 2:15). God in Christ has triumphed over the powers in the cross and resurrection. They are shown up as usurpers of God's power, unmasked as false gods, disclosed as desperate and unjust and hopeless pretenders to divine power. It is God who is God, not these powers. It is Christ who is

> **Gods of the Cosmos**
>
> When Hitler took the helm in Germany in 1933, the powers of *Volk*, race, and state took a new grip on men. Thousands were grateful, after the confusion of the preceding years, to find their lives again protected from chaos, order and security restored. No one could withhold himself, without utmost effort, from the grasp these Powers had on men's inner and outer life. While studying in Berlin (1937) I myself experienced almost literally how such Powers may be "in the air." [See Eph. 2:2.] At the same time one had to see how they intruded as a barrier between God's Word and men. They acted as if they were the gods of the cosmos.
>
> —**Hendrikus Berkhof**
>
> *Christ and the Powers*, trans. John Howard Yoder (Scottdale, PA: Herald Press, 1962), 25.

Lord, not these powers. They are disarmed because their violence is shown up as powerless against God. They are disarmed because the cultures of enmity they nurture in their own self-interest are disclosed as deceptions. Disarmed and unmasked, they lose their tight-fisted hold on humanity. They are put in their place, denied their claims to ultimacy.

To be sure, the cross looked like the victory of the powers, not like a victory over them. But just when the power of sin and death and the powers of empire seemed to have won the battle, God vindicated both his own faithfulness and Jesus, raising him from the dead—and to sovereignty over the powers.

Let it be admitted that it did not look like much had changed. Pontius Pilate still sat on his little throne on the day after Easter. The Roman emperor still gave his little orders commanding his generals not to worry about a little collateral damage. Neither the earthly rulers nor the angelic powers that stand behind them simply and suddenly admitted defeat. The struggle continued (6:12). But the outcome was certain. These Christians of the Lycus Valley did see Jesus, a "new humanity." And they were invited to participate in his "body," in that "new humanity," in the community that is freed from enslavement to the "powers." In that freedom the church could submit to the authorities when they served as ministers of God preserving some little good or avoiding some great evil, but in that freedom they were ready also to hold them in derision when they acted like gods or resisted God's cause (Ps. 2; Acts 4:23–31).

Freed from enslavement to the powers Christians were to display a politics of their own, a politics of peaceable difference, and they were to resist the formation of their community and character by the cultures of enmity nurtured by the powers, including the Roman Empire. They looked to God to secure their lives and their common life. They formed friendships across the barriers that divided people. And they acknowledged that they were called to serve God's cause in the world, to make manifest to the powers themselves the secret, the plan of God to renew all things, even them, even the powers (Eph. 3:9–10). The church has been let in on the secret of the true source of order in the world. It knows the secret of genuine politics, a common life that conforms to God's plan. But it is a secret not yet fulfilled. In the meanwhile, the church is called to a politics that is new and different, to a politics that displays the firstfruits of God's good future. It is called to a common life that makes manifest something bigger than the church, something going on in the whole creation.

Ephesians had a social ethic, a political posture that may neither be separated from the life of the church nor reduced to it. We grant that we do not typically think of angelic (or demonic) forces as standing behind political powers and events. The concept of the "powers" seems to those of us who take pride in our scientific and secular accounts of the world to call out for demythologizing. And it may be noted that Paul may have set us on that path in a preliminary way, at least in comparison to apocalyptic literature.[7] He puts the stress much more on the governing function of these powers than he does on their being personal angelic beings. It is a secondary point, however, and no one in the first century would have made a tidy split between "spiritual" and "secular." Indeed, perhaps our political reflection should take spiritual realities more seriously. But the primary point is that as strange as it sounds to us, this was the way both Jew and Gentile talked politics in the first century. And Ephesians does not avoid or eliminate such political language. On the contrary, with the language available to its hearers Ephesians insists on the political relevance of the gospel. It does not reduce the gospel to the salvation of souls, not even to the salvation of individuals, not even to the salvation of the church. It was the salvation of the world that they were looking for, a salvation that included the renewal of the institutions and the powers at work in the world. Ephesians talks about these "spiritual rulers" not because Ephesians is so spiritual but rather because it is so political.

7. So Berkhof, *Christ and the Powers*, 17–18.

2:1–10

Saved by Grace:
A New Social Reality

As the *berakot* had prompted Ephesians to reflect on Jew and Gentile and their common calling to live "to the praise of God's glory," so the prayer for the church we have just examined prompts attention to the relation of Jew and Gentile in this section. Paul is not changing the subject to more mundane things; he is bringing their knowledge and hope, their inheritance and the power of the resurrection, to bear on mundane things. The church has been let in on the secret. It knows something of God's plan to gather up all things in Christ, and Paul has prayed that they may know it more fully and live it more faithfully. The church knows what is going on in the world, even if it is hidden from the eyes of emperors and high priests. And those in the church are called to respond to what God has done and is doing and will do in Christ. They are to make the Christ manifest, to make the secret manifest, but how?

God's "plan for the fullness of time" is already happening in the churches. They can and should know what is happening in their very midst. The church is a new social reality, a stunning new thing, Jew and Gentile together in community. The old thing was division, fanned in the time surrounding the Jewish revolutionary war by cultures of enmity. What is going on in the world is that the principalities and powers still assert their doomed reign. What is going on in the churches is something else, the power of God asserting the same power that raised Jesus from the dead and to sovereignty over the powers. They are to make Christ manifest, the secret known, by being the church, by being this community of solidarity and mutual affection, this community of peaceable difference. They are to celebrate the resurrection and anticipate God's good future.

From Death to Life with Christ

Paul takes up the case of the Gentiles first this time. "You," he says, "were dead through [your] trespasses and sins" (2:1). It is a grim picture. Sin and death and the "ruler of the power of the air, the spirit that is now at work among those who are disobedient" (2:2), had hold of them and would not let them go. There is here no denial of the power of sin, death, and the devil. There is no hope for the Gentiles in such a denial. But there is hope in "the immeasurable greatness of [God's] power" that raised Jesus from the dead (1:19). Paul does not make that point immediately, however. He leaves the thought (and the sentence) unfinished in order to consider the Jews.

One can imagine a pious Jewish Christian who was not yet fully convinced that he should make peace with Gentile "sinners" interrupting the sentence with an "Amen, preach it, brother." At any rate, this grim picture of Gentile unrighteousness would not have been unfamiliar to the Jews. But without finishing his opening sentence, Paul includes the Jews in this grim picture. "All of us," he says, were sinners. All of them, the Jews no less than the Gentiles, were in the grip of sin and death. The Jews, "like everyone else," were "children of wrath" (2:3). Such an indictment, of course, was also familiar to the Jews. Amos, for example, after he had condemned the nations around Judah and Israel, aimed his sharpest criticisms precisely at the Jewish nations (Amos 1:3–2:8). Other prophets, too, had indicted Israel and Judah. And the Psalms could be cited to make the point (and they were cited by Paul in Rom. 3:10–18): "There is no one who is righteous, not even one." Jew and Gentile have this sad solidarity as "sinners."

"But . . ." (Eph. 2:4). It is a welcome "but." "But" that grim picture is not the end of the story or the final measure of their solidarity. God, "who is rich in mercy, out of the great love with which he loved us . . . made us alive together with Christ" (2:4–5). The grim picture is matched—and overmatched—by a picture of solidarity with Christ. Once death (2:1, 5), but now life (2:5). Once ensnared in "trespasses and sins" (2:1) and the "children of wrath" (2:3), but now, by God's "mercy," "love," and "grace" (2:4, 5), freed, "created in Christ Jesus for good works" (2:10). Once without hope, but now with an inheritance that surpasses the imagination. Once "you" and "we" in the sad solidarity of "sinners," now just "we" in glad solidarity with Christ.

This transformation is in accord with "the working of [God's] great power" (1:19) in raising Jesus from the dead. With a series of words compounded with *syn* ("with"), Ephesians makes clear that the God who raised Jesus from the dead and set him at God's right hand also "made us alive together *with* him . . . raised us up *with* him and seated us *with* him in the heavenly places" (2:5–6). It is by God's grace and by our solidarity with Christ that this remarkable transformation from death to life is accomplished—for both Jew and Gentile.

There is even a transition in style marked by the "But . . ." of 2:4. Before it the words are prose, heavy words to provide a dark picture. One can only imagine writing them or reading them or hearing them with a heavy countenance and with shoulders slightly slouched. But after the "but" the words are poetry. Indeed, some have suggested that 2:4–7, 10 is a liturgical hymn. That suggestion is plausible enough, but no more plausible than that Paul (and his language) got caught up in the creative power of God to give life to the dead. Words fail, but they can become poetry when caught up by the creative power of God that raised Jesus from the dead and that raises humanity with him.

Caught up with the Angels

Karl Barth once wrote that when the angels go about their official task of praising God, they play only Bach. But when they get together as a family with the door closed, they play Mozart, and "our Lord listens with special pleasure." In a similar way, when the church goes about its official task of doing theology, it leans heavily on the letters of the Romans and to the Galatians. But in the quiet moments, when it wants to praise God with joy and delight, it reads aloud Ephesians, and "our Lord listens with special pleasure."
—Charles B. Cousar

An Introduction to the New Testament: Witnesses to God's New Work (Louisville: Westminster John Knox Press, 2006), 81.

It *is* humanity that is raised! The citation of Psalm 8 in Ephesians 1:22 made that clear. But again one may ask, is it true? We see humanity under the power of sin and death and the devil. But . . . we do see Jesus, risen from the dead, seated at God's right hand, with sin, death, the devil, and the powers humbled. And Psalm 8 is true of humanity because it is true of Jesus. Humanity is exalted with Jesus. Indeed, not just humanity but "all things" are "gathered up" in Christ, renewed, fulfilling God's intention as creator and redeemer.

We are getting ahead of ourselves a little. It is not yet that good future of God. But the church is in on the secret, is in on Christ, is in on "the immeasurable greatness of [God's] power" (1:19). The church bears witness to a "new humanity" by looking to Christ and by displaying that "new humanity," that new social reality. One might think Paul is getting ahead of himself a little bit here too. The poetry may soar a little too much. In 2:5–6 the church has already passed from death to life, has already been raised with Christ, is already seated with Christ in the heavenly places. A little experience in the life of the church might suggest a little more emphasis on the "not yet" character of our lives and of our common life. Paul (or the Paulinist) surely has more than a little experience in the life of the churches; he is not ignorant of the failings of the churches, or given to denial. But however realistic he might be about the churches, he is more confident in God, ready to celebrate God's immeasurable power already displayed in Christ and at work in the church. He is realistic about what God has done and is doing and will do.

The church as a new social reality that displays the new humanity (and indeed the new humanity itself) is not simply some ideal that human beings must strive for; it is not some ideal that stands simply outside human history and reality. It is a reality in Christ, and that reality enables and demands a response; it renders us response-able and responsible. It is not yet God's good future, but we do see Jesus, and we do see the church "in Christ," the firstfruits of this "new humanity," itself a "pledge" (1:14) of God's plan for the fullness of time by the power of the Spirit. This is all God's work (*poiēma*, 2:10), God's gift (2:8). This reality, this salvation, this future, and the presence already of this future are not created by human "works" (2:9) but by God. By God's power and grace the church is given an identity and made a community, by God's grace it is empowered for "good works." "We are what [God] has made us, created in Christ Jesus for good works" (2:10). Such a life is what God intended from the beginning, and it stands in obvious contrast to the way of life described in the opening grim picture. (The same Greek verb, *peripateō*, is used in 2:2 and in 2:10, but the verbal echo is usually lost in translation. It is a concluding contrast with the grim picture with which this section began: once you "walked" a path of disobedience; now you may "walk" the path that is in accord with God's plan.)

The emphasis here surely falls on God as the agent of the redemption of humanity and the renewal of all things. The emphasis here surely falls on the "already," on the passage from death to life as having already taken place. (Even here, however, there is in 2:7 an acknowledgment that it is not yet the good future of God. There the present reality is taken as evidence that in "the ages to come" God will display the full riches of God's grace.) The emphasis here falls on the indicative, on the reality that God has established. It is tempting to say that here the emphasis falls on the gospel. It is gospel, to be sure; it is good news. But at its conclusion (2:10) the passage already hints that when the letter will later turn to emphasize human agency, when it will adopt the imperative mood, that is gospel too. We will come to those passages in due course. Here it is enough to observe that when Ephesians turns to exhortation, when it gives some account of the "good works" for which we are created in Christ Jesus and which God had prepared "to be our way of life" (2:10), that too is good news.

FURTHER REFLECTIONS
An Evangelical Ethic

God's agency does not eliminate human agency. God's grace enables and summons human agency. As in the *berakot*, God's blessings enable and invite humans to bless God. It is not that God's grace will take us only so far, and then human agency must complete the task. It is God's grace all along. It is God's Messiah who finally completes the task, "the one who fills [or completes] all things completely" (our translation of 1:23). God's grace enables and summons the church to agency, to bear witness to the reality wrought by God's great power and to respond to God's grace, to perform the gospel. That summons to agency will demand the imperative as long as it is not yet God's future. But it is still gospel, sometimes as here in the indicative mood, sometimes as later in the imperative mood.

Both moods, indicative and imperative, are appropriate, indeed integral, to the proclamation of the gospel. The gospel is, for Paul, "the power of God" that brings salvation to Jew and Gentile (Rom. 1:16), and the power of God is intentional and active. God is not some passive deity who simply watches his law-abiding creation run; he is actively at work in it to accomplish his plan. God intends the good; God's power stands opposed to what is evil. The relation of indicative and imperative is determined by Pauline eschatology. In the crucified and risen Christ God has acted to end the rule of sin and death and all the powers that subvert and destroy God's purpose. They have not yet, however, admitted defeat; they have been conquered but not yet vanquished; and they are not yet ineffectual, not even against the believer. God's good future is sure to be, but in the meanwhile the gospel, the power of God, stands in fundamental opposition to the powers of this age. And the one who receives the gospel is freed from the dominion of the powers to stand under the lordship of Christ, to stand within the purpose of God. That "standing" is now always both gift and demand, both indicative and imperative. (Compare Rom. 5:2 and 1 Cor. 15:1 with 1 Cor. 10:12, 16:13, and Eph. 6:10–14.)

The indicative mood has an important priority, as the insistence in this passage on "by grace you have been saved" (Eph. 2:5, 8) makes clear. That priority cannot, however, be understood as the establishment of an ideal or a principle that needs to be "actualized" or "realized" later and separately in human decisions about character and conduct, for there is also an important finality to the indicative, as the persistent references to God's promised future make equally clear. The indicative mood, then, has an important priority and an important finality in the proclamation of the gospel, but the imperative is by no means a mere addendum to the indicative. Solidarity with the crucified and risen Christ (the important priority of the indicative) and anticipation of God's good future (the important finality of the indicative) are here and now *constituted* by joyful obedience to God's will and way (the imperative).

The juxtaposition of the indicative and imperative, then, is possible—and necessary—because the present evil age continues while God's good future has already begun. The indicative mood describes the eschatological salvation already wrought by God in Christ and of which the Spirit is "the pledge" (1:14). But the imperative mood acknowledges that Christians are still threatened by "the spiritual forces of evil" (6:12), though their doom is sure, and that therefore they must "take up the whole armor of God" and "stand firm" (6:13). The imperatives are not the imposition of some alien duties; they are the gospel, the power of God, taking hold of lives and of the common life. They too are gospel.

Ephesians 2:1–10 points to the reality of a new humanity established by Christ and names the church as the display of that reality. The indicative is already subtly demanding. The good future comes to us as a gift, and the gift already subtly makes its claim upon us. Later on, Ephesians will be considerably less subtle about the demands and claims of that reality, but it will still be the gospel taking hold of life, to be received and performed with joy. That is part of what we mean when we call this an *evangelical ethic*.

From Death to Life and Justification

It should be noted, finally, that Ephesians talks here of the passage from death to life rather than of "justification." "Justification" is an image of some considerable importance to Romans and Galatians (see especially Rom. 1:16–5:21; Gal. 2:16–3:24). That language has come to be so associated with the Pauline gospel that it is difficult for some to think of Ephesians as Pauline (see the introduction). It may be responded that "justification" does not seem to be as central for Paul as it is for certain readers of Paul. He does not include it, for example, in his account of what he had announced to the Corinthians "as of first importance" (1 Cor. 15:3–8). That was the message of the death and resurrection of Christ. That was the saving event for Paul, and "justification" was one way (but not the only way) he had for talking about it. Moreover, when Paul did talk of "justification," he was consistently making the point that is being made in Ephesians as well. The language of justification in Paul always occurs in the context of discussions of the relation of Jew and Gentile in the church. (See especially Rom. 1:16–17; 3:27–31; Gal. 2:16–3:29.) Paul uses that language to insist on a new social reality, a reality in which "there is no distinction" between Jew and Gentile (Rom. 3:21–25). Finally, the pattern of the argument in Romans and Galatians echoes in

> **Justification as a Social Event**
>
> Justification is a social event. It ties human to human together. Justification by works would segregate people because each person would select his/her own arbitrary criterion of good works. Justification by grace, however, brings people together in reconciliation, even those of alien background, like the Jews and Gentiles.
>
> —Markus Barth
>
> "Jews and Gentiles: The Social Character of Justification in Paul," *Ecumenical Studies* 5 (1968): 241.

Ephesians even without the language of justification. There is the sad solidarity as "sinners" (Rom. 3:9–18, 23; Gal. 2:15–18) and the glad solidarity of being "one in Christ Jesus" and joint "heirs according to the promise" to Abraham (Gal. 3:28, 29; see also Rom. 4:16–25). And as Romans forbade boasting because it denied our dependence upon God's grace and because it undercut this new social reality of the church, so does Ephesians (see Rom. 2:17–24; 3:27–31; Eph. 2:8–9). And in its exuberant delight in the gospel and in its rejection of boasting Ephesians here echoes what surely must be regarded as Pauline slogans, "by grace you have been saved" (2:5) and "by grace you have been saved through faith" (2:8).[1]

In Romans "the obedience of faith" (1:5; 16:26) meant the performance of this new social reality in practices of hospitality (14:1; 15:7).[2] In Galatians "the truth of the gospel" (2:14) was at stake

---

1. None of this proves, of course, that Paul is the author, but it does make it clear that the author, if not Paul himself, is a faithful Paulinist.
2. See Paul Minear, *The Obedience of Faith: The Purposes of Paul in the Epistle to the Romans,* Studies in Biblical Theology 2/19 (Naperville, IL: Allenson, 1971), 7–17.

in the performance of a table fellowship between Jew and Gentile Christians that reflected that new social reality. Now in Ephesians the gospel—and that new social reality, threatened by conditions surrounding the war—must be preserved and performed in the midst of "cultures of enmity."

FURTHER REFLECTIONS
Dead Men Walking: Saved by Grace

"Most Americans are Pelagians, as far as I can tell," observed the theologian.

Pelagians? This was the heresy that St. Augustine condemned. Pelagius contended that down deep we are basically good people who are capable of making progress. The function of theology is to appeal to our better motives, to motivate us to be the sort of people we know we ought to become.

St. Augustine rejected this too optimistic assessment of humanity. We are sinners. We are prone to do and to be wrong. God must therefore do for us what we cannot do for ourselves. We are saved by grace, not by our own works. Our salvation is an act of God, not the result of our earnest efforts.[3]

It was not just Augustine who "rejected this too optimistic assessment of humanity." So did the writer of Ephesians. "You were dead through the trespasses and sins in which you once lived" (Eph. 2:1–2), he said. That is hardly an optimistic assessment of the human condition. To borrow a phrase from Sister Helen Prejean's engaging book and movie, we were "dead men walking," dead women walking.[4] Our lives only made manifest the rule of death.

The walking dead have been captured in modern fiction in characters such as Willy Loman in *Death of a Salesman* by Arthur Miller and John Updike's character in the Rabbit series. T. S. Eliot gives us a vivid description of the walking dead in "The Hollow Men":

3. William H. Willimon, "Don't Be Too Conscientious," *Pulpit Resource* 37, no. 2 (2009): 48.
4. Helen Prejean, *Dead Man Walking: An Eyewitness Account of the Death Penalty in the United States* (New York: Random House, 1993).

> We are the hollow men
> We are the stuffed men
> Leaning together
> Headpiece filled with straw. Alas!
> Our dried voices, when
> We whisper together
> Are quiet and meaningless
> As wind in dry grass
> Or rats' feet over broken glass
> In our dry cellar.[5]

In this human condition we are neither aware of our condition nor capable of changing it. We are left to the mercy of the powers, which are only too ready to claim ultimacy and to tell us who we are and whose we are, only too ready to nurture enmity toward those who are different. Our identities, indeed our very lives, are at the mercy of powers "in the air" and beyond our control.

Only God can rescue us from this condition. The walking dead can find life only by God's breath and Spirit. The "hollow men" must be filled with Christ. But this is the good news. God has rescued us from this condition, liberated us from the hold of the powers. "But God, who is rich in mercy, out of the great love with which he loved us even when we were dead through our trespasses, made us alive together with Christ" (Eph. 2:4–5). That is our new situation, and it is ours not by birth or by right but by the grace of God; "by grace you have been saved" (2:5).

"Saved"! When some hear this word, an alarm goes off inside. Some of us have negative responses because we have been the victims of zealous evangelists who have inquired about the state of our souls. "Are you saved?" they asked, challenging us to name the time and place that we made "a decision for Christ." But we are not saved by our decisions. We are saved by God, by God's grace. "Are you saved? If you were to die tonight, would you spend eternity in heaven or hell?" they asked, suggesting that salvation is simply a matter of whether an individual person gets into heaven.

5. T. S. Eliot, "The Hollow Men," *The Complete Poems and Plays: 1909–1950* (New York: Harcourt, Brace & World, 1962), 56.

It is not just the zealous evangelists who assume that salvation is an individual achievement and an individual's reward for an individual "decision." Such an account of salvation is deeply rooted in our culture. But it is not the account provided by Ephesians (or the rest of Scripture).

In the first place, Ephesians would certainly join the theologian cited by Will Willimon in the quotation above (and Augustine) in regarding this account as a form of Pelagianism. In Ephesians 2 the agent of our salvation is not some individual and his or her "decision" but God. It is God who intervenes on our behalf out of love for us. By the "rich mercy" of God we are made alive together with Christ (2:4–5). "By grace you have been saved" (2:5). And to underscore the point, it is repeated, "For by grace you have been saved through faith, and this is not your own doing; it is the gift of God—not the result of works, so that no one may boast" (2:8–9). Salvation is not a human achievement; it is a gift from God. It is not something we earned or deserved, not the result of works, not even the work of a "decision." God rescues us from death and sin, from the hold the powers have on us, and this rescue is traced not to a human decision but to God's sovereign freedom and steadfast love. The initiative belongs to God and to God alone in healing the brokenness of the cosmos and of humanity. This truth underscores our dependency on God. It keeps us from boasting in our own abilities to save ourselves. In a culture in which the market is flooded with self-help books and we are proud of how spiritual we are, gratitude and humility are essential in response to the generosity of God made known to us in Jesus Christ. The emphasis should not fall on "how I found God" or "turned my life over to Christ"; the emphasis belongs where Ephesians puts it, on God's grace and gift. It is that grace that makes us agents ready and able to praise God's glory and to participate in the good future that is God's plan and our "salvation."

But that brings us to a second, and even more important, corrective that Ephesians offers to our culture's account of salvation. It is not just a matter of whether an individual gets into heaven. In the biblical story and in Ephesians salvation is a matter of the cosmos being renewed, of humanity being restored, of "all things" being gathered up with Christ as head (Eph. 1:10). To be sure, we are privileged to have that salvation as our "inheritance" by the grace of God. Ephesians can even speak of our being rescued from the dead with Christ and "seated . . . with him in the heavenly places" (2:6). But those "heavenly places" are not some otherworldly realm; it is where the cosmic conflict between the "powers" and God is waged; it is where the victory of God is already assured; it is where Christ sits in sovereignty over the powers (1:20–23). Those who have been made alive "in Christ" already experience the blessing of God's good future. The future is present, even while it remains future (2:7).

It is present, according to Ephesians, in the church. The good future of God is not something that we enter alone; no, never alone. We only enter that future, that salvation, "with Christ," in solidarity with this Jewish Messiah. And we only enter that future, that salvation, with others, with Israel and the church, in solidarity with the church and in solidarity with the new humanity created by Christ.

Let Go of My Onion

Once upon a time there was a peasant woman and a very wicked woman she was. And she died and did not leave a single good deed behind. The devils caught her and plunged her into the lake of fire. So her guardian angel stood and wondered what good deed of hers he could remember and tell to God; "She once pulled up an onion in her garden," said he, "and gave it to a beggar woman." And God answered: "You take that onion then, hold it out to her in the lake, and let her take hold and be pulled out. And if you can pull her out of the lake, let her come to Paradise, but if the onion breaks, then the woman must stay where she is." The angel ran to the woman and held out the onion to her. "Come," said he, "catch hold and I'll pull you out." He began cautiously pulling her out. He had just pulled her right out, when the other sinners in the lake, seeing how she was being drawn out, began catching hold of her so as to be pulled out with her. But she was a very wicked woman and she began kicking them. "I'm to be pulled out, not you. It's my onion, not yours." As soon as she said that, the onion broke. And the woman fell into the lake and she is burning there to this day. So the angel wept and went away.

—**Fyodor Dostoevsky**

The Brothers Karamazov, book 7.3, at http://www.freebooks.biz/Classics/Dostoevsky/Karamazov_VII03_4.htm.; cited by William T. Cavanaugh, "Pilgrim People," in *Gathered for the Journey: Moral Theology in Catholic Perspective*, ed. David Matzko McCarthy and M. Therese Lysaught (Grand Rapids: Eerdmans, 2007), 89.

Indeed, that solidarity with others, that peace with others, that community of peaceable difference, is no small part of the salvation God brings. Our preoccupation with our self-interest, even our pre-occupation with our own individual salvation, our getting to heaven someday, is a preoccupation of sinners, of "dead men walking."

Salvation is cosmic and communal, not otherworldly and indi-vidual. That we are gathered as the church is the first effect of the new humanity created by Christ. The church is not some voluntary society, like a chess club or the Rotary, which individuals with similar interests join. It is the creation of God, a gathering of diverse people who by God's grace are members of the body of Christ, in solidarity with Christ, and "members of one another" (4:25), in solidarity with one another.

And this community has a role to play in God's plan to save the cosmos. God makes this community and its members agents in mak-ing known "the secret." They make it known by telling it, of course. But to the telling of it, the response of many Jews and pagans was surely to scoff. "Ha. These Christians want to tell us that this Jesus, who was put to death on a Roman cross, was raised from the dead. Ha. They claim that at that place and time everything changed, that then and there the creation was made new. Ha. It's pretty clear that nothing much has changed. Caesar still rules. Enmity and violence still reign." The only response that Christians could make to that sort of mockery was to point to com-munities where things had in fact changed, where enmity no longer ruled, where the "powers" were not regarded as ultimate, where people were united in peaceable difference. "Look there, scoffers. The Jerusalem community (Acts 2:44–47) was a community of friends. They shared their goods. There was not a needy person among them. There the hopes of both Jews and Gentiles were realized. Look here, mockers. Our own communities are

---

The Church as Visible Sacrament

God has gathered together as one all those who in faith look upon Jesus as the author of salvation and the source of unity and peace and has established them as the Church, that for each and all she may be the visible sacrament of this saving unity.

—Second Vatican Council

Walter M. Abbott, SJ, ed., *The Docu-ments of Vatican II* (New York: America Press, 1966), 26.

evidence that things have changed. Jews and Gentiles live together in peaceable difference. This is not our accomplishment. This is God's work in Christ." Their own lives and their common life was the only proof they had to offer. The church was the visible sign of God's salvation of the world. Indeed, it may not be too much to call the church "the visible sacrament" of God's salvation.

What God has done in Christ to save the world must already shape the lives and the common life of Christians. The verb "to save" is in the perfect tense here (*sesosmenoi*; 2:5, 8). Many have suggested that this is radical departure from Paul's usage, and indeed, there is no other time that Paul uses "to save" in the perfect tense. Nevertheless, it seems to us not so much a radical departure as a way to call attention to the continuing effects of what God has done for us in Christ. The good future of God is already making its power felt in the churches. We—and everyone (3:9)—may see some token of God's good future, which will surely come to fruition in God's good time.

This does not mean that the church is already perfect. It has a lot of growing to do before it reaches "the measure of the full stature of Christ" (4:13). The gospel must still also be announced in the imperative mood. And it does not mean that the Spirit of God is not at work outside the church in the world. But it does mean that the church has a role to play in making the secret manifest in and to the world. It does mean, as Ephesians says, that "we are [and are to be] what [God] has made us, created in Christ Jesus for good works, which God prepared beforehand to be our way of life" (2:10).

The tension between grace and good works that has been presupposed in many sermons and in much theology disappears when we see them in their proper relationship. Good works are not done in order to get on God's good side or to earn God's affection. By God's grace we are made agents in God's cause; by God's grace we are called and enabled to live "to the praise of his glory"; by God's grace we may live as we were created to live; by God's grace we may do good works. Although both Jews and Christians have sometimes boasted about their good works, both Judaism and Christianity know better. It is the grace of God at work, creating and recreating the very freedom by which we respond to God and to God's cause.

For the Christians of the Lycus Valley and for us, good works are not simply a supplement to our salvation. They are, rather, part of that salvation. They give concrete expression to our identity and community in Christ for the world. They are not the means to our salvation, not even our own idea. They are the embodiment of what "we are," of what God "has made us." God prepared them "beforehand to be our way of life" (2:10). It is a lovely thought that doing good works is God's good idea in the rescue of us, making us alive.[6]

FURTHER REFLECTIONS
Easter Chickens

In his book *Brother to a Dragonfly*, Will Campbell, a noted Baptist preacher and theologian, recounts a conversation with his irreverent friend P. D. East. The conversation takes place in Alabama during the civil rights movement. They had just heard of the killing of a young seminarian, Jonathan Daniel, who had been registering black citizens to vote. East complained about the role of the church in those turbulent times; he said the church reminded him of an "Easter chicken." He then described the baby chicken he had given his little daughter, Karen. The Easter chicken was dyed a deep purple. Will interrupted his friend to remind him that white is the liturgical color for Easter, but P. D. ignored him.

P. D. went on to describe how the baby chicken started feathering and the new feathers were Rhode Island Red. They took the half-purple and half-red chicken and put it into the chicken yard with the other chickens. At first, the little chicken was different and the others knew it was different. It did not bother the others or enter into their fights. But little by little it began behaving just like the rest of the chickens. It would peck and fight, knock other chickens down to catch a bug. "And now," said P. D., "you can't tell one chicken from

---

6. Andrew Lincoln is helpful when he points out that salvation is not "by works" but "for works." "The new creation, which in its widest sense includes the summing up of all things in Christ (cf. 1:9, 10) has already begun as a movement in history in the lives of men and women. These lives are to be characterized by good works" (*Ephesians*, Word Biblical Commentary 42 [Dallas: Word Books, 1990], 114).

another. They're all just alike. The Easter chicken is just one more chicken."

"Well, P. D.," Will responded, "the Easter chicken is still useful. It lays eggs, doesn't it?" It was what P. D. wanted Will to say. "Yea, Preacher Will. It lays eggs. But they all lay eggs. Who needs an Easter chicken for that? And the Rotary Club serves coffee. And the 4-H Club says prayers. The Red Cross takes up offerings for hurricane victims. Mental Health does counseling, and the Boy Scouts have youth programs."[7]

Ephesians calls us to be an Easter people, not Easter chickens. The resurrection calls us to be a people who no longer follow "the course of this world" (Eph. 2:2), who no longer conform to the "warring madness" of this world or the selfish materialism of a culture that leaves us "rich in things and poor in soul."[8] In "the course of this world" difference means enmity. The way of the world is to understand ourselves over against those who are different from us, whose heritage, customs, nationality, or skin color makes them different from us, and to condemn and despise them for their differences. Ephesians calls us to be different, to be an Easter people, not Easter chickens, but the mark of that difference is peace rather than hostility, love rather than enmity, in response to difference. As Christ broke down the dividing walls between Jesus and Gentiles, creating a new humanity, so we are encouraged to see ourselves as members of a new social reality, as belonging to what Martin Luther King Jr. called "the beloved community."[9]

We have been given a new identity by our baptism into Christ, into the church, and into a new humanity. The cultures of enmity

---

7. See Will D. Campbell, *Brother to a Dragonfly* (New York: Seabury Press, 1977), 219–20.
8. The phrases are from Harry Emerson Fosdick's wonderful hymn, "God of Grace and God of Glory," in *Rejoice in the Lord*, ed. Erik Routley (Grand Rapids: Eerdmans, 1985), no. 416. In *Cadences of Home: Preaching Among Exiles* (Louisville: Westminster John Knox Press, 1997), Walter Brueggemann uses the metaphor of "exile" to describe the situation of the church in the United States. He calls attention to the militarism and materialism of the culture and calls the church to hear the gospel and its call to a different identity. "I suggest," he says, "an evangelical dimension to exile in our context. That is, serious, reflective Christians find themselves increasingly at odds with the dominant values of consumer capitalism and its supportive military patriotism" (p. 2).
9. Dr. King used this phrase often in his sermons and addresses. It was central to his vision. See Kenneth L. Smith and Ira G. Zepp, *Search for the Beloved Community: The Thinking of Martin Luther King, Jr.* (Valley Forge, PA: Judson Press, 1974).

that surround us are no less expert at "identity theft" than the cultures of enmity in the first century. The church has been too often conscripted into the service of nationalism, racism, and sexism. The new identity we have in Christ is not simply a pleasant alternative to the frustrations of the world. It is the gift of God to the church for the world. It is part of God's plan for the fullness of time and for the restoration of all things in Christ. And it is a calling to lives and a common life that conform not to the "warring madness" of our cultures of enmity but to the new humanity.

We are an Easter people, not Easter chickens. We must protect ourselves from identity theft—for the sake of the world. We must remember who we are by God's grace, and whose we are. "For we are what he has made us, created in Christ Jesus for good works, which God prepared beforehand to be our way of life" (Eph. 2:10). Then we may live "for the praise of [God's] glory" (1:12, 14), and others may see the secret (cf. 3:9).

The script calls us to performance. It calls us to a new way of life. Remembering what God has done in Christ and anticipating the good future of God, we live by grace. That is, we trust in God to provide for our needs, and we share what we have because God assures us there is enough. Our relationships are characterized by forgiveness instead of revenge, and we work as agents of God's reconciling love. Our lives and our common life are marked by hope, oriented toward a future that we know in Christ, a future that God is sure to bring.

2:11–22

Peace!

The passage begins, "So then, remember." Permit us to use that phrase as a pretext to remind ourselves of a few things we have talked about already and that seem to us to be important to understand this passage.

We have talked about "cultures of enmity" in the Roman Empire, about a "holy enmity" between Jewish and Gentile populations within the Roman Empire. The Jewish Dispersion had resulted in more Jews living outside Palestine than within it.[1] They were about 10 percent of the population of the entire empire, and they were a significant minority also in Asia Minor, including the Lycus Valley.

The relations between Jew and Gentile were not always or uniformly marked by suspicion and enmity. There were voices calling for peace on both sides of the aisle. From the side of the Roman Empire, the Pax Romana was hailed as a great accomplishment. It had been achieved by the strong hand of a superpower and its military (like "the Pax Americana," and like "the Pax Americana" it was as much war as peace), but this peace was hailed by Virgil, for example, as the golden age.[2] Stoic philosophers had extolled peace,

---

1. G. A. Van Alstine, "Dispersion," *The International Standard Bible Encyclopedia*, ed. G. W. Bromiley, rev. ed. (Grand Rapids: Eerdmans, 1979), 1:962–68.
2. See Virgil, *Eclogues* IV, 4–52 in *Virgil*, I, trans. H. R. Fairclough, Loeb Classical Library (Cambridge, MA: Harvard University Press, 1999). There is no irony in Virgil, but Tacitus makes the irony plain in a speech he attributes to Calgacus of Britain, "To plunder, butcher, steal, these things they misname empire; they make a desolation and call it peace" (cited by Klaus Wengst, *Pax Romana and the Peace of Jesus Christ*, trans. John Bowden [Philadelphia: Fortress Press, 1987], 52).

both in the form of "contentment," or peace of mind, and in the form of cosmopolitanism, or international peace. Epictetus, for example, had said, "The universe is but one great city, . . . full of beloved ones, . . . by nature endeared to each other."[3]

From the side of the Jews, there was already Jeremiah's advice to Jews in exile: "Seek the welfare [Hebrew *shalom*, 'peace'] of the city where I have sent you into exile, and pray to the LORD on its behalf, for in its welfare [*shalom*] you will find your welfare [*shalom*]" (Jer. 29:7). There were as well, of course, the great prophetic visions of peace, of *shalom*, at the end of the age. And among the rabbis of the first century there were voices calling for peace, notably Gamaliel: "By three things the world is sustained: by justice, by truth, and by peace."[4]

There were voices calling for peace, human spirits yearning for peace, but in the times surrounding the war of 66–73 those voices seemed to be crying in the wilderness of a world gripped by powers of enmity and division. There were louder voices on both sides that nurtured resentment and suspicion and that called for violence in the name of all that was "holy" on one side or the other.

Remember also where we are in Ephesians. Remember the greeting: "Grace and peace." It was God who gathered the Christians of the Lycus Valley as a community and God who blessed them with "grace and peace." We observed already that that greeting is matched at the closing of the letter with "peace and grace," so that this blessing of God provided an envelope for the letter. And when we open the envelope and read the body of the letter, we find again "grace" and "peace." In the section examined in the last chapter we found an emphasis on "grace," including the Pauline slogan, "By grace you have been saved." In this section the emphasis falls on "peace."

Remember the great *berakot*, the prayer to God blessing God for all God's blessings, and especially for letting this community in on the secret, the revelation of the mystery of God's "plan for the

---

3. Epictetus, *Discourses* 3.24, in *The Works of Epictetus. Consisting of His Discourses, in Four Books, the Enchiridion, and Fragments*, ed. and trans. Thomas Wentworth Higginson (Boston: Little, Brown, 1866), 266.

4. *Pirke Abot* 1.18; *The Living Talmud: The Wisdom of the Fathers*, ed. Judah Golden (New York: New American Library of World Literature, 1964), 75.

fullness of time," to unite all things in Christ. That good future of God was already making its power felt in that both "we" and "you," both Jew and Gentile, were called "to the praise of God's glory," to doxological existence.

Remember the prayer that the churches would know the greatness of the hope that could only be measured by the greatness of God's power in raising Jesus from the dead and to sovereignty over the principalities and powers. Already there with reference to Psalm 8 we called attention to Christ as "the new humanity." Remember that it was as head of all things that Christ was given to the church, which is his body, the way Christ is made manifest and is at work in the world.

Remember the grim picture of the solidarity of Jew and Gentile as sinners, with its reminder that *all* of us are "sinners." And remember the glad solidarity of Jew and Gentile "in Christ," with its grand announcement that *all* of us are made alive together with Christ. The grace and power of God created a new social reality in the church. That passage began by addressing "you," reminding the Gentiles that they were under the power of sin, death, and the devil, but it broke off midsentence in order to include the Jews, to remind them that "sinner" is not just a term for the Gentiles but for "all of us." When that passage made its stunning transition from solidarity as sinners to solidarity in Christ (marked by the great "But . . ." of v. 4), it talked of everyone, but the primary audience, we think, remained the Jewish Christians (and the Gentile "Judaizers") of the Lycus Valley. At least the warning against boasting seems particularly apropos to that audience (see Rom. 2:17–24; 3:27–31). Paul can warn against "boasting" by any faction of the church (e.g., 1 Cor. 1:29), but the reference later to the epithet "the uncircumcision" suggests that the "boasting" here belonged especially to a Jewish Christian faction.

Earlier we imagined that a pious Jewish Christian who was not yet fully convinced that he should make peace with Gentile "sinners" might well have interrupted the reading of the letter at the end of Ephesians 2:2 by shouting, "Amen, preach it, brother." At least Paul abruptly turned his attention to the Jews. At Ephesians 2:9, when Paul chided those who would boast, one might also imagine that a Gentile Christian who resented the boasting of the Jews might well have uttered those same words of approval. At any rate here in 2:11 Paul turns his attention back to those whom he began to address in 2:1, back to "you," back to "you Gentiles." The glad solidarity in Christ, the happy transition from death to life, the new social reality created by the fact that we are "made alive together with Christ" (2:5), is now developed in terms that are explicitly political.

From Aliens and Strangers to Fellow Citizens

"So then," he says, "remember that at one time you Gentiles . . ." (2:11). Paul will go on to remind the Gentiles both of the grim picture with which the chapter began and of the glad passage from death to life in Christ. First, however, there is a little aside still intended for the Jewish believers. "Remember," he says, "that at one time you Gentiles by birth [*en sarki*, literally 'in the flesh'], called 'the uncircumcision' by those who are called 'the circumcision' . . ." (2:11). The Gentile Christians are obviously addressed, but the little parenthetical remark that follows is just as obviously intended for the Jewish Christians and for the Judaizers among the Gentiles. The parenthetical remark is a reminder that circumcision is not all that important, a "physical [cutting] made in the flesh [*en sarki*] by human hands" (2:11). It is surely not as important as the decision of God to unite all things in Christ, surely not as important as the spiritual reality that Paul has announced and will continue to proclaim. This too is familiar enough to the Jews schooled by the Torah and the Prophets, which insisted on a circumcision of the heart (e.g., Deut. 10:16; 30:6; Jer. 4:4; 9:25–26). It is familiar also in Paul (e.g., Rom. 2:25–29; Col. 2:11).

After this little aside, Paul reminds the Gentiles that "you were at that time without Christ, being aliens from the commonwealth of Israel, and strangers to the covenants of promise, having no hope and without God in the world" (2:12). "That time" is itself a reminder of that grim picture with which the chapter began, when "you were dead" (2:1). The grim picture is revisited, but it is now described particularly in terms of their being "without Christ," Gentiles without the Jewish Messiah. The Messiah belongs to Israel and fulfills the promises of covenant with Israel. At "that time" they were outside Israel, aliens, not fellow citizens of Israel, strangers to the covenants with Israel. They had no share in those promises and therefore no hope. One might regard this as an exaggeration, and a chauvinistic exaggeration at that. Surely the Gentiles had hopes, but they did not have the messianic hope. They did not have the hope for God's good future. They were without God (*atheoi*, "atheists"). Again, the Gentiles were hardly atheists, but they did not know the God of Israel, the God of promise; they were "without God" no matter how many gods they may have worshiped. The grim picture here is precisely that the Gentiles are not Jews. One can imagine another "Amen" rising from the side of the "circumcised."

"But now . . .," Paul says, marking again the transition from death to life, from being "without Christ" to being "in Christ," "in Christ Jesus you who once were far off have been brought near by the blood of Christ" (2:13). Once you were strangers to Israel, to its covenants and promises, "but now" you are in Christ, and in this Jewish Messiah you Gentiles have been united with Israel; now you have a share in that inheritance, in God's good future. Once you were "aliens from the commonwealth of Israel, strangers to the covenants of promise" (2:12), "but now" you are "no longer strangers and aliens, but you are citizens . . . and members of the household of God" (2:19). Once you were hopeless, "but now" in the Jewish Messiah, in Christ Jesus, you Gentiles have been given a hope that is a fulfillment of the ancient promises to the Jews and in accord with God's power in raising Jesus from the dead.

If it was especially the Jewish Christian who needed to be reminded earlier that *all* are "sinners," not just the "uncircumcised," not just the Gentiles, and that *all* are brought from death to life by the gift of God's grace, not by "works" of the law, the Gentiles are now reminded of the promises *to Israel* and that it is in the Jewish Messiah that they are given a share in them. Then let the Jews not condemn the Gentiles as "sinners," and let the Gentiles not despise the Jews into whose promises they enter (cf. Rom. 14–15).

Paul borrows the language of "far" and "near" from Isaiah 57:19, "Peace, peace, to the far and the near, says the LORD." Paul boldly read "the far" as a reference to Gentiles. Isaiah may have simply meant to include both those Jews returning from exile and those who remained in Judah, but Paul's reading is not an outrageous stretch. The prophet was capable of a vision of God's future—and of God's peace—in which the Gentiles would be welcomed. Consider, for example, Isaiah 2:2–4:

> In days to come the mountain of the LORD's house shall be established as the highest of the mountains . . .; all the nations shall stream to it. Many peoples shall come and say, "Come, let us go up to the mountain of the LORD, to the house of the God of Jacob; that he may teach us his ways and that we may walk in his paths." For out of Zion shall go forth instruction, and the word of the LORD from Jerusalem. He shall judge between the nations, and shall arbitrate for many peoples; they shall beat their swords into plowshares and their spears into pruning hooks; nation shall not lift up sword against nation, neither shall they learn war any more.[5]

And in Isaiah 56:3–7, just one chapter before the passage of Isaiah alluded to, is another oracle promising the inclusion of "the foreigner":

> Do not let the foreigner joined to the LORD say, "The LORD will surely separate me from his people"; and do not let the eunuch say, "I am just a dry tree." For thus says the LORD: To the eunuchs . . . I will give, in my house and within my walls, a monument and a name better than sons and daughters; I will give them an everlasting name that shall not be cut off. And the foreigners who join themselves to the LORD, to minister to him, to love the name of the LORD, and to be his servants, . . . these I will bring to my holy mountain, and make them joyful in my house of prayer . . . for my house shall be called a house of prayer for all peoples.

"The foreigner" here would come to be understood as the proselyte, but "proselyte" itself (derived from Greek *proserchomai*) means "one

---

5. Consider also, for example, Mic. 4:1–4, where this oracle is repeated; Isa. 40:22–25; Isa. 42:6; 49:6; 52:10; also Zech. 8:20–23, etc.

who comes near."[6] The proselyte was to be welcomed. To be sure, there were requirements, and on the basis of Genesis 17:12–14 circumcision was usually regarded as a requirement.[7] The ellipses in the quotation above mark the requirements that eunuch and foreigner "keep my sabbaths" and "hold fast my covenant" and bring sacrifices. Those requirements may or may not include circumcision, but the point is only that, given both the scope of Isaiah's vision and the tradition of welcoming the proselyte, Paul's reading of "the far" as a reference to Gentiles is not an excessive stretch.[8]

Paul's reading of Isaiah 57 remains, however, a bold interpretation, a radical transformation of the tradition of the proselyte, the one who "comes near." What makes it radical is this: that those who "were far off have been brought near" not by the blood of circumcision but by the blood of Christ. And this: that this blood was shed when the Gentiles were still "dead," still "following the course of this world" (2:1–2), still "sinners" (Rom. 5:8), not when "God-fearers" piously kept sabbaths or observed "the law with its commandments and ordinances" (Eph. 2:15). And this: that the peace proclaimed is not just peace with God, but peace between Jew and Gentile, a new and peaceable social reality. The Gentiles are included in the promises to Israel, but they do not and need not act like Jews.

Paul will use the language of Isaiah 57 again in 2:17. The two allusions to Isaiah frame what is the climactic passage of this chapter, and perhaps of the whole letter (2:13–18).

> But now in Christ Jesus you who once were far off have been brought near by the blood of Christ. For he is our peace; in his flesh he has made both groups into one and has broken down the dividing wall, that is, the hostility between us. He has abolished the law with its commandments and ordinances, that he might create in himself one new humanity in place of the two, thus making peace, and might reconcile both groups to God in one body through the cross, thus putting to death that hostility

6. Barth, *Ephesians 1–3*, 276.
7. Numbers 9:14, which permits the "alien" to celebrate Passover, however, makes no mention of a requirement of circumcision.
8. See further Barth, *Ephesians 1–3*, 276–79.

through it. So he came and proclaimed peace to you who were
far off and peace to those who were near, for through him both
of us have access in one Spirit to the Father.

Once more, as in the transition at 2:4, the grim picture is overmatched by the gospel. Once more the style shifts to something like
liturgical poetry. Once more the transition is attributed to the grace
and love of God. But whereas 2:5 focused on God, who "made us
alive together with Christ," here the focus falls on the Christ and
on his death, on his "blood" (v. 13), his "cross" (v. 16). Of course,
there is no understanding of the cross without the resurrection, but
neither shall we understand the resurrection apart from the cross. It
is not just that Christ is made head of all things in the resurrection
but that he was made the head of all things as one who was willing to
bear the cost of fidelity to God and to the cause of God, to the "will"
or "plan" of God (1:9, 10), even the great cost of his death.

God has brought the Gentiles into his covenant and its promises
"by the blood of Christ." By referring to Christ's death in this way,
Ephesians adopts the language of sacrifice. There are a variety of sacrifices in the Old Testament, but the reference in 2:12 to "covenants"
prompts consideration, first of all, of "the blood of the covenant"
(Exod. 24:8).

Moses sealed the covenant between God and Israel at Sinai by
sacrificing oxen "as an offering of well-being to the Lord." (Hebrew
zebach shelamim might also be translated—significantly in our context—as "peace offering.") Then "Moses took the blood and dashed
it on the people, and said, 'See the blood of the covenant'" (Exod.
24:3-8). An offering of well-being, or a peace offering (Lev. 3:1-
17), is distinguished from a sin offering (Lev. 4:1-5:13). The peace
offering seals the covenant and creates community. Certain parts
of the sacrificed animal were burned on the altar, but the rest was
consumed in a common meal. Against this background God seals a
"new covenant" in "the blood of Christ." And in that "new covenant"
there is a new community, a community of both Jew and Gentile, a
community that shares the memory of Christ and the hope of God's
promises with a common meal. Against the background of Exodus
24, "[Christ] is our peace [offering]" (Eph. 2:14).

The Works of the Messiah Making Peace

Ephesians goes on then with a burst of phrases describing the work of Christ. We risk losing the exuberant joy of this catalogue of Christ's work when we pause over each of them, but each is rich with the promise of a new social reality and with the reality of God's promise.

"In his flesh he has made both groups into one" (2:14). He has made Jew and Gentile, "the circumcision" and "the uncircumcision," into one. That is the new social reality. Given the cultures of enmity, it was a radically new idea. Yet it was also an old idea. It may be announced as the fulfillment of human hopes, both the hopes of Israel (e.g., of Isaiah), and the hopes of the Gentiles (e.g., of Virgil). And it was an old idea in the Pauline churches. The baptismal formula quoted often by Paul, for example in Galatians 3:27–28, made the point quite clearly,[9] "There is no longer Jew or Greek, there is no longer slave or free, there is no longer male and female; for all of you are one in Christ Jesus."

But this was not merely an idea, as the reality of baptism makes clear. This was not merely an ideal that exists outside history and toward which we must strive. This was and is a reality wrought in Christ on the cross and displayed in the churches when God initiates diverse people into Christ and into the church. Ideals are powerless against the forces in this world that divide and abuse, against the principalities and powers that nurture cultures of enmity. But those forces are and will be finally powerless against the promise and reality of God's future.

"He has broken down the dividing wall, that is, the hostility between us" (2:14). This is related to the previous item in this catalogue of the works of the Messiah. He made us both one by breaking down the wall that divided us. Like many if not most biblical scholars, we take this "dividing wall" to refer to the stone wall of the Jerusalem temple that stood about five feet tall and beyond which no Gentile was permitted to go. On the pillars of this wall there were inscribed warnings to Gentiles that to go further into the temple was

9. See Richard Longenecker, *New Testament Social Ethics for Today* (Grand Rapids: Eerdmans, 1984), 31–33, for the argument that Gal. 3:28 is a baptismal tradition.

a capital offense. Those who were "far off" could come no nearer than this wall allowed. That wall was a vivid image of the division between Jew and Gentile, and to tear down that wall would be a vivid image of the new unity and equality of Jew and Gentile. It would be a powerful image as well for the point to be made in 2:18 that both Jew and Gentile now have access to God. If Ephesians was written after Paul's death and after the destruction of the temple in 70 CE, then that wall had in fact been broken down. The identification of the "dividing wall" with that stone wall of the Jerusalem temple is reinforced, we think, when at the end of this chapter the church is described as "a holy temple." In that temple there is no wall limiting the access of Gentiles.

Breaking down "the dividing wall" is a vivid image for overcoming the division between Jew and Gentile. It happens when the Christ breaks down the "hostility" between them—and in response these churches must be about overcoming that hostility, that enmity. Those who hear Ephesians are not called to go to Jerusalem to break down the barriers. They are called to break down the walls and to perform this new social reality by forming friendships with the people on the other side of the aisle, or on the other side of town.

"He has abolished the law with its commandments and ordinances" (2:15). It was not really some five-foot wall that stood in Jerusalem that divided Jew and Gentile in the Lycus Valley. That was

---

God Hates Walls

God hates walls and divisions and intends to save the world by breaking them down. If we want to stay close to God, we need to participate in this barrier-breaking project, not frustrate it. Churches, for all their awful mistakes, have a unique power to do that. . . . The community of God has no barriers to membership, not even sin. Christ died for us *while* we were yet sinners. He didn't wait until we got over it. . . . When the church lives up to its charter, nothing divides its members. . . . People who wouldn't come together for any other reason, who don't share nationality, race, opinions, who don't even like each other, can draw close to each other here, because God chose all of them.
—Barbara G. Wheeler

Who Needs the Church? Price H. Gwynn Church Leadership Series (Louisville: Geneva Press, 2004). Also available online at http://www.ppcbooks.com/pdf/price_gwynn/whoneedsthechurch.pdf.

only an image for their hostility, their enmity. But one thing that did divide them in the Lycus Valley was the Jewish law with its commandments and ordinances. It was that law that prompted Jews to boast and to condemn the Gentiles as "sinners." And it was such boasting self-righteousness that provided a "justification" for the Gentiles to despise them. But that law too Christ has broken down, indeed, abolished (2:15)! Ephesians here echoes Paul in Galatians 2:15–21. There too Paul talked about tearing down what had divided Jew and Gentile, and there too it was the law. Some Jewish Christians had evidently regarded Gentiles as "sinners" (Gal. 2:15, 17) and themselves as the "righteous." Some Gentile Christians had their own epithets. They called the Jews "weak" and regarded themselves as "strong," not encumbered by any scruples about the law. In Galatians it is Paul (in solidarity with Christ) who tore down that wall. The law itself, as Paul had insisted, lets us know that we are *all* "sinners" (Rom. 3:19–20). And it is by the grace of God we are *all* "righteous."

The same point is made here. Lest we think that because the law is broken down we may be unconcerned about "righteousness," Paul had already reminded the Ephesians that we are "created in the Messiah Jesus for good works" (2:10, our trans.). The law is still useful to point the way to God's intentions, but it is not to be used as a weapon to defend ourselves as "the righteous" and to condemn others as "sinners." It is not the law any longer that is to be constitutive of our identity and community or determinative for our discernment. It is Christ.

One can imagine again that pious Jewish Christian in the corner lifting his voice to interrupt again in response to this phrase about the law being abolished, but this time he would interrupt not to say "Amen" but to say "What?!" And we might join him in asking for some clarification. This is not the first time that Paul had had to reply to such an inquiry. "Do we overthrow the law by this faith? By no means! On the contrary, we uphold the law," he had said (Rom. 3:31). That sounds a little different than abolishing the law. He had announced to Jewish believers in Rome (7:1) that in Christ they had "died to the law . . . so that you may belong to another, to him who has been raised from the dead in order that we may bear fruit for God" (7:4). But in that very context he had insisted that "the law is holy, and the commandment is holy and just and good" (7:12). That too sounds a little different than "[Christ] has abolished the law with its commandments and ordinances." Perhaps Paul has contradicted himself, or perhaps some Paulinist has departed from Paul on this point, or perhaps some further clarification is in order. We think that some further clarification is in order.

Ephesians cannot mean that the Torah is abolished. Only a few verses before Ephesians had not discredited but honored the "covenants of promise" that one learns of in the Torah (2:12). And the author took the promises given in the Torah to be fulfilled in Christ, not abolished by this Jewish Messiah. It is in the Torah, after all, that one reads that the blessing on Abraham included finally a blessing on all the nations. So one clarification would be that Paul distinguishes the story from statutes, the promise from ordinances, the commandment from the commandments, and that he gives hermeneutical priority to the story completed in Christ, to the promise fulfilled in Christ, and to the commandment to love God and the neighbor. That seems right, but another clarification may also be necessary.

Paul never suggested that Jewish believers are to cease being Jews, to begin to act like Gentiles. He himself evidently usually observed the law. But he also never suggested that Gentile believers need to cease being Gentiles or that they must begin to act like Jews. Indeed, he insisted that Gentiles need not keep the ordinances and commandments in order to be fully partners in the life of the church. It is not the law itself but two specific functions of the law, two functions especially tied to ordinances and commandments, that are abolished. The first abrogation is this: it is no longer in the power of the law to condemn (e.g., Rom. 8:1; 2 Cor. 3:7–11). And the second "like unto it" is this: the Jews may not condemn the Gentiles on the basis of the law (e.g., Rom. 2:1); it is no longer in the power of the law to divide Jew from Gentile. Because these two uses of the law are abrogated, the law itself is abrogated as the principle of identity, abrogated as constitutive of the community, and abrogated as the final test for the community's discernment.

Such a clarification is confirmed in the next phrase. He "abolished the law with its commandments and ordinances, that [Greek *hina*, or 'in order that'] he might create in himself one new humanity in place of the two" (2:15). By robbing the law of its power to condemn and to divide, the Messiah can gather up the two into one, creating one new humanity. This is the new social reality, one new humanity. This is the fulfillment of Psalm 8 in Christ. The risen Christ and his cross are the new principle of identity, constitutive of a new community, and the new test for a community's discernment.

The next phrase, "thus making peace" (2:15), is both summary and climax, retrieving as it does the theme of peace and the text from Isaiah. But it is not the end of this catalogue. The little catalogue of the works of the Messiah continues, adding phrase to phrase. It is pleonasm again, but the theme of the Messiah making peace is worthy of it.

In parallel to "that he might create in himself one new humanity" stands the next phrase: "and might reconcile both groups to God in one body through the cross" (2:16). Among the works of the Messiah is also this one: the Messiah reconciles. Ordinarily in Paul it is God who reconciles, but here it is the Messiah. It is according to the plan of God "to gather up all things in [Christ]" (1:10), but it is still here counted among the works of the Messiah. Who is reconciled? The two groups, Jew and Gentile. To whom are they reconciled? They are both reconciled to God, but reconciled to God, they are reconciled to each other. Where are they reconciled? In the "one

---

Chrysostom on Jew and Gentile

Don't you see? The Greek does not have to become a Jew. Rather both enter into a new condition. His aim is not to bring Greek believers into being as different kinds of Jews but rather to create both anew. Rightly he uses the term *create* rather than *change* to point out the great effect of what God has done. Even though the creation is invisible it is no less a creation of its Creator.

—Chrysostom

Homily on Ephesians 5.2.13–15, quoted in *Galatians, Ephesians, Philippians*, Ancient Christian Commentary on Scripture: New Testament 8, ed. Mark J. Edwards (Downers Grove, IL: InterVarsity Press, 1999), 140.

body," in Christ and in the body of Christ, the church (1:23). And how are they reconciled? Through the cross. The blood of Christ (2:13) was the seal of a new covenant, the sacrifice of the cross our "peace offering," and it is celebrated in a common meal in which we remember his death and anticipate God's good future, discerning and displaying "one body." And the cross is the paradigm for reconciliation in community. Later Ephesians will urge these Christians to "live in love, as Christ loved us and gave himself up for us, a fragrant offering and sacrifice to God" (5:2). The significance of the cross as paradigmatic for reconciliation in the community does not stand in competition with the language of sacrifice and covenant but on the foundation of the works of the Messiah.

The next phrase follows naturally, "thus putting to death that hostility through it" (2:16). This phrase stands parallel to "thus making peace." "Hostility" has been mentioned once before in this little catalogue (2:14). There it was explicitly the hostility between Jew and Gentile, in apposition to the image of the "dividing wall" between Jew and Gentile. Here the meaning of "hostility" is broadened but not changed. It is broadened because the Messiah reconciled both groups *to God*. In the grim picture of Gentile and Jewish unrighteousness (2:1–3) it was clear that both groups were "sinners" and had made themselves the enemies of God and of God's cause. Both groups needed to be brought from death to life; both needed to share in the death and life of the Messiah. But the meaning of "hostility" has not changed; it still includes (and has as its primary referent) the enmity of Jew and Gentile. They were reconciled "in one body," and the hostility is put to death "through it," through that one body of Christ, the church.[10]

The Messiah reconciled Jew and Gentile "through the cross, thus putting to death that hostility" (2:16). This wonderfully ironic combination of phrases displays the reversal so characteristic of the cross in the light of the resurrection. What looks like the defeat of the

10. Reading *en autō* (2:16) as a neuter (like NRSV) and "body" as its antecedent. It is also possible to read it as a masculine and Christ as its antecedent, "in himself," like the parallel in 2:15. If he put hostility to death "in himself," the reconciliation still displays itself in his body, the church.

Christ ends up in victory. What looks like triumph for the powers is really their defeat. What looks like the hour of his humiliation is, as John says, the hour of his glory (John 12:23; 17:1–5). And in his dying he puts "hostility" to death. The love that is displayed on the cross—and the love that fits the paradigm of the cross—is patient, kind, not envious or boastful; "it does not insist on its own way; it is not irritable or resentful"; it does not rejoice in the wrongdoings of others (1 Cor. 13:4–6). It puts enmity and hostility to death. Hostility, too, like the rest of the grim picture, is overmatched.

The final item in this catalogue of the works of the Messiah is that he "came and proclaimed peace to you who were far off and peace to those who were near" (Eph. 2:17). Once more the language of Isaiah 57:19 is retrieved, "Peace, peace, to the far and the near, says the LORD." The Messiah is the Lord, the "prince of peace" (Isa. 9:5–6), who has come "proclaiming peace" (cf. 52:7). The story of Peter and Cornelius is helpful here. Cornelius was an uncircumcised "God-fearer" (Acts 10:2), the first Gentile convert in Acts. Peter may have been a little reticent to visit him, fearing it was "unlawful for a Jew to associate with or to visit a Gentile" (10:28), but God had shown him in a vision that he "should not call anyone profane or unclean" (10:28). So he went "without objection" (10:29) and said to Cornelius, "I truly understand that God shows no partiality, but in every nation anyone who fears him and does what is right is acceptable to him. You know the message he sent to the people of Israel, *preaching peace by Jesus Christ*—he is Lord of all" (10:34–36, italics added). As Peter continued his conversation with Cornelius, celebrating the spread of that message, remembering Jesus, and reaching the point where he affirmed with "all the prophets" that "everyone who believes in him receives forgiveness of sins," the Spirit "fell upon all who heard the word, . . . even on the Gentiles" (10:43–45). And then Peter knew that the grace of God could reach farther than he had imagined; then he knew that the message of peace included also the Gentiles; and then the Gentiles were baptized (10:48). He knew, as Ephesians puts it here, that both Jew and Gentile "have access in one Spirit to the Father" (2:18).

All the other works of the Messiah on this list are tied to the cross. It may be a little awkward chronologically to think of his coming and his preaching as references to the ministry of Jesus before the cross, but it is surely appropriate. His coming was greeted with the songs of angels, "praising God and saying, 'Glory to God in the highest heaven, and on earth peace'" (Luke 2:14). He came announcing "the kingdom of God," the good future of God. He not only announced it; he made that future present in his works of power and his words of blessing. When the sick (both Jew and Gentile) were healed, God's good future and its *shalom* (wholeness, well-being) made its power felt. When the waters of chaos were calmed at his command, "Peace! Be still!" (Mark 4:39), there was a display of God's good future. When he blessed the peacemakers (Matt. 5:9), he blessed them because in the peace they make we see a little token of God's future; in the peace they make we see some little token of Christ and of the secret, the mystery, of God's plan for the fullness of time. He announced the kingdom and healed those who were far as well as those who were near, "sinners" as well as the righteous, Gentiles like the centurion (Matt. 8:5–13) as well as Jews, the least as well as the greatest. His table fellowship with "sinners" gave reason for the accusation that he was "a friend of sinners" (e.g., Matt. 11:19; Luke 7:34), an accusation that Jesus was evidently happy enough to let stand. He called for—and displayed—a radical inclusiveness. It was no shock that the "sinners" and Gentiles and others on the margins of society, "the least," heard him most gladly.

Given the awkwardness chronologically, however, perhaps we are to think of the risen Christ greeting the disciples with the words, "Peace be with you" (John 20:19, 21). But however we think of it, the claim of Ephesians is that among the works of the Messiah is this one, that he proclaims peace.

All of this is accomplished "in [Christ's] flesh" (2:14).[11] This is not the work of some docetic redeemer, some spiritual apparition who provides an esoteric and otherworldly knowledge; this is the work of the Jewish Messiah. It may also be a reference to the cross,

---

11. It is difficult to know to which of the phrases this "in his flesh" belongs. It is found at the end of 2:14 in the Greek and might belong to what precedes it in v. 14 or to the phrase or phrases that follow it in 2:15–17. NRSV puts it at the beginning of 2:14, immediately following "he is our peace," as if it covers all these works of the Messiah. That seems right to us.

like "blood" (2:13), or to the incarnation, as in John 1:14. But it surely must be read in conjunction with two previous times in this chapter that "in the flesh" (Greek *en sarki*) is used. In Ephesians 2:11 the Gentiles are addressed as "you Gentiles *en sarki*" (NRSV "by birth"), and circumcision is described as a cutting by human hands *en sarki* (NRSV "in the flesh"). The only hope is when the Jewish Messiah works "in *his* flesh" to bring fulfillment to "the covenants of promise" (2:12), which from the beginning included the promise that "all the families of the earth shall be blessed" (Gen. 12:3). This Jewish Messiah has now provided for both Jews *en sarki* and Gentiles *en sarki* "access in one Spirit to the Father" (Eph. 2:18). There is no reason for boasting, no basis for confidence in the flesh, but there is hope in the one who was the Messiah in the flesh. And if he has done all of this "in his flesh," then the unity he gives and the peace he makes are fleshly too. The church may not be content with some docetic unity or some "spiritual" peace; it must look for and work for some fleshly consequences of that unity and peace.

The catalogue of the works of the Messiah is completed: the Messiah makes both one, breaks down the dividing wall, abolishes the power of the law to condemn and divide, creates in himself one new humanity, makes peace, reconciles both Jew and Gentile to God, puts hostility to death, and proclaims peace. Little wonder that the passage begins with that powerful declaration not about the works of the Messiah but about his person. "He is our peace!"

FURTHER REFLECTIONS
Performing Peace—Breaking Down the Walls

A new social reality has been accomplished by God in Christ. Christ has broken down the dividing wall. He has created a new humanity. He has made peace. He *is* our peace. That new social reality makes claims upon us and upon our life together. What does it mean to perform this peace, to practice it in the world?

There is a magnificent description of the church in the *Book of Order* for the Presbyterian Church (U.S.A.). In the section on the mission of the church, the church is called "a provisional demonstration of what God intends for all of humanity."[12] In the field of agri-culture, demonstration plots are places where new crops are culti-vated and nurtured so that others may observe their growth and development for the benefit of the whole community. Sometimes those new crops provide essential produce for those in need of nourishment.

The church is a demonstration plot for the new humanity brought about by God's reconciling work in Jesus Christ. To be the church is to be a people who respond to God's work with joy and praise, who display something of what God intends for all of humanity in their common life. The church is called to provide an alternative to the cultures of enmity at work in the world. It is to be a community that resists efforts to build up again those walls of division and enmity that Christ has broken down. It is to be a place of hospitality to the stranger, a place of peaceable difference. It is to demonstrate the new human community that Christ has made. It is to put God's work and cause on display. God knows the world des-perately needs to see it. Ephesians calls us in the church to reclaim our identity as peacemakers in the spirit of Christ, who is our peace, and to be about the business of breaking down the dividing walls.

The urgency of this vocation was evident when University of Notre Dame offered President Barack Obama an honorary doctorate in May 2009. The announcement of the degree and the invitation to give the graduation address to the class of 2009 ignited a protest by those who thought it was inappropriate for a Catholic university to honor someone whose views and policies concerning abortion differ from the teachings of the Roman Catholic Church. Address-ing the students in his introduction of the president, Father John Jenkins, president of Notre Dame, described the situation in which we live this way: "The world you enter today is torn by division—and is fixed on its differences." Differences must be acknowledged, and in some cases cherished. But too often differences lead to pride in one's self or in one's little tribe and contempt for others. Too often differences lead to hostility and enmity. Too often difference ends

---

12. *The Constitution of the Presbyterian Church (U.S.A.), Part II, Book of Order (2005–2007)* (Louisville: Office of the General Assembly, 2005), G-3.0200.

up with two sides taking opposing views of the same difference and demonizing each other. Whether the difference is political, religious, racial, or national, trust fails, anger rises, and cooperation ends— even for the sake of causes all sides care about. "More than any problem in the arts or sciences—engineering or medicine—easing the hateful divisions between human beings is the supreme challenge of this age. If we can solve this problem, we have a chance to come together and solve all the others."[13]

President Obama then called upon his audience to join him in taking on this most difficult challenge we face in the twenty-first century. "We must find a way to reconcile our ever-shrinking world with its ever growing diversity—diversity of thought, diversity of culture, and diversity of belief. In short, we must find a way to live together as one human family."[14] Obama then told about his personal journey to the practice of peacemaking. He was not raised, he said, in "a particularly religious household," but his mother instilled in him a sense of the importance of service and empathy. That led him to become a community organizer. In that role he began to work with Catholic and Protestant churches, Jewish and African American organizations, and with working-class residents of the community, black and white and Hispanic. It was, he said, "an eclectic crew, all of us with different experiences, all of us with different beliefs. But all of us learned to work side by side because all of us saw in those neighborhoods other human beings who needed our help—to find jobs and improve schools. We were bound together in the service of others."

Then he reported something else that happened in the time he spent in those neighborhoods: he was drawn to the church.

> Perhaps because the church folks I worked with were so welcoming and understanding; perhaps because they invited me to their services and sang with me from their hymnals; perhaps because I was really broke and they fed me. Perhaps because I witnessed all of the good works their faith inspired

13. The full transcript of Fr. Jenkins's speech may be found at http://frates.wordpress .com/2009/05/18/full-transcript-fr.jenkins-notre-dame-speech/.
14. The full transcript of President Obama's speech may be found at http://www.Chicagotribune .com/news/politics/obama/chi-barack-obama-notre-dame-speech,0,6345947.story.

them to perform, I found myself drawn not just to work with the church; I was drawn to be in the church. It was through this service that I was brought to Christ.

"But now in Christ Jesus you who once were far off have been brought near by the blood of Christ" (Eph. 2:13). Practicing peace can lead to the one who is our peace and who has broken down the dividing wall. In a deeply divided world, which threatens each day to come apart over differences of every kind, it is an evangelical moment when people with little in common find common ground. For Christians, that common ground is at the foot of the cross. There we discover the good news that our differences need not divide us. There the cultures of enmity and exclusion were and are called into question. And by the power of the resurrection and the gift of the Spirit, people began to perform a new social reality.

Ephesians reminds the churches of the Lycus Valley of their identity, reminds them of what God has done in Christ, so they can live into God's good future with hope. The world was—and is—threatened by our habits of dividing the world into the predictable little tribes who fear and despise the other tribes. Despite the cynicism and weariness that characterizes our time, some still hope that there is another way. Performing peace offers a new possibility. If the church simply practices the same old enmities, performing the scripts provided by cultures of enmity, why would anyone sign on for more of that behavior? Ephesians calls us to live in solidarity with Christ and a new humanity, to live in accord with that reconciled condition, putting hostility to death and proclaiming peace to those far off and to those who are near.

A church proclaiming and practicing peace is an evangelical church with a message that is good news to the weary world. Proclaiming the good news of peace in a war-torn world is not something the church does to find comfort. Peacemaking is hard work and can be dangerous. Nevertheless, the church is called upon to be faithful to the identity it has been given in Christ and to share the good news of a new humanity with the world.

The call to perform peace put Martin Luther King Jr. to work building "the beloved community." It was a religious vision and a religious calling.[15] He had a dream, and he had that dream because he saw Jesus. "There is a great event that stands at the center of our faith," he said, the great event of the cross and resurrection, "which reveals to us that God is on the side of truth and love and justice."[16] It was the same "great event," he said, that calls for nonviolent resistance to the lies of enmity and injustice, the same "great event" that calls the church to be transformed, not to be conformed to the present age.[17] The "beloved community" is the reality of reconciliation introduced by the cross and resurrection and still calling to us from the future. When King spoke about the goals of the civil rights movement, he said, "the end is reconciliation, the end is redemption, the end is beloved community."[18] The "beloved community" knows no boundaries apart from "the solidarity of the human family." As he said in his "Letter from Birmingham Jail," "we are caught in an inescapable network of mutuality, tied together in the single garment of destiny."[19]

This "beloved community" stands in stark contrast to segregation and to all the cultures of enmity whose creed is divide and conquer. "It is still true," King said, "that in Christ there is neither Jew nor Gentile (Negro nor white) and that out of one blood God has made all men to dwell upon the face of the earth."[20] And we still face a choice between conformity to the cultures of enmity in our age and the good future of God, between "march[ing] to the drumbeat of conformity" and "listening to the beat of a more distant drum."[21]

---

15. King was quite candid about the Christian character of his vision and calling. See Charles Marsh, *The Beloved Community: How Faith Shapes Social Justice, from the Civil Rights Movement to Today* (New York: Basic Books, 2005), 11–50. See also Richard Lischer, *The Preacher King: Martin Luther King Jr. and the Word That Moved America* (New York: Oxford University Press, 1995).

16. Martin Luther King Jr., *The Papers of Martin Luther King, Jr.*, vol. 3, *Birth of a New Age: December 1955–December 1956*, ed. Stewart Burns, Susan Carson, Peter Holloran, and Dana L. H. Powell (Berkeley: University of California Press, 1997), 327, cited in Marsh, *Beloved Community*, 44.

17. Marsh, *Beloved Community*, 44.

18. King, *Papers*, 3:452, cited in Marsh, *Beloved Community*, 1.

19. Martin Luther King Jr., "Letter from Birmingham Jail," in *Why We Can't Wait* (New York: Signet Book, 1964), 77.

20. King, *Papers*, 3:17, cited by Marsh, *Beloved Community*, 45.

21. Martin Luther King Jr., "Transformed Nonconformist," in *Strength to Love* (New York: Pocket Books, 1968), 18.

That march, that pilgrimage, will require love and justice. Love, agape love, is the fundamental requirement for King, and not simply as some "impossible ideal." It is "the only way to create the beloved community."[22] But love partners with justice. Justice is essential if we are to live together in peace. King made clear that the beloved community is built upon a commitment to work for justice, not for one race or class, but for all:

> Let us be dissatisfied until rat-infested, vermin-filled slums will be a thing of a dark past and every family will have a decent sanitary house in which to live. Let us be dissatisfied until the empty stomachs of Mississippi are filled and the idle industries of Appalachia are revitalized. . . . Let us be dissatisfied until our brothers of the Third World of Asia, Africa and Latin America will no longer be the victims of imperialist exploitation, but will be lifted from the long night of poverty, illiteracy and disease.[23]

And he often said: "Injustice anywhere is a threat to justice everywhere."[24]

King saw Jesus, and because he saw Jesus, he also saw something of the vision in Ephesians of one new humanity; he called it "the beloved community." And he answered the call of Ephesians to put that vision on display in the world. Reading Ephesians again in the churches may provide the "spectacles" (to use Calvin's image) that we need to see it for ourselves. And with our vision corrected, perhaps we may also hear a little better the call to put that vision on display. The vision in Ephesians given to churches of the Lycus Valley and to us is too good to miss. And the call in Ephesians to put it on display is a call that we ignore at our own peril. But if we can see that vision, heed that call, and embrace the work of performing peace, we may witness to a peace the world desperately needs.

We do not yet see all things united and renewed in Christ. But we too can see Jesus, and occasionally we catch a glimpse of this community where the walls of hostility are broken down. After the

22. Martin Luther King Jr., "Loving Your Enemies," in *Strength to Love*, 48.
23. Martin Luther King Jr., "Honoring Dr. Du Bois," in *Freedomways* 8 (Spring 1968): 110–11.
24. For example, in his "Letter from Birmingham Jail."

On Knowing We Are in Church

The First Presbyterian Church of Durham established a memorial garden in 1984 as a sacred space to place the ashes of church members. The names of the saints "who from their labors rest" are displayed on plaques that hang on the wall in the garden. One day a devoted member and a lay leader of the congregation, Gran Uzzle, who owned a successful automobile dealership, asked me to join him in the memorial garden.

As we stood beneath the wall of names, he pointed to two plaques. One was a plaque for George Watts Hill, a lifelong member and part of a highly respected North Carolina family, a prominent business and civil leader, and a philanthropist. The other was a plaque for Richard Vereen. Richard was an African American who grew up in Andrews, South Carolina, until he was drafted and served in the U.S. Army in Vietnam. During his tour of duty, he became addicted to drugs. In his mid-thirties, upon his release from service in the Army, he settled in Durham. As he struggled valiantly to overcome his debilitating illness, Richard joined our congregation and was an active member. When a seizure took his life, the congregation, who had become his family, held his memorial service.

When Gran Uzzle pointed to those two plaques, he said, "Every time I come into this garden and see these two plaques near each other, I know I am in church."

—Joseph S. Harvard, Pastor of First Presbyterian Church

---

march to Montgomery in the spring of 1966, King tells about waiting with some of his fellow marchers for a plane to arrive: "As I stood with them and saw white and Negro, nuns and priests, ministers and rabbis, labor organizers, lawyers, doctors, housemaids and shopworkers brimming with vitality and enjoying a rare comradeship, I knew I was seeing a microcosm of the mankind of the future in this moment of luminous and genuine brotherhood."[25]

It is clear that for the writer of Ephesians and for King, the creation of this beloved community is due to divine intervention. King said, "above all, we must be reminded anew that God is at work in his universe. As we struggle to defeat the forces of evil, the God of the universe struggles with us."[26] So when the vision of God's good

---

25. Martin Luther King Jr., *Where Do We Go from Here: Chaos or Community?* (New York: Harper & Row, 1967), 9.
26. Martin Luther King Jr., *Strength to Love* (New York: Harper & Row, 1961), 64.

future seems dim, we should listen again to the story of peace in
Ephesians 2:11–22 or see that story performed when a diverse congregation of God's beloved community lifts a common voice and
sings,

> God of our weary years,
> God of our silent tears,
> Thou who has brought us thus far on the way;
> Thou who has by Thy might
> Led us into the light,
> Keep us forever in the path, we pray.[27]

The Building that Grows

In that good news of the peace that Jesus is and brings, the grim picture of the Gentiles as "aliens" and "strangers" and "hopeless" and
"without God" is overmatched. Now "through Christ" the Gentiles
are "no longer strangers and aliens" (2:19). In a happy jumble of
metaphors, they are "citizens" of a heavenly kingdom that includes
Jews and Gentiles, "members" of God's household, and part of a
building.

It is not just any building, of course. This building has Christ
Jesus as its keystone.[28] This building has Christian apostles and
prophets as a foundation. This building "grows"; it is a living thing.
Its "growth" is not simply a matter of numbers. It grows into something fitting to Christ, into "the measure of the full stature of Christ"
(4:13). It is not yet what it must become, but it grows. It grows into
a holy temple, not built by hands (cf. 2:11). And Christians are part
of it, part of this temple made of Jew and Gentile joined together to

---

27. James Weldon Johnson, "Lift Every Voice and Sing," *Presbyterian Hymnal* (Louisville:
Westminster John Knox Press, 1990), no. 563.

28. "Keystone" is the marginal reading in the NRSV of Eph. 2:20. The text has "cornerstone." A
cornerstone can mean a foundation stone, as it does in Isa. 28:16, but the foundation here
is otherwise provided. Moreover, "cornerstone" has come to mean a stone at the corner of
a building that is laid or disclosed with a special ceremony. That seems insufficient to the
significance of Christ. A "keystone" is the wedge-shaped stone at the crown of an arch that
holds all the other pieces in place.

Christ and to each other, fitted together in ways only a master crafts-man could manage, built together in the Spirit. This building is the church, already the dwelling place for God, and called to grow into something worthy of God's dwelling (2:20–22).

When Solomon prepared to dedicate the temple, "the glory of the Lord filled the house of the Lord" (1 Kgs. 8:11). In Ezekiel's vision of a restored temple "the glory of the Lord filled the temple" once again (Ezek. 43:5). But according to the *berakot* at the end of Psalm 72, the same glory would fill the earth: "Blessed be the Lord, the God of Israel, who alone does wondrous things. Blessed be his glorious name forever; may his glory fill the whole earth. Amen and Amen" (Ps. 72:18–19). This temple, too, the church, is filled with the presence, the glory, of the Lord, who is the one who will finally and completely fill all things. The conclusion of this chapter thus echoes the conclusion of chapter 1 (at least as we translated it). There the church was described as Christ's body, not as a temple; but that body, like this temple, is filled by the one who finally and completely fills and fulfills all things.

There is no place for ecclesiasti-cal triumphalism here. Apart from its head the body will wither. Apart from its keystone the building will fall apart. The church is not yet what it is called and destined to be. It must grow into that. "For this reason" (3:1) Paul turns again to prayer for the church.

St. Francis's Prayer

Lord, Make me an instrument of your peace. Where there is hatred, let me sow love.

—Francis of Assisi

3:1–13

A Prayer Resumed—
and Interrupted

In Ephesians we have frequently found Paul praying. It started in the magnificent *berakot* of the first chapter, blessing God for God's blessings. It continued with the report of Paul's thanksgiving for the churches' faith and love (1:16). Paul turned immediately then to petition. Beginning in 1:17 he prayed that the church would know its immeasurably great hope. The church already knew it, of course. That was one of the blessings Paul had counted earlier: that the secret, the mystery of God's good future in the fullness of time, had been made known to the church. But he prayed that the church would know it more fully, see it more clearly. That immeasurably great hope he then tried to measure by the immeasurable power of God that raised Jesus *from* the dead and *to* sovereignty over the powers. That was the basis of the hope, and the object of hope was nothing less than a new humanity established in Christ—indeed, nothing less than the renewal of "all things" in him.

Those "spiritual blessings" and that hope for the future were not something remote from this earth or from the present. It was not some "pie in the sky by-and-by." The knowledge for which Paul prayed—and for which these Christians prayed as the letter was read in the churches—was not some gnostic knowledge, not some esoteric knowledge of our truly spiritual origin and destiny. These "spiritual blessings" and our hope do not dismiss our life in the body and in community; they do not make life in the flesh and in the present insignificant and trivial. On the contrary, the "spiritual blessings" have worldly consequences, fleshly consequences. And the good future of God, the inheritance of the church, is already real and present in the Spirit and in the work of the Spirit in the churches.

So Paul paused in his prayer to call attention to the share that these Christians, Jew and Gentile, have in Christ already: "made alive together with Christ" (2:5), saved by grace and so rendered one community, a harbinger of a new humanity in Christ. In the midst of cultures of ethnic enmity Christ made the two one community. Christ is our peace. Already Jew and Gentile may live in peaceable difference. These blessings, like the blessings counted in chapter 1, do not confer upon the church a status about which they might now boast. They confer upon them a calling, a calling to bless God, a calling to agency in response to God's blessings and a calling of loyalty and service to God's cause. They have not yet measured up to that calling. They must grow.

Now Paul is poised to resume his prayer. "This is the reason that I Paul . . ." (3:1) pray for the church. But wait! In 3:1 he does not pray. He does not turn to prayer until 3:14. There he repeats this opening phrase, "For this reason I bow my knees before the Father . . ." and makes petition for the church. In 3:1 Paul is ready to turn to prayer again, but he interrupts himself.

Paul as Paradigm

It is an extended interruption, a long parenthesis. In it Paul describes his ministry, his own calling. We need to try to figure out what is going on here. How does Paul describe his ministry? But also, why describe it *here*? Why *interrupt* his turning to prayer?

It will help to observe that Paul does this now and then in his other letters too. In 1 Corinthians 9, for example, he interrupts his answer to the question about eating meat that had been sacrificed to idols by talking about himself, about his "rights" as an apostle, and about his freedom not to make the claims that are his to make when forgoing those claims serves love. The "interruption" there advances his argument and provides a model for the Corinthians. The Corinthians are invited *to imitate* Paul, to affirm freedom but not to insist on their own "rights" about eating meat or not. "Be imitators of me, as I am of Christ," he says (11:1).

Something similar is going on here, we think. He interrupts his turn to prayer in order to remind the Christians of the Lycus Valley of the burden and the glory of Paul's calling—and of their own. Paul's calling provides a model for their own, and when they see it, they will be ready to pray more earnestly for the strength to perform it. In this long parenthesis, he calls attention to himself and, indeed, to his apostolic authority, but not to boast. Or if we must call it boasting, at least we must also observe that it is a paradoxical boasting, a boasting about his weakness, about his being "least," about the grace of God (3:8).[1]

The passage reminds its hearers of what they surely know of Paul, that he was imprisoned, for starters (3:1). But why is he in chains? They knew that too, of course. It was not because he was a felon, not because he had stolen or killed, not because he had led an armed rebellion against the state. (It is worth observing that they may have known that Paul was in prison because of events in Jerusalem after he delivered the collection, that sign of the unity of Jew and Gentile in the churches, but Paul makes no explicit mention of it.) They knew, or could be expected to know, that Paul was imprisoned for his proclamation of Jesus as the Jewish Messiah "for the sake of you Gentiles" (3:1). He was, in a sense, a prisoner of this Christ rather than of the Romans. His imprisonment was related to his work as an apostle. He was in chains, and this was God's grace at work! It is a curious boasting, if that is what it is. He has to *endure* his blessing. His being blessed and called by God got him what? Imprisonment. One might reasonably have responded, "Uh, thanks but no thanks. Thanks for thinking of me, God, but can your gifts be returned for cash?" Paul makes no such response. His response to God's call is empty of two things: triumphalism and self-pity. It is empty of the sort of triumphalism that supposes that God calls us to a path that ends with a pleasant little lunch with the emperor. And it is empty of

---

1. Parenthetically, this section seems to us to be one of the best arguments for thinking Paul was indeed the author—not just because the author says, "I, Paul . . ." but also because a later Paulinist would likely have celebrated Paul a little less paradoxically than this passage does. If it is by a later Paulinist, he understands Paul's understanding of his own apostleship quite well—and evidently shares it.

the sort of self-pity that supposes that the story is all about me. He interrupts the turn to prayer to tell his story, but he tells it as God's story, as a story that reveals something of God and the cause of God, not as a story about himself to which God is a footnote.

God let Paul in on the secret (3:3), and God called him, sent him, to make it known to the Gentiles. That gift and calling, the gift and calling of being made an apostle to the Gentiles, was not easy. It involved hardships and imprisonment, but there is no self-pity here. Indeed, it is closer to boasting. He was a revolutionary in a way, not an insurrectionist, but he, along with other Christians, as Acts says, was "turning the world upside down" (Acts 17:6). He had an eschatological role to play; he was an important character in the drama of history. By God's grace and his apostleship, he stood at the turning of the ages in the service of the cause of God, the creation of a new humanity. He was given that role, commissioned to be an apostle, by the grace of God. It was not something about which he could boast. He was let in on the secret, the mystery of God's good future, and he was blessed and called to make it known.

Telling the Secret

Lest these Christians of the Lycus Valley (or any other readers) forget, he reminds them ("as I wrote above," 3:3) that the "secret" is this: "the Gentiles have become fellow heirs, members of the same body, and sharers in the promise in Christ Jesus [that is, in Jesus, the Jewish Messiah] through the gospel" (3:6). In Greek those phrases are all created with the prefix *syn-*. If we tried to translate it more literally, using "co-" as the English equivalent of *syn-* here, it would be "co-heirs, co-corporate, and co-partakers." We know "co-corporate" is a made-up word, but so it appears was Paul's word, *syssōma*, the word translated "members of the same body." We did not report this just to show off a little Greek. These words created with the prefix *syn-* echo an earlier set of words using the same prefix. Back in 2:5 and 6 there was another set of words with *syn-* prefixes: "made us alive together *with* him . . . raised us up *with* him and seated us *with* him" (italics added). In that context it was *with Christ* that they (both Jew and Gentile) were made alive, raised up, and seated. Here in 3:6

it is the Gentiles who are made heirs, members of the community, and given a share in the promises *with the Jews*.

There is no setting aside of the Jews. And if Gentiles pretend that they *rather than* the Jews are now the beloved children of God, the pretense is to be traced to racism, not to the gospel. Indeed, it contradicts the gospel. It—and all racism—contradicts the secret that God revealed to Paul and the church. There is a new humanity in Christ. Christ is our peace. That is the gospel in the midst of cultures of ethnic enmity.

The Jews need not set aside their own Jewishness, nor Gentiles adopt a Jewish identity. Christ is our peace not by enforcing a culture of oppressive homogeneity but by inviting a culture of peaceable difference. Each is to practice hospitality to the other. Such hospitality must be distinguished from its counterfeit, the attitude that pretends to hospitality while adopting the role of the noble benefactor to a needy beneficiary. Such counterfeit "hospitality" may also be called "charity," but it is a counterfeit charity too, marked and marred by "the conceit of philanthropy." The counterfeit hospitality divides the world—and the church—into two great camps, the noble benefactors and the needy beneficiaries. The counterfeit hospitality always comes with a reminder of on which side of that great divide one stands, with the benefactors or with the needy. And it usually comes with the expectation that each will stay on the side of that great divide where they belong. But Paul has made clear with his grim picture of both Jew and Gentile that both are needy. It is God alone who is the great benefactor, and God has blessed both Jew and Gentile in Christ. Any kindness or patience or forgiveness or hospitality in their relationship is like a simple prayer of thanksgiving, just gift answering to gift, a glad response to the gospel that announces peace.

Paul's Ministry, God's Gift, and the Church's Calling

Of that gospel, Paul says, he has "become a servant" (3:7). He does not boast about his being an apostle. It is, he says, "the *gift* of God's *grace* that was *given* me by the working of [*God's*] power" (3:7, italics added). He is, he says, "the least of the saints" (3:8; or more literally, if ungrammatically, the "leastest"), but *"grace* was *given"* (3:8, italics added) to make him an apostle to the Gentiles, announcing to them "the news of the boundless riches of Christ" (3:8; cf. 1:18). By piling on these reminders of gift and grace, there are no loopholes left for boasting. Still, what a glorious calling! It is an eschatological existence, a life at the turning of the ages, a *doxological* existence. Paul lives to the praise of God's glory, and it fills him when he brings to the Gentiles the news of their immeasurable riches in Christ, their great hope in Christ, an inheritance that surpasses their imagination but that nothing can destroy or wither.

Moreover, by bringing to the Gentiles this good news, this gospel, there is an unveiling of God's secret—and "everyone" (Jew as well as Gentile) may come to see the plan of God to unite all things in Christ (3:9). That is, the success of the gospel among the Gentiles will display by the Spirit's power the budding of a new humanity and of peace between Jew and Gentile. Everyone, not just the Gentiles to whom Paul preaches, will be able to see the new social reality created as the firstfruit of God's good future.

Then he makes a transition to the church, a transition from talking about his apostleship to talking about the church's apostolicity. It remains God's story, but the church no less than Paul has a role in it. The church is called to serve God's plan, to make the secret known, "that through the church the wisdom of God . . . might now be made known to the rulers and authorities in the heavenly places" (3:10).[2] The church has a calling of cosmic proportion. This calling cannot be reduced to saving souls from the world. It is closer to "bringing the world in for repairs," closer to caring for the cosmos. It has this calling only because the work of Christ has cosmic significance, only because the plan of God is "to gather up all things in [Christ]" (1:10).

2. The ellipsis here is "in its rich variety." We are not quite sure what to make of this phrase. We are quite sure that it does not refer here to things like visions, oracles, and the like, the "rich variety" of ways revelation comes to people. We think it is rather an acknowledgment—and celebration—of the diverse ways in which different people with different gifts (and different communities in different contexts) may display something of God's wisdom. If we are right about that, it would be another indication that God's peace does not impose an oppressive uniformity but invites peaceable difference.

This—the ministry of Paul and the calling of the churches—is all in accord with the secret, with the mystery, the Creator's plan not to abandon the world but to renew it, to create a new humanity, to reconcile Jew and Gentile to God and to one another, to restore the peaceable difference of the creation.

That plan is not some ideal that stands outside our world and our history. It is not some ideal that would have no reality unless the church managed on the basis of its own fleshly powers somehow to accomplish it. That plan is already now a reality. It has already been accomplished by Christ. The cause of God has been "carried out in Christ Jesus our Lord" (3:11). He has been raised from the dead, raised to sovereignty over the principalities and powers, and there he sits at God's right hand, a new humanity in whom we can see the truth of Psalm 8 (Eph. 1:20–22a) and God's secret. It is not yet the good future of God, but that good future is already a reality in the risen Lord, not just an ideal, and it is already making its power felt also in the life of Paul and in the life of the church. It is only in the power of God that the church can either have or fulfill this cosmic calling. It is only when the church is filled with the works of the Messiah that it can itself work in the service of God's cause and calling. We take the "access to God" (3:12; cf. 2:18) that we have in Christ to be a synec-doche for all the works of the Messiah catalogued in 2:14–17, to be the part that stands for the whole of the work of the Messiah. When we remember Jesus, the Messiah, our Lord, and his faithfulness, we discover resources for boldness and confidence and our own faith-fulness. Remembering is not simply recollection. Memory is consti-tutive of identity and community, and it is the basis of our hope. It is only forgetfulness that makes us think that the principalities and the powers properly rule our lives.

Indeed, there is hope even for the principalities and powers. (See pp. 65–71, "Further Reflections: The Powers.") They too were cre-ated, remember, but they had become arrogant, making idolatrous claims, nurturing enmity toward any who resisted their claims. But the church, by its being the church, by its performance of peace, by its rejection of enmity, by its display of the possibility and the promise of a new humanity, is to make God's good future present and real—and known! By its life and witness in faithfulness to the

Jewish Messiah, in the power of the Spirit (and yes, in imitation of the apostle), the "apostolic" church is to let even the principalities and the powers in on the secret. That will require resisting their pretentious claims, being a bone crossways in their throat when they would devour any who resist their pretensions, humbling them. It will require the humble and patient display of an alternative culture, one body of Jew and Gentile, a more excellent way. And if Paul's story is a clue, it will also require the church to bear some burdens, to endure some suffering. And that is why Paul prays that they will not lose heart over Paul's suffering (3:13). If they do, they will lose courage. They should rather think of Paul's suffering for them as their "glory" (3:13). If they do, they will not lose courage. Rather, they will come to understand that their readiness to bear the burden of this calling is their "glory" because it leads to God's glory.

The church, no less than Paul, has a glorious calling! Like Paul, the church lives an eschatological existence, a life at the turning of the ages, a little beachhead for God's good future. As Paul is blessed and called by God to be an apostle, to make the secret known to the Gentiles, *so* the church is blessed and called by God to make the secret known to the principalities and powers. As Paul's calling is to

---

The Church as Pioneer and Representative

In ethics [the church] is the first to repent for the sins of a society and it repents on behalf of all. When it becomes apparent that slavery is transgression of the divine commandment, then the Church repents of it, turns its back upon it, abolishes it within itself. It does this not as the holy community separate from the world but as the pioneer and representative. It repents for the sin of the whole society and leads in the social act of repentance. When the property institutions of society are subject to question because innocent suffering illuminates their antagonism to the will of God, then the Church undertakes to change its own use of these institutions and to lead society in their reformation. So also the Church becomes a pioneer and representative of society in the practice of equality before God, in the reformation of institutions of rulership, in the acceptance of mutual responsibility of individuals for one another.

—H. Richard Niebuhr

"The Responsibility of the Church for Society" and Other Essays, ed. Kristine A. Culp (Louisville: Westminster John Knox Press, 2008), 74–75.

him both blessing and burden, *so* the church is both blessed and burdened by its calling. As Paul suffered for it, *so* the church may expect to suffer by its refusal to participate in the cultures of enmity. As Paul acknowledges that his calling is a gift of the grace of God, leaving no room for boasting or triumphalism, *so* must the church. As Paul lived boldly, *so* must the church. As Paul lives to the praise of God's glory, *so* must the church, Jew and Gentile, live to the praise of God's glory. It is a *doxological* existence. Loyal to the cause of God and faithful to their calling to make the secret known, even to the principalities and powers, the church is filled by Christ and the Spirit, who will completely fill all things finally.

That is the end of the parenthesis. The prayer has been interrupted just long enough for Paul and his hearers to be ready to pray for strength for their task. That is the next chapter.

3:14–21

The Prayer for the Church,
Part Two

"For this reason. . . ." Paul repeats the phrase he used in 3:1 before he interrupted himself to tell the story of his apostleship and to invite the church to something like the same story, to play a role in God's story. Here, however, he finally continues with his prayer, bowing his knees and invoking God as "Father." There is nothing terribly unusual about that invocation. God was regularly invoked as "Abba," "Father," "our Father," and a number of variants, including the "God and Father of our Lord Jesus Christ," which is found at the beginning of the *berakot* (1:3, and here in some manuscripts). But this particular variation is unusual: "Father, from whom every family in heaven and on earth takes its name" (3:14–15).

The Father of All

There is a play on words between "Father" (Greek *patera*) and "family" (Greek *patria*), and that may be enough to make the claim that every "family" "takes its name" from the "Father." But "takes its name" also suggests something more, something like the tradition of patronymy, the tradition of sons taking the names of their fathers. For example, the patronymic name of Simon Peter is Simon son of Jonah (*bar-yonah*; Matt. 16:17). Then "every family" would have God as "Father," and every tribe and nation would be counted among the children of God. Then the invocation could be translated, "Father of all families [or tribes or nations]." It is clearly not a biological relationship that is affirmed, but the care a father takes to supply the needs of his family, as when God is praised in Psalm 68:5 as the "father of orphans," the father of the fatherless. The scope of God's parental care is not limited to those who know to call God "Father." Its reach extends beyond those who are near, and even beyond those who have been brought near.

This is no tribal deity, no local god, not just the god of our ancestors. This God is not just committed to the flourishing of a particular culture, country, or family. This God is the God of "all the families of the earth," the God of "all things." And to this God alone the Jews and Gentiles of the Lycus Valley—and we—owe ultimate loyalty.

The universality of this God does not render God an unknowable cipher behind any and every particular deity. It is the God of Israel who is invoked here. It is the God and Father of our Lord Jesus Christ who is "the Father from whom every family . . . takes its name."

And this universality does not deny the significance of history. It does not sacrifice the significance of the particular to some gnostic spiritual universality. It surely does not diminish the significance of God's adopting Israel. It does not undercut the importance of Israel and its covenants and promises. Nor does it do away with the church or its "adoption as his children through Jesus Christ" (1:5). But it sets that history of Israel and the church in the context of God's "plan" from the beginning to "gather up all things in [Christ]." We honor that history by saying that it was God's plan from the beginning to care for all the families of the earth, and that God carried out that plan first by blessing Abraham that he might be a blessing to "all the families of the earth" (Gen. 12:1–3) and finally and decisively in the Jewish Messiah. And the church now also has a particular role in that plan. That is what prompts this prayer for the church.

Three Petitions Governed by the Cause of God

The prayer is one long (and complex) sentence from 3:14 through 3:19. It contains three petitions.[1] Each is governed by the cause of

---

1. Each is marked at the beginning with *hina*, "that." The NRSV inserts "I pray" at two of the three, but takes the third to introduce a purpose clause related to the second petition. That is surely also possible.

God. Each petition asks, in effect, that the kingdom may come, that the good future of God may establish already some little foothold in the life of the church, displaying itself already in the ordinary stuff of their common life. Each simply asks God to act in accord with God's character and plan. That is why, we think, the first petition first says, "according to the riches of [God's] glory" (3:16). Those "riches" are the riches of our inheritance (1:18), the inheritance to which Jews and Gentiles are "co-heirs" (3:6). In the *berakot* that inheritance prompted both Jews and Gentiles to "live for the praise of his glory" (1:12, 14), and in each of these petitions Paul prays to God that the church may have the strength to do precisely that, to live in accord with God's glory and their hope.

In these petitions "you" is consistently plural. They are petitions for the church, not (at least not first of all) petitions for individuals within the church. This is immediately relevant at the beginning of the first petition. There Paul asks God, according to the NRSV translation, to "grant that you may be strengthened in your inner being with power through his Spirit" (3:16). It is tempting to read "inner being" as some spiritual part of an individual (perhaps Plato's soul or Freud's superego?) and to understand the prayer as a prayer for the strengthening of that part of an individual. But that is, we think, a temptation of individualism. It fits neither with the consistent use of the plural "you" nor with Pauline anthropology. A more literal translation would be a petition that God "grant to you [plural] the power to be strengthened through his Spirit into [*eis*] the inner man [*anthrōpon*]." It is a prayer that the church will "grow" (cf. 2:21), not here "into [*eis*] a holy temple" (2:21), but "into the inner man." Still, what or who is this "inner man"? It is Christ, the "new man" (4:24), who establishes a new humanity. The petition is that the church will be empowered by the Spirit to grow into Christ. Ephesians 4:15 turns the petition into an exhortation, "We must grow up in every way into him who is the head, into Christ."

That reading is confirmed and clarified as the first petition continues. There is no "and" in the Greek (as in NRSV). It is not another petition but a restatement of the first one, "that Christ may dwell in your hearts through faith" (3:17). If the church is to be strengthened, as in the first part of this petition, it will only happen as Christ dwells among them. If they are to "grow into" a holy temple, it is only by the presence of God's "glory" and Christ and the Spirit. If they are to "grow into" Christ, it is only by the grace of Christ who "fills" the church, "which is his body" (1:23).

When Christ dwells among them, "fills" them, then they will be "rooted and grounded in love" (3:17). To be rooted in love is, according to the parallel in Colossians 2:7, to be rooted in Christ. Christ is the soil in which a new humanity can grow, and Christ is himself "the inner man," the new humanity, into which the church must grow. Our hope is not in the resources of our own "inner man"; our hope is in Christ. And Paul's first petition is that God will empower the church for service to its calling by strengthening it into what he calls it to be, a new humanity in Christ, into the social reality already established but still the object of our hope. This petition, like all the others, is governed by the good future of God that already made its power felt and its presence real in Jesus, the Messiah. It echoes the eschatology of the Lord's Prayer: "Your kingdom come. Your will be done, on earth as it is in heaven" (Matt. 6:10). In the heavenly places Christ is already the new humanity. As it is, we do not yet see this new humanity on earth. But we know Christ. We know the works of the Messiah and of his resurrection and exaltation. And by the power of Christ and of the Spirit, perhaps the church can provide some small token of that reality "on earth" and for the whole world.

But it will not be easy. The second petition also asks for strength, but the verb suggests a context of struggle and resistance. "I pray that you may have the power [*exischysēte*] . . ." (3:18). The verb *exischyo*, found only here in the New Testament, is formed by adding the prefix *ek* to *ischyo*, intensifying it. In 1 Maccabees 6:6, a similar intensifacation of *ischyo* (there with the prefix *epi*) is used to report that the Jews "had grown strong" for the battle against the Seleucids. The petition, we suggest, foreshadows the recognition of the "struggle" with the powers of this age in Ephesians 6:12. Moreover, the verb translated "to comprehend" (*katalabesthai*) may better be translated "grasp." "Comprehend" suggests a "comprehensive" knowledge, but that sort of knowledge seems impossible here. To "grasp" is not just to acknowledge some fact; it is not necessarily to be able to give a thorough and objective account of something; it is to "hold onto" some truth—and here, we think, to hold onto that truth as if one's life depended upon it. But what is it that we need strength to "hold onto"? What is "the breadth and length and height and depth"?

Many have attempted to identify these four dimensions. Augustine (*On Christian Doctrine* 2.41) suggests that they refers to the shape of Jesus' cross, with its four arms, and then, as Calvin reports it, "he makes the breadth to be love, the height, hope, the length, patience, and the depth, humility." It is clever, but we are instructed by Calvin's response, "All this pleases us with its subtlety, but what has it to do with Paul's meaning? No more, certainly, than the opinion of Ambrose, that it denotes the shape of a sphere."[2] Calvin goes on to identify it with the love of Christ, which comes next in this petition. We could be happy enough with that, except it seems that Calvin simply skips over these words. In the book of Job Zophar makes a powerful speech reminding Job that he cannot claim to be wiser than God.

> Can you find out the deep things of God?
> Can you find out the limit of the Almighty?
> It is *higher* than heaven—what can you do?
> *Deeper* than Sheol—what can you know?
> Its measure is *longer* than the earth,
> and *broader* than the sea.
> (Job 11:7–9, italics added)

The significance of the four dimensions is clear here. They refer to the inscrutable mystery of God. Zophar reminds Job that he cannot "comprehend" that mystery if "comprehend" means to understand it fully. Job cannot penetrate the "secrets of wisdom" (11:6). But neither can Zophar! He is in the wrong in accusing Job, as if Zophar had God figured out. Job finally "holds onto" God without claiming to understand God exhaustively. And that is the way we understand this petition. Paul pleads that the church will grow strong enough to hold onto the mystery of God without claiming to be able to understand

2. John Calvin, *The Epistles of Paul the Apostle to the Galatians, Ephesians, Philippians, and Colossians*, trans. T. H. L. Parker, ed. David W. Torrance and Thomas F. Torrance, Calvin's Commentaries (Grand Rapids: Eerdmans, 1963), 168.

that mystery fully. That is, after all, what "all the saints" (Eph. 3:18), including Job, did. And that reading is confirmed by what follows, "and to know the love of Christ that surpasses knowledge" (3:19a).

Again (as in 3:17) this is not a new petition, not another petition. Again it serves to clarify what preceded it. If a "comprehensive" knowledge seemed impossible before, here it is indeed said to be impossible. It is an oxymoron, "to know [what] surpasses knowledge." To know the unknowable makes as much sense as to describe the indescribable, to make effable the ineffable, or to measure the immeasurable. Of course, Ephesians has attempted to do exactly those things previously. Here, given the revelation of the "secret," the mystery of God and of the cause of God can be known in Christ, if "only in part" and "dimly" (1 Cor. 13:9, 12). What is known when the mystery of God is known is Christ and his love. Zophar had it wrong. The inscrutable mystery of God is not his retributive justice in punishing "sinners," but his love. It is a petition, then, that the church will be strong enough to hold onto the "secret," the "mystery," the plan made known in the love of Christ, against the cultures of enmity that surround them. As Ephesians 4:15 had turned the earlier petition into an exhortation, so this petition becomes an exhortation in 6:10–11, "Be strong in the Lord and in the strength of his power. Put on the whole armor of God, so that you may be able to stand against the wiles of the devil."

The final and climactic petition revisits what was the climactic conclusion of the first prayer for the church, the announcement that God "has put all things under his feet and has given him [that is, Christ], the head of all things, to the church, which is his body, filled by the one who fills [or completes] all things completely."[3] Here Paul prays that the church will in fact be "filled with all the fullness of God" (3:19b), that is, with Christ (cf. Col. 1:19; 2:9), in whom the secret was made known and who will bring the plan of God to complete fruition. That grace, that glory, that love is not created by human beings, but it exalts human beings. It creates and restores humanity, and it strengthens the church to respond to God's grace and glory and love, to be responsible agents in service to God's plan.

---

3. Our translation of Eph. 1:22–23. See above, p. 61 n. 1.

No Future Without Forgiveness: Desmond Tutu's Prayer

O God of justice, mercy and peace. We long to put behind us all the pain and division of apartheid together with all the violence which ravaged our communities in its name. And so we ask You to bless this Truth and Reconciliation Commission with Your wisdom and guidance as it commences its important work of redressing the many wrongs done both here and throughout our land.

We pray that all those people who have been injured in either body or spirit may receive healing through the work of this commission and that it may be seen to be a body which seeks to redress the wounds inflicted in so harsh a manner on so many of our people, particularly here in the Eastern Cape. We pray, too, for those who may be found to have committed these crimes against their fellow human beings, that they may come to repentance and confess their guilt to almighty God and that they too might become the recipients of Your divine mercy and forgiveness. We ask that the Holy Spirit may pour out its gifts of justice, mercy, and compassion upon the commissioners and their colleagues in every sphere, that the truth may be recognized and brought to light during the hearings; and that the end may bring about that reconciliation and love for our neighbor which our Lord himself commanded. We ask this in the holy name of Jesus Christ our Savior. Amen.

—Desmond Tutu

No Future Without Forgiveness (New York: Image, Doubleday, 2000), 113.

Doxology: The Praise of God's Glory

There were three petitions "according to the riches of [God's] glory" that the church would have the strength to live "to the praise of God's glory," to live doxologically. Now the prayer itself breaks into doxology. "Now to him who by the power at work within us is able to accomplish abundantly far more than all we can ask or imagine, to him be glory in the church and in Christ Jesus to all generations, forever and ever. Amen" (3:20–21).

The power of God is immeasurable (1:19). God displayed that power, "put this power to work," in raising Jesus from the dead, exalting him to God's right hand, making him sovereign over the principalities and powers. There he is the new humanity in fulfill-ment of Psalm 8 and the "head over all things" (1:20–22). Little wonder, then, that here that immeasurable power is described as capable of things beyond our imagination or our petitions. But here that immeasurable power is described as "at work within us" (3:20), at work in the church. That too retrieves the climactic conclusion of the first prayer for the church and the climactic final petition of this prayer. The power of God is at work in the church "filled" with Christ. Does an end to the hostility between Jew and Gentile seem like too much to ask? Is peaceable difference beyond our imagining? Given the cultures of enmity, perhaps so. But it is not beyond God's power. And that power is at work in the church.

So let the church say and display God's glory, the glory that has been and will be and is displayed in Christ, the glory that is peace. Once more we pause to say that this is not a mere ideal. It is a reality that empowers and summons the church to response and to responsibility. And the first response is simply doxology, to say "Blessed be the God and Father of our Lord Jesus Christ," to say "Glory to God," to say "Amen" to God's cause.

It is not enough just to say "glory," of course. It is not enough to say "Amen" at the close of a doxology. The church, Jew and Gentile together, must "live to the praise of his glory" (1:12, 14). They must perform praise. They must *be* praise. They must live doxologically. The praise of God's glory must be embodied. And so, "therefore. . . ." But that is the next chapter.

4:1–16

Therefore, the Performance of Peace

What is the most important word in the vocabulary of the Christian life? What word could the Christian life not do without? There are a number of good candidates, of course. Some would undoubtedly answer, "love." And it is difficult to think of the Christian life without the word "love." Indeed, it comes up more than once in this section. Some of the wisest among you may have answered "humility." And that word too comes up in this passage. There are many other plausible suggestions; there are many words whose destruction would make it difficult to think or talk about the Christian life. But surely among that list of words—and perhaps heading the list—is the word "therefore."

Therefore

Throughout Scripture "therefore" often signals the link between its talk of God and its talk of human conduct. Even when it is not mentioned, it is usually to be understood. In Scripture, after all, human conduct is measured and motivated by who God is and what God has done. Ethics is fundamentally a matter of response to God. For example, the Decalogue begins with an announcement of what God has done, "I am the LORD your God, who brought you out of the land of Egypt, out of the house of slavery" (Exod. 20:2). And when the commandments follow, the presence of an implied "therefore" is clear enough. Leviticus announces that God is holy and insists that the people of God should, therefore, be holy too: "You shall be holy,

for I the LORD your God am holy" (Lev. 19:2, cf. also 20:7; 1 Pet.
1:15–16). Everywhere the pattern is the same. God loves us; therefore, we should love one another (cf. 1 John 4:11). Jesus died to sin;
therefore, we too should die to sin. Jesus was raised from the dead;
therefore, we too should walk in newness of life. God sent the Spirit;
therefore, let us walk by the Spirit (cf. Gal. 5:25).

In the letters of Paul "therefore" frequently marks a transition
from theological exposition to moral exhortation. The point was
made long ago by C. H. Dodd. Dodd called attention to the division of Paul's letters "into two main parts. The first part deals with
specifically religious themes—deals with them, in the main, in the
reflective manner which constitutes theology—and the second part
consists mainly of ethical precepts and admonitions."[1] The first part
is, according to Dodd, related to *kerygma* (or proclamation), and
the second, to *didache* (or ethical teachings). The pattern, he says, is
"first *kerygma*, then *didaché*," first the proclamation of the gospel and
then moral exhortation.[2]

The transition in Ephesians is clear, and many have observed that
the first three chapters are theological exposition and the final three
chapters are moral instruction. That is both right and wrong. It is
right because this "therefore" in Ephesians 4:1 does indeed mark a
transition from theological exposition to moral exhortation. But it
is wrong because it suggests that these are two altogether different
things. The contrast is drawn too sharply. The problem with Dodd's
account is that he fails to see this "therefore" not only as a transition but also as a link. He so sharply distinguishes proclamation and
exhortation, *kerygma* and *didache*, theology and ethics, that he fails
to make sense of the link. The exhortations are cut off from the gospel; they become "a new law." In Ephesians (and in the Pauline Epistles generally) "therefore" signals a link, not just a transition. It is a
moral theology in the first three chapters, announcing the "immeasurable greatness of [God's] power" (1:19), attentive to the grace

---

1. C. H. Dodd, *Gospel and Law: The Relation of Faith and Ethics in Early Christianity* (New York: Columbia University Press, 1951), 5. He cites Romans, Galatians, Colossians, and Ephesians as especially good examples of this division. Note the "therefore" in Rom. 12:1, Gal. 5:1, Col. 3:1 (NRSV "so"), and Eph. 4:1.
2. Ibid., 10.

and the cause of God, but always already with an eye toward the implications of the gospel for the lives of Christians and the common life of the churches. And it is a *theological* morality in the last three chapters, announcing the gospel now in the imperative mood, attentive to the sort of conduct, character, and community that are empowered and required by God's grace and cause.

The pattern is not, as Dodd says, first *kerygma*, and then *didache*. The pattern is rather that the gospel comes to us in both the indicative mood and in the imperative mood.[3] To be sure, the indicative is frequently (and appropriately) first and the imperative second, but in both the gospel is proclaimed. As an apostle and as a pastor Paul was always proclaiming the gospel, "the power of God for salvation to everyone who has faith" (Rom. 1:16). He did not stop proclaiming the gospel when in Romans 12:2 he urged the Roman Christians to "be transformed by the renewing of your minds," or when in Romans 15:7 he urged them to "welcome one another." Such imperatives are not a mere addendum to the gospel. They are the gospel in the imperative mood, calling for "the obedience of faith" (Rom. 1:5; 16:26), summoning the churches to perform the gospel.

And if Ephesians is written by a Paulinist rather than by Paul himself, the author seems to have learned that lesson well. Indeed, Dodd's hard division of *kerygma* and *didache* is especially inept as an account of Ephesians. The *berakot* at the beginning counts the many blessings of God, and among them is the cause of God that "we" and "you" "might live for the praise of [God's] glory" (1:12). Indeed, the grace of God and the power of God render the community agents in God's cause, enabling them by the Spirit to "bless God" by joining the *berakot* and by living lives and a common life that are doxological. The doxology of 3:20–21 celebrates "the power of God at work within [the church]." It is that doxology that provides the immediate context for the transition in 4:1 to moral instruction, and marks that instruction as a *doxological ethic*. The prayer that the church might "know" the great power of God (1:17–19) was not that they might know it intellectually but that they might be formed by this knowledge. Ephesians 4:22–24 will make that clear. The transition

3. See pp. 76–78, "Further Reflections: An Evangelical Ethic."

from life to death, announced confidently in the indicative in 2:4–6, was already aimed at the "good works, which God prepared beforehand to be our way of life" (2:10). The "one new humanity" and the "peace" (2:15) that Christ has created and proclaimed quite clearly demanded "the obedience of faith." And the prayer for strength, coming as it does on the heels of the vocation of the church to make the secret "known to the rulers and authorities" (3:10), clearly presupposes the agency of the church, which is itself God's gift. There is in Ephesians an obvious and intimate relationship between *kerygma* and *didache*, between the indicative and the imperative, between the proclamation that God "raised us up with [Christ]" (2:6) and the command, "Sleeper, awake! Rise from the dead" (5:14).

God's power is the source and summons for human agency. God does not destroy human agency to achieve God's plan; God engages it. God calls people to participate by their lives and their common life in God's good future. That is no small part of the good news, and it is marked by the use of the imperative mood.

As God intends the good and stands opposed to the powers of death and sin and to the cultures of enmity, so God summons the church to agency in service of God's cause. As God in Christ has made the secret known, so God empowers the church by God's Spirit to make that secret known even to the principalities and powers. In the interval between Christ's resurrection and the final renewal of all things, the "spiritual forces of evil" still threaten. They have not yet admitted defeat. "Therefore," Ephesians says, "take up the whole armor of God" (6:13). Those who receive the gospel, the power of God, are freed from the dominion of the powers. They are enabled and summoned to live in accord with the gospel.

The gospel frees us for lives "to the praise of [God's] glory." In the Heidelberg Catechism, at the transition from its account of grace to its account of the human response and responsibilities of gratitude, the question is asked, "Why then must we still do good?" The catechism allows this question without sympathizing with it. In answering it, the catechism insists that our deliverance, our participation in Christ's righteousness, is our renewal as well as our redemption. "Christ by his Spirit is also renewing us to be like himself, so that in all our living we may show that we are thankful to God for all [God] has done for us, and so that [God] may be praised through us" (Q & A 86). That is it exactly. God's grace and power and "Christ by his Spirit" renews us, transforms us, renders us agents so that we "may" do good. We do good not so much because we must but because we may. Our participation in Christ is our permission in "all our living"—in our marrying, working, saving, spending, managing, consuming, playing, politicking—to show that we are thankful and to "live to the praise of [God's] glory."

God gives permission to live faithfully. Indeed, he permits nothing else. But the demands of God are not less gospel than the announcement of the gospel in the indicative mood. Or to reverse the point, the announcement of the gospel in the indicative mood is not less demanding than the demands announced as imperatives. This bond between gift and claim, between grace and gratitude, between *credenda* and *agenda*, between theology and ethics, between *kerygma* and *didache* (whatever terms one might prefer for these "parts"), is signed and sealed by this "therefore." It is an *evangelical ethic*, a *doxological ethic*.

The Apostolic Encouragement

Paul exhorts the Christians of the Lycus Valley to "lead a life worthy of the calling to which [they] have been called" (4:1). This exhortation provides a heading for all that follows in the rest of the letter, but it leads here and immediately to the encouragement to perform the unity that the Christ has created, the peace that the Messiah has made.

Paul "begs" them to lead such a life. Given Paul's apostolic authority, one might expect him to command these Christians of the Lycus Valley to lead such a life, but instead he uses the language of polite request, *parakalō*, which is here translated "beg," a little too self-effacing, perhaps, but a nice and obvious contrast to "I order you." Indeed, *parakalō* and *paraklēsis* when used by Paul may sometimes best be translated as "comfort" or "encourage" and sometimes as "exhort." In Philippians 2:1 the "encouragement [*paraklēsis*] in Christ" comes to expression in the exhortation to "let the same mind be in you that was in Christ Jesus" (2:5). Again we may note that there can be no sharp division between the proclamation of the gospel and moral exhortation. Paul "encourages" these Christians to a life worthy of the calling to which they were called. He honors them by his exhortation, expecting of them the performance of the gospel he has proclaimed. He does not burden them with demands; he appeals to their standing in Christ. He regards these churches, as he did the Roman churches, as "full of goodness, filled with all knowledge, and able to instruct one another" (Rom. 15:14). That is another item in the ecclesiology of this letter. The churches are places for mutual encouragement and instruction, for moral discourse and discernment. By this turn to *paraklēsis* Paul contributes to that communal discernment; he does not provide a substitute for it.

This is not to set aside Paul's apostolic authority but to exercise it. He is, after all, an apostle of Jesus Christ. Christ is the source of his authority—and the pattern for it. It is the authority of a servant, not the authority of a despot handing out commands and enforcing them with threats. The pattern is not provided by the principalities and powers of this world but by Christ.

Paul reminds them at this transition to exhortation that he is a "prisoner in the Lord" (4:1). That reminder itself is a link to what has gone before. In chapter 3 Paul had interrupted his turn to prayer to talk about his imprisonment and about his apostleship. It was not to boast but to offer himself as a model for the churches. It was a "gift of God's grace" that had made Paul an apostle, a "servant" of the gospel (3:7). That gift and calling were demanding, to be sure, but Paul devoted himself to the cause of God and, on the model of Christ, endured suffering for the sake of God's cause in the world. In chapter 3 already it was clear that, as Paul had a calling by the grace of God to serve the cause of God and to make it known, so did the church (3:10). It had a calling to be the community of peace in the midst of cultures of enmity, to be a place of peaceable difference, so that even the principalities and powers might know God's secret.

Here, as Paul turns to exhortation, this reminder of his imprisonment is also a reminder of his apostolic authority. As Calvin says, "He claims . . . a greater authority from his chains. . . . The apostle's prison is more to be revered than all the pomps and triumphs of kings."[4] His apostolic authority is not exercised in despotism but in service. As Christ is the pattern for Paul's suffering for the sake of God's cause in the world, so Christ is the pattern for the exercise of authority in the church. That point will be revisited soon, but first we return to the opening exhortation.

The Performance of Peace: An Ethic of Peaceable Difference

They are "to lead a life worthy of the calling to which [they] have been called." What is this calling, this vocation? It is clearly not simply one's job or one's profession (although those things too might be transformed by this calling). There is a link again to what has gone before. In Ephesians 1:18 it was Paul's prayer that the church might "know the hope to which [God] has called you." We are called to a great hope. It is not simply that we are called to be "hopeful," surely not simply that we are called to be optimistic. It is rather the substantive hope of God's good future to which we are called, a future already established when God raised Jesus from the dead to sovereignty over the powers (1:20–21), a new humanity in Christ, peace (2:15). The church was made an agent in the unveiling of that good future (1:22b; 3:10). That is its calling, its hope. And now they are

---

4. Calvin, *Ephesians*, 171, on Eph. 4:1.

The Hope of Faith

But our hope is different in kind; for it is the hope of faith. This hope does not rise and fall as ours does. Its nerve-centre lies not in human capacity, but in the capacity and purpose of God. Such hope, then, possesses a real purpose by which its content is shaped and cannot be *confounded* or *put to shame* . . . , even though all hope be removed. It endures, when we have lost all power of endurance. It is approved, when we are not approved. Therefore we *glory in hope*. . . , precisely because it is not an achievement of our spirit, but the action of the Holy Spirit, and because the love of God has been shed abroad in our hearts through the Holy Spirit which was given to us.

—Karl Barth

The Epistle to the Romans, trans. Edwyn C. Hoskyns (London: Oxford University Press, 1933), 157.

here encouraged to a common life that is worthy of that calling, that is in accordance with that hope, that is fitting to that gospel.

Little wonder, then, that this opening sentence of paraenesis concludes with an urgent exhortation to make "every effort to maintain the unity of the Spirit in the bond of peace" (4:3). This unity is in accord with the plan of God to "gather up all things" in Christ (1:10); it is created by Christ, who makes Jew and Gentile into one community (2:14–18); it is the work of the Spirit, the pledge of God's future (1:14), in whom through Christ both Jew and Gentile have access to the Father (2:18). It has been announced in the indicative, but now this gospel comes as an imperative, as an urgent imperative. The church is not the creator of this peace, but it is called to display it, to make it manifest, to perform it.

The community maintains and performs this unity when the members of the community practice "humility and gentleness [and] patience, bearing with one another in love" (4:2). These are virtues for living in community with those who are different from you. These are virtues to make and maintain communities of peaceable difference.

"Humility" (*tapeinophrosynē*) heads this little catalogue of virtues. And rightly so, according to Calvin, who comments that humility is the "first step" to unity. It will be useless to exhort people to gentleness or patience or forbearance or love or unity, he says, "unless we have begun with humility."[5] Humility stands in obvious contrast to the boasting that is unworthy of the gospel (cf. 2:9). It is not arrogant in relation to others. It is not "puffed up." It does not use difference to destroy community.[6]

---

5. Ibid., 172–73.
6. It is worth observing that there is a transformation of the Greek vocabulary at work here. *Tapeinophrosynē* was not regarded as a virtue among the Greeks; it suggested a lack of self-respect, an inappropriate self-abasement. Even in the New Testament the word can still be used with negative connotations. It is used in Col. 2:18 and 23 to capture the "self-abasement" of the spiritually elite. This "humility" belongs to the "flesh" and is of no help against it (Col. 2:23). The same word soon occurs again in Colossians, however, in 3:12 (parallel to Eph. 4:2) in a list of character traits that Christians are to "put on." There it is evidently a quality of the "new self" (3:10). This transformation of vocabulary suggests, first, that "humility" (or *tapeinophrosynē*) is evidently not some free-standing virtue that names some character trait that has a purely rational foundation and is universally commendable. But second, this

It is paired here with "gentleness" (*prautēs*). If humility stands in contrast to arrogance by not boasting, gentleness stands in contrast to arrogance by not condemning or despising the other for being different. If humility is not "puffed up" by one's own righteousness (or knowledge or ethnic heritage or religious pedigree), gentleness treats the other—in his or her particularity—gently. It is not hard on the other. It is not rude. It does not demean or despise the other for being different. It does not judge the "faults" of another too severely. Even when admonition or correction is required, it is to be done in a "spirit of gentleness," eager for community (so Gal. 6:1 and 2 Tim. 2:25). Difference is not to be an occasion for boasting. It is to be an occasion for gentleness. Both humility and gentleness are skills for maintaining peaceable difference.

A third characteristic is commended then, "patience" (*makrothymia*). Etymologically *makrothymia* is to be "long-tempered." It can mean either the patient "endurance" of suffering or the patient "forbearance" of another (for example, 1 Thess. 5:14). The second meaning is preferable here, for such patient forbearance helps to maintain unity in the midst of difference. To be patient is to be magnanimous, broad-minded, big-hearted, to tolerate the quirks of Jews or Gentiles for the sake of community. It is to be ready to "endure" a little discomfort for the sake of community with others rather than to assert one's own way and rights. This social construal of patience as forbearance is confirmed by the fourth item in this catalogue, "bearing with one another in love."

It is more literally "bearing one another in love." We prefer that literal translation because it suggests quite clearly that the other can

---

transformation of vocabulary—and the meaning of "humility" here—can only be traced to the power of the gospel. The humility commended in Ephesians stands in obvious continuity to the "encouragement in Christ" in Philippians (2:1), which prompted exhortations to unity and humility (2:2–3). It stands in conformity to the pattern of Christ, who "did not regard equality with God as something to be exploited, but . . . humbled himself" (2:6, 8). And that pattern can be traced still further back to Jesus of Nazareth, who announced the coming kingdom with axioms of reversal, like "all who exalt themselves will be humbled, and those who humble themselves will be exalted" (Luke 14:11; 18:14; Matt. 23:12). This Jesus was among us as one who was "gentle and humble [*tapeinos*] in heart" (Matt. 11:29) and as one who served. And this Jesus, after he had humbled himself to the point of death on the cross, was exalted by God (Phil. 2:9).

be and sometimes is a burden. The exhortation is not just, like Galatians 6:2, that we should "bear one another's burdens"; it is that we should bear the other, even if and when the other is a burden to us. There were times, we suppose, when Jewish Christians and Gentile Christians found it difficult to bear the other. The cultures of enmity were quick to insist that Gentiles were a burden to Jews or that Jews were a burden to Gentiles, quick enough to suggest that Jew or Gentile be discarded or excluded or eliminated in hostility. But the peace created by Christ and a new humanity in Christ required and empowered them to "bear one another"—and more, to bear one another "in love." That would fulfill "the law of Christ" (Gal. 6:2).

"Love" (*agapē*) is humble and gentle; it is not boastful or arrogant. It is patient, magnanimous; it is not irritable or resentful; it bears all things (cf. 1 Cor. 13:4–7). Love is the gift of the Spirit, and the mark of God's good future, but once again that good news comes to us as both indicative and imperative. Love is, according to Colossians, what "binds everything together in perfect harmony" (3:14). In Ephesians the "bond" is "peace" (4:3), but the way to peace is through the gift and the performance of love. Forbearance and bearing one another in love are skills for maintaining a community of peaceable difference, equipping the saints for their efforts "to maintain the unity of the Spirit in the bond of peace" (4:3).

Ubuntu

Ubuntu is very difficult to render into a Western language. It speaks of the very essence of being human. When we want to give high praise to someone we say, "*Yu, u nobuntu*"; "Hey, so-and-so has *ubuntu*." Then you are generous, you are hospitable, you are friendly and caring and compassionate. You share what you have, it is to say, "My humanity is caught up, is inextricably bound up, in yours." We belong in a bundle of life. We say, "A person is a person through other persons." It is not, "I think therefore I am." It says rather: "I am human because I belong. I participate, I share." A person with *ubuntu* is open and available to others, affirming of others, does not feel threatened that others are able and good, for he or she has a proper self-assurance that comes from knowing that he or she belongs in a greater whole and is diminished when others are humiliated or diminished, when others are tortured or oppressed, or treated as if they were less than who they are.

—Desmond Tutu

No Future Without Forgiveness (New York: Image, Doubleday, 2000), 31.

FURTHER REFLECTIONS
Unity, Equality, and an Oppressive "Sameness": A Response to Boyarin

Against those who read Paul as opposed to the "liberation of slaves and women" and as a prop for the anti-Judaism of the Christian churches, Daniel Boyarin insists that Paul envisioned a universal and inclusive community of equality. He regards Galatians 3:28–29 as the fundamental clue to Paul's vision of unity and equality. Paul was, Boyarin says, "a passionate striver for human liberation and equality."[7] Boyarin gives Paul credit for his passion for unity and equality, but he objects to what he takes to be Paul's strategy for achieving them. Paul's passion for equality was corrupted, he says, by his tendency "to equate equality with sameness" (p. 9). And by that equation Paul's social thought was "deeply flawed" (p. 9). He would achieve universality and equality by sacrificing difference. Paul devalued particular identities and valorized a *spiritual* unity and equality. Boyarin traces that tendency and strategy to Paul's "dualism of the flesh and the spirit, such that while the body is particular, marked through practice as Jew or Greek, and through anatomy as male or female, the spirit is universal" (p. 7). The result, he says, is an abstract universality and an empty equality.

Worse than that, the result of Paul's "dualism" in this world of embodied difference has authorized dominant groups to celebrate a "spiritual" equality while refusing to honor or celebrate the differences that mark the other as other. Particular ethnic and gender identities have been threatened by the dominant culture, which can claim universality and pressure others to conform. Where equality is equated with "sameness," whatever cultural group has hegemonic power can enforce conformity while it pretends to acknowledge equality and to favor integration. According to Boyarin Paul challenged "tribal allegiances," but his account of equality and universality "has been a powerful force for coercive discourses of sameness, denying . . . the rights of Jews, women, and others to retain their

---

7. Daniel Boyarin, *A Radical Jew: Paul and the Politics of Identity* (Berkeley: University of California Press, 1994), 9. The references that follow in the text are to this book.

difference" (p. 233). Boyarin finds in Paul "the seeds of an imperialist and colonizing" culture (p. 234).

We agree with Boyarin that Paul had a passion for human libera- tion, for equality, for inclusion in a universal community. Ephesians can be used to make the point no less than Galatians 3:28–29. And we agree that when equality is equated with "sameness," a subtle oppression of minority cultures and identities can be authorized. But we disagree both with Boyarin's claim that Paul equated equal- ity with sameness and with his account of Paul's "dualism of the flesh and the spirit." When Boyarin traces the problem to Paul's "dualism of the flesh and the spirit," he seems to neglect the difference between Paul and the Platonic tradition of dualism. Paul's dualism of "flesh" and "spirit" does not map onto Plato's dualism of body and soul, or Boyarin's embodied difference and "spiritual" unity. Paul uses "flesh" not as a simple reference to the "body" but as a reference to the susceptibility of whole persons, embodied and communal and spiritual beings, to the powers of this present evil age. And he uses "spirit" to refer not to simple transcendence over the body or to absorption into Plato's "the One," but rather to the liberating effects of God's power and Spirit upon whole persons and their commu- nities. When Boyarin says, "the commitment to 'the One' implied a disdain for the body, and disdain for the body entailed an erasure of 'difference'" (p. 231), it sounds to us more Platonic than Pauline. In Paul, and explicitly in Ephesians, "the One" who is our peace (2:14) is not a disembodied transcendence over particular bodies and cul- tures. He is the incarnate one, the crucified and risen Jewish Messiah. "In his flesh" (2:14) he makes peace and puts hostility to death (2:16). This Jewish Messiah had and has a body, a body that suffered on a Roman cross, a body that was raised from the dead and to sover- eignty over the powers. Paul finds the grounds for unity and peace in the particularity of that body of Jesus. The unity he envisioned was not a denial of particularity, not the elimination of embodied difference; it was a unity of peaceable difference. The problem with our world as Paul saw it was not difference but enmity.

There is plenty of evidence for Paul's appreciation of difference. For example, he celebrated the diverse gifts within Christian com- munities (e.g., 1 Cor. 12–14; Rom. 12:4–5; Eph. 4:14–16). There is "one new humanity," but it is not in Paul "a third race" that eliminates Jewish identity or Gentile difference; it is made up of Jew and Gentile. Jews need not act like Gentiles nor Gentiles like Jews. But each must give up the enmity, the "hostility," that marked and marred their relationship (e.g., Rom. 14:1–15:12; Eph. 2:14–16). Boyarin's claim that Paul equated equality with sameness seems to be as mistaken as the claim that Paul was opposed to human liberation, equality, and unity.

Similarly, Boyarin claims on the basis of Galatians 3:28 that Paul locates the unity and equality of male and female "in the spirit" (p. 193) and that he devalues the body, where difference is found. We must admit that Galatians 3:28–29 does say, "no longer male and female," which seems a "cancellation" of Genesis 1:28. Boyarin takes Paul's vision to be "a state of androgyny, a cancellation of gender and sexuality" (p. 195). But Paul does not work within an anthropological dualism, and there is nothing in Paul's instructions to the churches that presupposes an abstract unity of pure spirits or souls without gender. On the contrary, what is cancelled is not our existence as male or female but the culturally formed norms that have been attached to gender. It is, for example, no longer an obligation for men to marry and to procreate. Women may perform functions in the church that had been regarded as appropriate only for men. The striking equality of men and women within marriage in 1 Corinthians (7:3–5, 12–16) is quite clearly not a "cancellation" of embodied sexuality. And in Ephesians the ideal is plainly not an androgynous humanity that erases the difference between male and female; the paradigm is rather the embodied self-giving love of Christ, who "loved the church and gave himself up for her" (5:25). Paul recognizes and celebrates the duality of male and female. That celebration of duality can easily slip and slide into a celebration— or at least an acceptance—of inequality. It is surely the case that the recognition of difference has frequently been accompanied by claims about the superiority of men and the inferiority of women. But Paul does not draw that inference—nor does he take refuge in "sameness."

While we acknowledge that Paul does sometimes seem to slip into an acceptance of inequality, his strategy for achieving unity and equality is not to deny difference but rather to insist on the inter-dependence of male and female. As he says in a passage where he seems to slip some, "Nevertheless, in the Lord woman is not inde-pendent of man or man independent of woman" (1 Cor. 11:11). Moreover, this interdependence and equality does not have some "spiritual" basis; it has a quite specifically embodied and physical basis: "For just as woman came from man, so man comes through woman; but all things come from God" (1 Cor. 11:12). This is not a denial of embodied difference; it is not an erasure of gender and sexuality for the sake of some spiritual "third gender," some androg-ynous "sameness," which is neither male nor female. The recognition of interdependence should help when one gender is tempted to dominate the other, when it is tempted to disparage the other and manipulate the other. Once again, however, it is not difference that is the problem but enmity and the self-serving readiness to reduce the other to a means to achieve our own ends. The recognition of interdependence will need to be supplemented—and in Paul's strategy it is supplemented—by self-giving love, by the self-giving love that finds its paradigm in the embodied love of Christ for the church (Eph. 5:25). Such self-giving love in the context of interde-pendence is not to lose one's self; it is to find it. It does mean an end to self-centeredness and self-absorption, but it does not mean an end to self. Such self-giving love "nourishes and tenderly cares" for the other (5:29). It seeks to allow the other to flourish, to be truly themselves in relationship. The strategy on display in Ephesians is mutual submission (5:21).

There is no guarantee of an end to enmity or to the ways in which cultures have nurtured enmity between the sexes, allowing one to dominate and conscripting the submission of the other. The viola-tion of patterns of interdependence, self-giving love, and mutual submission will need to be persistently resisted and corrected. But the point is that Paul's passion for equality, liberation, and solidar-ity is not, as Boyarin claimed, corrupted by the equation of equality and sameness. It is not a purely "spiritual" unity that leaves embod-ied relationships untouched, nor is it an equality that authorizes an oppressive "sameness."

The Unity Creed

In a remarkable creed in Ephesians 4:4–6 the author reminds the churches of what they surely already know. It is ordered quite beautifully, if somewhat surprisingly. There are seven items, each preceded by an emphatic "one." These seven items are arranged in a triadic structure. The first triad is "one body and one Spirit, just as you were called to the one hope of your calling." The second triad is "one Lord, one faith, one baptism." The seventh item stands climactically alone, "one God and Father of all, who is above all and through all and in all."

It is, as has often been observed, Trinitarian in its structure, the first triad belonging to the Spirit, the second to the Lord, and the third to the Father. Trinity itself points the way toward social relations of self-giving love, of unity and peaceable difference. The order, however, is a bit surprising. One would expect a reverse order, beginning with God the Father and ending with the Spirit and the Spirit's work in the church. It is doubtful that this creed existed before the writer of Ephesians penned it. It is, we think, an original creedal statement, not older than Ephesians itself, but its excellence is not its originality but its power to remind these churches of what they already knew and, by that reminder, to call them to unity and to service.

> **A Binding Confession**
>
> Those uttering the confession are bound by its implications. They speak as the "body" animated by the "Spirit" and appointed to march on the way of "hope." "Faith" and "baptism" tie them to the "Lord." "In all things" and persons they are willing to recognize the dominion, presence, and operation of "God the Father."
>
> —Markus Barth
>
> *Ephesians 4–6*, 466.

That is the reason for beginning with "one body." There *is* "one body." It can be announced and affirmed in the indicative. It is the church "which is [Christ's] body" (1:23). The Gentiles, as Ephesians has previously announced, are "members of the same body [*syssōma*]" (3:6). But this announcement comes to them—and to us—also as an imperative. To be sure, this unity is a gift, not the accomplishment of either Jews or Gentiles (as if either could boast), but it is gift that must be performed. It is a gift of the Spirit, the "one Spirit." That is the second item in this list. That one Spirit is "the pledge of our inheritance" (1:14), the guarantee of God's good future. The Gentiles, as again previously announced, have been made "fellow heirs" (3:6) of that inheritance. In the gift of that "one Spirit" both Jew and Gentile have access to God (2:18) and a share in God's good future. And in the gift of that "one Spirit" the community is strengthened (3:16), empowered for a life worthy of its calling (4:1). That calling, or the "one hope of [their] calling," is the next item in this creed. That "one hope" is God's good future, *shalom*, all things gathered up in Christ, a new humanity. Again, Ephesians has previously insisted that the Gentiles have become "sharers in the promise in Christ Jesus" (3:6). The "unity of the Spirit" is a foretaste of that future, that "one hope," and by the gift of the Spirit the community is empowered to be "one body," equipped for its efforts to "maintain the unity of the Spirit in the bond of peace" (4:3).

"One Lord" stands first in the second triad, and that "one Lord" is clearly the Christ, the one in whom the "secret" was revealed and in whom the plan of God is accomplished (1:9–11). The "one Lord" is the Christ exalted to the right hand of God (1:20–22), the crucified Messiah who is "our peace" (2:13–18). This Christ is the basis of unity, and to deny or disrupt or destroy that unity prompts the question Paul asked the divided Corinthians, "Has Christ been divided?" (1 Cor. 1:13). The answer, of course, made emphatic here, is no. There is "one Lord," one Christ, and any division in the church, any denial or disruption or destruction of its unity, is unworthy of the gospel. The point about the unity of Jew and Gentile in the Lord here simply echoes Romans 10:12, "there is no distinction between Jew and Greek; the same Lord is Lord of all."

That message is received in faith, and as there is "one Lord," so is there "one faith." There are those who take "faith" here to refer to a deposit of doctrine, a creedal statement. It is not impossible, given that the reference comes in the context of a creedal statement. But we consider it much more likely that the use of "faith" here (and in 1:15 and 2:8) follows the more common usage of Paul. Abraham's "faith" was his confidence in the promises of God and his faithfulness, his loyalty, to God's cause. By that "faith" he left his country and his kindred, his culture, and began a journey toward God's future, toward God blessing "all the families of the earth" (Gen. 12:1–3). By that "faith" he became the "father of all who believe," Gentiles as well as Jews (Rom. 4). And that faith, that confidence in the plan of God and that loyalty to the cause of God, is "one faith," shared by all in the church.

"One baptism" completes this triad, the concrete practice of the church by which diverse Christians are welcomed into Christ the "one Lord" and into the community. Baptism is the public act in which we are made "one in Christ." As Galatians 3:27–28 (or the baptismal liturgy quoted by Galatians[8]) says, "As many of you as were baptized into Christ have clothed yourselves with Christ. There is no longer Jew or Greek, there is no longer slave or free, there is no longer male and female; for all of you are one in Christ Jesus." To be baptized is to pass from death to life, to "put off" the "old self" and to "put on" a new humanity in Christ. Ephesians will make use of the traditions of moral instruction that accompanied baptism soon enough. Here it is enough to list it as a sign and seal of the unity in Christ Jesus, the "one Lord," and joyfully confessed in "one faith."

> **A Definition of Faith**
>
> Now we shall possess a right definition of faith if we call it a firm and certain knowledge of God's benevolence toward us, founded upon the truth of the freely given promise in Christ, both revealed to our minds and sealed upon our hearts through the Holy Spirit.
>
> **—John Calvin**
>
> *Institutes of the Christian Religion* 3.2.7.

Both the gift of the Spirit and the gift of Christ can be traced to the love and grace of God, the "one God and Father of all, who is above all and through all and in all" (4:6). This is the seventh and climactic item in this unity creed. And it sets the unity of the church in the context of God's "plan for the fullness of time, to gather up all things in [Christ]" (1:10).

---

8. Richard Longenecker, *New Testament Social Ethics for Today* (Grand Rapids: Eerdmans, 1984), 31–33.

> Or is God the God of Jews only? Is he not the God of Gentiles also? Yes, of Gentiles also, since God is one: and he will justify the circumcised on the ground of faith and the uncircumcised through that same faith.
> —Romans 3: 29–30

Calvin does well to trace "the Spirit of sanctification" and "the government of Christ" to their source in God the Father, but he limits the scope of "God's government and presence" to the church.[9] Calvin makes this move in part because in his version the conclusion was "in all of you," "in you all."

But the earliest manuscripts (and the best) have simply "in all." Calvin's reading is, we think, a misreading. And it can lead to a bad performance. It suggests a narrower vision than Ephesians and this passage require. From the beginning Ephesians had a vision of "all things" being "gathered up" (1:10), of "all things" under the rule of the risen and exalted Christ (1:22), of "all things" being filled (1:23). From the beginning Ephesians had celebrated the blessings of God upon the church not as a status that it could boast about but as a calling. The church was made an agent in the world, to bless God and to serve God's plan for "all things." This passage stands in that context and requires that the Spirit and the Christ—and the church's life and unity—be understood in that context. This passage requires a cosmic vision.

This "one God and Father" is, of course, the "God and Father of our Lord Jesus Christ" (1:3), but that "one God" is also the "Father, from whom every family in heaven and on earth takes its name" (3:14), and is here identified as the "one God and Father of all, who is above all and through all and in all." The "oneness" of the triune God is the fundamental basis for the church's unity, but the "secret" of this one God's plan reaches beyond the church to all humankind and to all things. Any narrowly ecclesiological vision is unworthy of the calling of the church. The church is the firstfruits of God's power, but it is not the full harvest. It is, by God's grace and power, an agent in God's plan, but not by limiting its horizon or by building an ecclesiological empire against the world. It is an agent in God's plan by lives and a common life worthy of its calling.

9. Calvin, *Ephesians*, 173; he acknowledges that in other passages of Scripture God's governance and presence extends to "all creatures."

As the structure of this unity creed reminds us, this "one God" is the Trinity (cf. also the Trinitarian references in the *berakot*, 1:3–14). God's oneness is itself a community of three "persons," a social unity. God's unity is not uniformity; it is the unity of self-giving love. And the self-giving love that constitutes the interior life of God first graciously creates the world as "other" from God, summoning the world into existence in its own free and fertile otherness, and then reaches out to it, summoning it to fellowship and service. To use the wonderful image of Irenaeus, the Son and the Spirit are the two arms of God by which the Father reaches out to embrace humanity and the whole creation (*Against Heresies* 5.6.1). The unity of God is the unity of peaceable difference and self-giving love. And the unity of the church finds its paradigm not in uniformity but in the triune God, in self-giving love and in peaceable difference. It does not deny or denigrate or destroy the diversity of its members—or of their gifts.

> **An Ironic Confession**
>
> The color line has been drawn so incisively by the church itself that its proclamation of the gospel of the brotherhood of Jew and Greek, of bond and free, of white and black has sometimes the sad sound of irony and sometimes falls upon the ear as unconscious hypocrisy—but sometimes there is in it the bitter cry of repentance.
> —H. Richard Niebuhr
>
> *The Social Sources of Denominationalism* (Cleveland: Meridian, 1957), 263.

FURTHER REFLECTIONS
Baptism in Ephesians and the Church

Within this unity creed we find the only time baptism is explicitly mentioned in Ephesians, "one baptism." It is hardly shocking that "one baptism" should find its way into this unity creed; baptism is a mark of the unity of diverse members of the church in the baptismal formula that is echoed in Galatians 3:26–28 and 1 Corinthians 12:12–13. It is more shocking that this is the only time baptism is explicitly mentioned, for baptism is evidently of great significance to Ephesians. Indeed, Nils Dahl regarded Ephesians as a letter to the churches of the Lycus Valley that was intended to remind these young churches of the meaning of their baptism.[10] And such an account is quite plausible.

Although "baptism" is explicitly mentioned only here, there are implicit references to baptism throughout the letter. In 5:25–27, for example, in the analogy between the relation of Christ and the church and the relation of husband and wife, there is an allusion to baptism. "Christ loved the church and gave himself up for her, in order to make her holy by cleansing her with the washing of water by the word, so as to present the church to himself in splendor." The figure may come from the bride's ritual bath of purification in Jewish marriage customs (cf. Ezek. 16:8–14), but "the washing of water" surely would have been (also) understood as a reference to baptism. Again, the references to "the seal of the Spirit" are most likely references to baptism. "In him you also, when you had heard the word of truth, the gospel of your salvation, and had believed in him, were marked with the seal of the promised Holy Spirit" (Eph. 1:13; cf. also 4:30, and note the combination of "hearing" and "believing" with baptism in Acts 8:12; 16:14–15; 18:8).[11]

These references to baptism, however, do not yet begin to mine the significance of baptism in Ephesians. Some have claimed that Ephesians 2:1–10 is a commentary on a baptismal hymn (or at least on a piece of a baptismal liturgy).[12] That claim has not won wide assent, but there can be little doubt that those who heard those verses would be reminded of their baptism.[13] Our participation in the death and resurrection of Christ is central both to the baptism liturgy (cf. Rom. 6:4–11; Col. 2:12–13) and to that passage.

10. Nils A. Dahl, "Addresse und Proömium des Epheserbriefes," *Theologische Zeitschrift* 7 (1951): 241–64.
11. See Kirby, *Ephesians*, 151–54.
12. G. Schille, *Frühchristliche Hymnen* (Berlin: Evangelische Verlagsanstalt, 1965), 53–60, cited by Lincoln, *Ephesians*, 88–89.
13. Lincoln makes this point clearly in his commentary on Ephesians: "There is no direct or explicit reference to baptism in Ephesians 2:1–10, but there is also no reason to deny that the way in which the writer talks about the contrast between pre-Christian past and Christian present, about the change brought by God's mercy, and about believers' participation in what happened to Christ, would have recalled to his readers the significance of their baptism" (p. 91).

Still more significant may be the use of moral traditions of the church that were associated with baptismal instruction, the tradition of "putting off" vices and "putting on" virtues (Eph. 4:22–5:2) and the tradition that believers were "children of the light" (5:8–20, a passage that contains what is widely regarded as a fragment of a baptismal hymn, "Sleeper, awake! Rise from the dead, and Christ will shine on you" [5:14]). We will turn to those passages in due course, but enough has been said to underscore the significance of baptism to Ephesians.

Here we would point to the significance of baptism as a practice of the continuing church. In baptism God gives to people a new moral identity and a new community. Christians are initiated into Christ's death and resurrection in baptism. They pass from death to life in baptism. Baptism by immersion, going down into the water and being lifted up out of it, provides a powerful enactment of this movement from death to life; but whether baptized by immersion or by sprinkling, to be baptized is to be identified with Christ and with his death and resurrection. Those who have been baptized into Christ are to regard themselves as dead to sin and as alive to God's righteousness (Rom. 6:1–11). But not alone; no, never alone. In Christ the baptized are also initiated into a new community. Baptized into Christ, they are "clothed with Christ," in whom "there is no longer Jew or Greek, . . . no longer slave or free, . . . no longer male and female; for all of you are one in Christ Jesus" (Gal. 3:27–28).

Baptism is first of all and fundamentally an act of God. But here again God renders the church an agent of God's work, so it is an act of the church. The church performs baptism. And then members of the church are also to *perform* this baptism in their lives and in their common life. It is not that baptism works magically to put a stop to old patterns of life and to initiate new ones, but it is the eschatological act of God (and of the community as the agent of God) by which God initiates people into Christ, into his death and resurrection, and into his one body, the church. Christians perform their baptism in lives that display the passage from death to life. And God will perfect their baptism at the last day, bringing them safely through the final judgment and giving them life. Until that time the temptations to various sorts of immorality are a series of identity crises.

In a short story by Flannery O'Connor a young man stands on a river bank while a preacher baptizes some others. When he indicates a desire to be baptized, the preacher picks him up in his arms and speaks words of warning (and promise), "You won't be the same again."[14]

"You won't be the same again." It is a bold claim about the power of baptism, but it is a claim, we believe, with which the writer of Ephesians would concur. If you listen carefully to the reference to dying and rising with Christ, you may hear the liturgy of baptism being uttered in the background. At the very least you will recognize a theme central to the theology of baptism.

When the Christian community performs a baptism to initiate one into Christ and into the church, all are instructed of who they are and whose they are. In the baptism liturgy the congregation is reminded to remember their baptisms. It seems a strange thing to say to people who were baptized as infants. Oh, there may be a baptismal certificate carefully kept in a scrapbook in a dresser drawer. The actual event of having been baptized may be remembered by family or in church records, but it is seldom a vivid memory to the one baptized. The admonition to "remember your baptism" is not a summons to recreate the scene with a child in a baptismal gown, with proud parents standing beside a pastor and representative of the congregation with a font of water to be doused upon the unsuspecting infant's head. Rather, it is a summons to remember that something has happened to you that has given you a new identity and that you will never be the same. It is a summons to perform your baptismal identity.

Unfortunately, the act of initiation into a distinct community has too often become a cultural ritual signifying nothing. If the church in the twenty-first century is to regain the transformative power offered in the gospel, a good place to begin is by recovering baptism as a formative event in the life of each church member and a collective resource to guide the life and mission of the community of faith.

---

14. Flannery O'Connor, "The River," *The Complete Stories* (New York: Farrar, Straus, and Giroux, 1971), 168.

During the height of the Cold War between the Soviet Union and the West, the National Council of Churches in the United States sent annual delegations of Christians from several denominations to visit the Russian churches and their members. It began when the Soviet Union was called "the evil empire," and it was an attempt to build bridges between our churches. Those trips provided some incredible experiences in which walls of hostility were broken down (cf. Eph. 2:14). Each group had a leader from the Russian Orthodox Church and a guide provided by the Soviet government. The guide was always a member of the Communist Party. At first, they were skeptical of the groups of American Christians. On many occasions after visiting numerous churches and church services, sharing conversation, meals, and tour bus rides, the guide would confide to a member of the group something that was troubling to the guide. One woman put it this way: "Traveling with you has been enjoyable for me, but also troubling. You know I am a Communist, but my grandparents are Christians; when I was very young, my grandmother took me to her church without my parents, who are also members of the party, and I was baptized. Getting to know you and hearing the Christian story in a positive way is forcing me to wrestle with my own baptism. What does it mean that I have been baptized?" These confessions almost always led to discussions late into the night.[15]

"What does it mean that I have been baptized?" A brief service in which words are said, questions asked to parents or the person being baptized and to the congregation, a prayer over the water, the mark of the cross placed on the head, and it is over. It does not seem so significant—but, "You are claimed by Christ and you are his

15. This account was given by Carlisle Harvard, who co-led nineteen groups of Christians from the United States to Russia since 1983. She is a member of the First Presbyterian Church in Durham and was director of the International House at Duke University for twenty-one years. She describes another moving experience when the guide, who had the microphone on the tour bus on the last day of the visit, was in tears as she thanked the group for what had been an incredible experience. She also said, however, that she would request not to be assigned again to such a group. She too had been baptized as a child, and she too reported that the conflict within her was painful. It took courage for parents and grandparents to have their children baptized in the Soviet Union. The possible consequences were staggering, but the story does seem to confirm the warning of Flannery O'Connor's preacher that if you are baptized, "you won't be the same again."

forever." This simple act has profound implications for the person baptized and the congregation—and "you won't be the same again." As Robert McAfee Brown wrote, "That baptism should be charged with such meaning is surely one of the surprises of grace. . . . Nothing the church does represents the gospel as a pure gift of grace more vividly than the baptism of an uncomprehending child. The sacrament shows that the initiative belongs wholly to God."[16] In the baptismal service of the French Reformed Church the pastor says, "Little child, for you Jesus Christ came into the world, he did battle in the world, he suffered; for you he went through the agony of Gethsemane and the darkness of Calvary; for you he cried, 'It is fulfilled'; for you he triumphed over death. . . . For you, and you, little child, do not yet know anything about this. But thus is the statement of the apostle confirmed, 'We love God because he first loved us.'"[17]

> **"I am baptized"**
>
> **In his moments of greatest doubt, Martin Luther would write in huge letters: "I am baptized."**
>
> **—Roland H. Bainton**
>
> *Here I Stand: A Life of Martin Luther* (repr. Peabody: Hendrickson, 2009), 381.

"What does it mean that I have been baptized?" It means that by the gracious promises of God I am included as a beneficiary of God's steadfast love. And it means that by the same grace I am included in the company of those "saints" throughout the ages and to the present moment who call us to worship and serve God. To be baptized is to be made a member of the body, to be incorporated into the Christian community.

Baptism takes place in worship, in the company of other members of the one body who promise to support and encourage the new member on the journey of faith. In a movie titled *About a Boy* the actor Hugh Grant played Will Freeman, a rich London playboy who has made it his goal to live only for himself. He has set out to prove John Donne wrong when he said, "No man is an island." Will

---

16. Robert McAfee Brown, *The Spirit of Protestantism* (New York: Oxford University Press, 1965), 148–49.
17. Cited in ibid., 149.

lived a shallow life devoted to clothes, videos, pop music, and other such stuff. Then he took on a sideline. He set out to seduce single moms. In pursuit of this goal, he meets the son of one of the women, an awkward twelve-year-old named Marcus. Marcus adopts Will. That is a twelve-year-old adopting a young playboy. Marcus goes on to teach Will valuable lessons of life. At one point in the story, when a crisis threatens to engulf both of them, Marcus, the twelve-year-old, says to Will, his new best friend, "Two is not enough. We need backup."

We all need backup. Many of us who grew up with the Lone Ranger were formed by the myth of the rugged individual, the independent hero who can deal with the "bad guys" by himself. But even the Lone Ranger had Tonto, and as Marcus said, "Two is not enough. We need backup." We were created to live in community, and the myth of the rugged individual is another form of identity theft. When we remember our baptism, our true identity is affirmed. We, like the person being baptized, are claimed by God and called to live in the community of God's people. There we are reminded of and called to display God's good future.

In baptism, moreover, the community of which we are made members is a community that transcends the boundaries that separate us from those who are different from us because of background, geography, race, class, sexual orientation, and any other dividing walls. The point is underscored by the passage of Scripture that is often read at the beginning of the rite, "There is one body and one Spirit, just as you were called to the one hope of your calling, one Lord, one faith, one baptism, one God and Father of all, who is above all and through all and in all" (Eph. 4:4–6). For the writer of Ephesians it is clear that we are all in this together and what binds us together is stronger that anything that would divide us.

John Buchanan, pastor of the Fourth Presbyterian Church in Chicago and editor of *Christian Century*, tells about a trip he made to Cuba as a member of a delegation of American Christians. They were visiting the First Presbyterian Church in Havana. Buchanan was scheduled to preach, and a baptism was also scheduled. The Cuban pastor invited John to participate in the baptism. He did, saying, "Anibal, I baptize you . . ." in English after the Cuban pastor had said the words in Spanish. Buchanan said it was a powerful experience for all present, displaying that baptism overcomes barriers of nationality, history, language, politics—all the barriers that separate the human race. The congregation in Chicago also celebrated the baptism of Anibal Quesada, who in her baptism belongs to Jesus Christ forever and is part of the great family of God's people, everywhere, the body of Christ.[18]

The message of Ephesians echoes from the baptismal font. The script of Ephesians is written on our foreheads with the mark of the cross that brands us forever. The move from death to life, signed in baptism, is the story of our lives and of our identity. It is God's gracious gift, which offers us forgiveness of our sins and calls us to live into the good future of God.

When the worship leader leads the Confession of Sin and Declaration of Pardon from the baptismal font, she is performing the script of Ephesians and calling us to remember our baptism. Remembering our baptism is to remember our identity as those who are claimed by God in the waters of baptism and empowered to live the newness of life given us through the death and resurrection of Jesus Christ.[19] Remembering our baptism is to remember who we are by the grace of God. It is to remember that our lives and our common life have been claimed by Christ. It is to be summoned to faithfulness to the identity we have been given by God's grace.

A Declaration of Faith captures all of this eloquently:

> We believe that in Baptism
> the Spirit demonstrates and confirms God's promise
> to include us and our children in God's gracious covenant,
> cleansing us from sin,
> and giving us newness of life,
> as participants in Christ's death and resurrection.

---

18. John M. Buchanan, *A New Church for a New World* (Louisville: Geneva Press, 2008), 62.
19. In a study entitled *Holy Baptism and Services for the Renewal of Baptism: The Worship of God*, Supplemental Liturgical Resource 2 (Philadelphia: Westminster Press, 1985), 1–21, the argument is made that the baptismal crisis is at the core of the challenge facing churches today: "Those 'outside' the church cannot always identify characteristics of Christian living among the baptized that distinguish the baptized from the nonbaptized. It is entirely possible that the crisis of the church is really not qualitatively different from the baptismal crisis" (p. 20).

> Baptism sets us in the visible community of Christ's people
> and joins us to all other believers by a powerful bond.
> In baptism we give ourselves up in faith and repentance
> to be the Lord's.
> For both children and adults, baptism is a reminder
> that God loves us long before we can love him.
> For both, God's grace and our response to it
> are not tied to the moment of baptism,
> but continue and deepen throughout life.[20]

The act of being baptized takes just a few minutes, but the consequences last forever, they "continue and deepen throughout life." In a complex and transient world, this provides a secure identity with staying power. Baptism does not have an expiration date.

A Diversity of Gifts

The unity of the church does not require an oppressive uniformity. It requires self-giving love and peaceable difference. That is the way and the will of the triune God, the "one God and Father of all, who is above all and through all and in all" (4:6). The unity of the church includes diverse people, and it is nurtured and sustained by a diversity of gifts.

Indeed, hard on the heels of this account of the cosmic scope of God's rule and of God's presence "in all" comes an account of the concrete and particular gift of grace to each. "Each of us was given grace according to the measure of Christ's gift" (4:7). The passive suggests a divine giver, the "one God and Father of all." And the gift is grace (*charis*), which God has distributed to each according to the measure of the gift of Christ (*tēs dōreas tou Christou*). The phrase has a wonderful ambiguity about it. Is Christ the gift or is Christ the giver of gifts? He is both, first gift and then giver of gifts. As gift Christ is the measure of God's immeasurable grace; it is an

---

20. *A Declaration of Faith* (1976), Presbyterian Church in the United States, in *Reformed Witness Today: A Collection of Confessions and Statements of Faith Issued by Reformed Churches*, ed. Lucas Vischer (Bern: Evangelische Arbeitsstelle Oekumene Schweiz, 1982), 255.

extraordinarily generous grace, and an extraordinarily demanding grace. As Paul was made an apostle "according to the gift of God's grace" (3:7; cf. also 3:2, 8), so each member of the church is given grace and called to service. Not all are called to be apostles, but each is given grace and summoned to the work of ministry (4:12). As giver of gifts Christ does not give the same gift to all or all gifts to any, but out of his "boundless riches" (3:8) he gives gifts to each. Because Christ does not give all to any, each needs the other; no one is sufficient unto herself or himself, not even Paul. The unity of the church is not only consistent with diversity; it requires it. The diversity of gifts is the way the one God works unity.

One might expect the author to repeat Paul's response to the inquiry of the Corinthians "concerning spiritual gifts" (1 Cor. 12:1). It would surely be apt. "Now there are varieties of gifts, but the same Spirit; and there are varieties of services, but the same Lord; and there are varieties of activities, but it is the same God who activates all of them in everyone. To each is given the manifestation of the Spirit for the common good" (1 Cor. 12:4–7). Each is gifted; even the one easily regarded as a spiritual clod, the one who sits in back but joins in the joyful confession that "Jesus is Lord," is gifted (cf. 12:3). The test for spiritual gifts is not ecstasy but the manifestation of the cause of God made known in Jesus, the manifestation of what Ephesians calls "the secret," and the self-giving love and humble service displayed on the cross. Then there is no place for boasting or for envy, no place for elitism. What there is is a call to community, a call to be the "one body" (12:12–27), a call to love (chap. 13).

To be sure, that reply to the Corinthians echoes in Ephesians 4:7, "Each [hekasto] of us was given grace according to the measure [metron] of Christ's gift." Each is gifted for the common good, and Christ is the measure. That these different gifts are to serve the common good is evident in the conclusion of this section in 4:16 which contains a verbal echo of 4:7 that is lost in translation. There the working of "each [hekasto] part . . . properly [en metro] promotes the body's growth in building itself up in love." Unlike Paul's reply to the Corinthians, however, Ephesians will turn next not to the *charismata* but to Christ's gifts to the church of the various leaders listed in Ephesians 4:11.

"Ascended on High";
"Descended into the Katōteros"

First, however, Paul cites and comments on Psalm 68:18. One can read smoothly from Ephesians 4:7 to 4:11, leaving out 4:8–10. But we should not leave that passage out—as much as we might like to (for it is among the most difficult passages we have so far encountered in Ephesians). It comes almost as a parenthesis between 4:7 and 4:11.

> Therefore it is said, "When he ascended on high he made captivity itself a captive; he gave gifts to his people." (When it says, "He ascended," what does it mean but that he had also descended into the lower parts of the earth? He who descended is the same one who ascended far above all the heavens, so that he might fill all things.)

To understand this passage and its relevance to the context is no easy matter. We are "needful of the minds of others"[21] and appreciate the diverse gifts that exist in the community that struggles to interpret and to perform the Scripture.

The "therefore" clearly indicates that this parenthesis is related somehow to the giving of gifts. But what is that relationship? The problems begin with the citation of Psalm 68:18 itself, "You ascended the high mount, leading captives in your train and receiving gifts from people." Psalm 68 is, according to the notes in the Oxford Annotated Bible, "the most difficult of the psalms to interpret." The cited fragment, however, seems clearly to refer to God's ascending to his throne in the temple and to a celebration of God's victory over God's enemies. The people, "even those who rebel against the LORD God's abiding there" (as Ps. 68:18 continues), are forced to bring tribute to God. The victory may be a reference to some historical triumph during the time of David or to an anticipated eschatological triumph.

---

21. Among the "minds of others" here, we have profited especially from the commentaries by Markus Barth, Francis Beare, and Andrew Lincoln, even though we were not completely convinced by any of them. We found an article in *TDNT* 3:640–42, by F. Büchsel on *katōteros*, even more helpful—and convincing.

The problems multiply, however, because Ephesians does not quote Psalm 68:18 exactly. It changes "you" to "he," indicating Christ. Instead of God's ascending "the holy mount," the text becomes a reference to Christ's ascending "on high." Instead of receiving gifts of tribute, Christ "gave gifts to his people." Even Calvin acknowledged that "Paul has twisted this quotation somewhat from its true meaning."[22]

Calvin knew of certain Jewish interpretations of this psalm that took it to refer not to God but to David, but he had less sympathy for those interpretations of Psalm 68 than he did for the reading of the psalm in Ephesians. Nevertheless, the tradition of Jewish interpretation may help us to see both that Ephesians stood in that tradition and how the citation of Psalm 68 may advance the argument Ephesians makes.

There was evidently a tradition of interpretation that transferred to the son of David (whether to the current king or to the messianic king) attributes ascribed to God in the enthronement psalms. It was a small step from that transfer to understanding David to be the one who "ascended" in this psalm, going up "the high mountain" of Zion, in the aftermath of his triumph over his enemies to establish Jerusalem as a place for the throne of God, bringing the ark of God to Jerusalem. Psalm 68 does seem to invite liturgical celebration at the temple (see vs. 24–27), and worship at the temple would surely connect with the earlier image of the church as "a holy temple," a "dwelling place for God" (Eph. 2:21, 22).

There was, however, another tradition of interpreting this psalm that transferred what was said of God to Moses. In this tradition Moses is the one who ascended the high mount, and the mount is Sinai.[23] That was evidently the view of a number of ancient Jewish interpreters, in part because the passage was read at the Jewish festival of Pentecost, celebrating the gift of the law. It found its way into the Targum on Psalm 68 (an Aramaic translation or paraphrase

---

22. Calvin, *Ephesians*, 174.
23. See W. H. Harris, "The Descent of Christ in Ephesians 4:7–11: An Exegetical Investigation with Special Reference to the Influence of Traditions about Moses Associated with Psalm 68:18" (Ph.D. diss., University of Sheffield, 1988), especially 110–92. Harris shows, moreover, that in some of these traditions Moses ascends not just to Sinai but also to the heavens and not just to receive the law but also heavenly visions. For the evidence associating this psalm with Pentecost, see Harris, 195–234.

that was read in synagogue worship). The Targum not only identified Moses as the one who "ascended," it also paraphrased "received gifts" as "you have learned the words of the Tora, you gave them as gifts to the sons of men."[24]

Ephesians reads this psalm christologically; it transfers to Jesus the Messiah what is said of God in the psalm. The Messiah is the one who "ascended"—and not to a mountain, whether Zion or Sinai, but to the heavens. Ephesians stands in the Jewish tradition of interpretation and extends it. This Jewish Messiah, this one who is greater than Moses or David, this one who brings the story of Moses and David to fruition and fulfillment, "ascends" and both receives the tribute of the principalities and powers and "gives" gifts.

At another point Ephesians does follow the Hebrew text—rendering a Hebrew phrase quite literally, "he took captivity captive." A more idiomatic translation would be something more like "he took captives in his train" (cf. Ps. 68:18 NRSV). The reading in Ephesians suggests that Christ's ascension marked (as in 1:20–21) Christ's sovereignty over the principalities and powers, his sovereignty over the powers that held us captive to sin and death and the law—and to enmity. Christ has taken the principalities and powers captive (as in Col. 2:15 and 1 Cor. 15:24–26), and in that he has taken our captivity captive too. He has liberated us from the dominion of the powers. He has delivered us from death. In him, remember, we pass from death to life (Eph. 2:4–6). The verses of Psalm 68 that follow immediately upon this citation are surely relevant here: "Blessed be the LORD, who daily bears us up; God is our salvation. Our God is a God of salvation, and to God, the Lord, belongs escape from death" (Ps. 68:19–20).

But we are not yet done with the problems here. Ephesians comments on this psalm by drawing an inference that may seem obvious: if he ascended, then he also descended. It makes sense to say of David that after he ascended to Zion he came back down, and to say of Moses that he ascended to Sinai and then descended with the gift of the law. The inference here, however, is that the Christ "descended into the lower parts of the earth [*katōtera merē tēs gēs*]" (4:9). What does that mean?

24. As cited by Barth, *Ephesians 4–6*, 475.

The conventional answer has been that this "descent" refers to the Son being sent by the Father into the world, as John would so often put it. That account of "descent" has frequently included especially reference to Christ's death on the cross. As Paul had put it in Philippians 2:5–8, the Son did not count equality with God a thing to be grasped but "emptied himself," and "being found in human form, he humbled himself and became obedient to the point of death—even death on a cross." But neither of these seems quite apt as an account of "the lower parts of the earth."

To say Christ descended to the "lower parts of the earth" seems to us different than saying that he descended to the earth. The language (*katōtera merē tēs gēs*) resembles the language that the Septuagint used to refer to Sheol, to the "underworld," the realm of the dead.[25] The Messiah descended into the realm of the dead by his death. He "was buried" (as the ancient confession in 1 Cor. 15:3–4 put it). He had descended "into the abyss" of death (Rom. 10:7). That is the presupposition for his resurrection from the dead and for his exaltation, his ascent, to his place at God's right hand, far above the powers, including the power of death. The Messiah was dead. He was in the realm of the dead. And he took even our captivity to death captive. Even the power of death can no longer hold us captive or separate us from God (cf. 1 Cor. 15:24–26; Ps. 68:20). All those held captive by death find their release, their liberation, in this Jewish Messiah (Eph. 2:4–6).

There is another possibility that shares with this last reading the understanding that he descended into Sheol, but understands that descent as a descent into hell. It is "the harrowing of hell." This interpretation, which was common among ancient commentators like Irenaeus and Chrysostom, bears some resemblance to the tradition in 1 Peter 3:19 and 4:6. There Christ "went and made a proclamation to the spirits in prison" and the "gospel was proclaimed even to the dead." Those passages themselves are notoriously difficult. They presuppose the story told in *1 Enoch*, a collection of five apocalyptic books that was quite popular and influential in the early Christian

25. See, e.g., Gen. 44:29; Pss. 63:9 (LXX 62:10); 139:15 (LXX 138:15); etc. See Buchsel, *TDNT* 3:641 n. 10.

Descended and Ascended

Sarah Sarchet Butter, now pastor of the First Presbyterian Church of Wilmette, led her congregation through an unspeakable tragedy. The husband of her administrative assistant and office manager shot and killed his wife and her son and then killed himself. Sarah had to lead and comfort and hold people together and preside and speak at a memorial service for mother and son. What in the world can you say in that situation? She chose wisely. She said there is one phrase in the Apostles' Creed that had always bothered her: that Jesus "descended into hell." She told how the pastor of the church in which she grew up was so bothered by that line that one time he went through all the hymnals where the creed was pasted inside the cover and with a large black marker crossed out "he descended into hell." Sarah said, "I grew up saying the creed without that line."

"But this week," she said, "I understood that phrase in the creed. We have descended into hell together. . . . Jesus Christ has gone before us, into every corner of it. The good news is that when life takes us there, when we have to go there, he goes with us.

"And the good news is that, on the third day, God raised him from the dead. And he ascended into heaven that we might be raised with him."

It was a powerful affirmation of our Christian faith in the midst of one of the most dreadful tragic situations imaginable. It was an affirmation of the good news of Easter, of Jesus Christ, dead, descended into hell, alive, strong, leading into a new future.

—John M. Buchanan

"Steadfast and Immovable," a sermon at Fourth Presbyterian Church of Chicago for Easter Sunday, April 12, 2009.

---

period. It is, for example, quoted in Jude 14–15 and in the *Epistle of Barnabas*, and it is alluded to in 1 Peter. In *1 Enoch* the strange story of Genesis 6:1–4 was retold, the story of the angels who came to earth and had sex (and offspring) with human women. In Enoch's retelling (*1 Enoch* 6–16), these rebellious angels and their offspring are directly linked to the evil that led to the flood, and Enoch is sent to the angels to announce God's verdict upon them. They are to be imprisoned. We will not say more about this story than that these angels still threatened to break loose and to wreak havoc. These "spirits in prison" were regarded as the powers behind heathen kings and tyrants (e.g., *1 Enoch* 67:4–69:1). First Peter—and perhaps Ephesians—makes Christ's victory over the powers a victory over these powers too, a victory that requires the descent to hell. Christ is Lord of every hostile spirit and of every spirit of hostility, even these.

The victory over the powers is associated surely with the ascension and perhaps also, if this reading is correct, with this descent. That victory guarantees the triumph of God's cause, the "secret" that all things are to be "gathered up" and restored by being brought under the lordship of this Christ, the "secret" that the church has been let in on, that is announced in the gospel and displayed in peaceable difference. The crucified and risen Lord, who "ascended on high" and "descended into the lower parts of the earth," is now in a position to "fill all things" (Eph. 4:10; cf. 1:23), to bring all things to completion and perfection, to the peace that is the good future of God. That Messiah is now in a position to receive God's praise and the praise of all, to receive the tributes of the powers, and to give God's gifts to the church. And give gifts he does (4:7, 11).

Both of these last two interpretations capture, in ways the conventional interpretations do not, the announcement in Ephesians of Christ's sovereignty over the power of death and over the "powers," those spirits that are at work in the world, at work in the structures and institutions of the world, at work in the cultures of enmity. That does not make either of these readings the required reading, but it does suggest that they are plausible readings.

But there is yet one more account of the "descent" that we ought to mention. It goes back to the reading of Psalm 68 at the Jewish Feast of Pentecost, and it supposes that it was adopted as a Christian Pentecost psalm, as a celebration not of Moses giving the law but of Christ giving the Spirit. In this account, after Christ ascends, it is the Spirit who descends.[26] There is throughout Ephesians an intimate connection between Christ and the Spirit. And this reading surely fits the giving of gifts. But an intimate connection between Christ and the Spirit is not an identification of the two. And this reading does not, in our view, take "the lower parts of the earth" seriously enough. Still, we appreciate the point that Christ's gift of the Spirit takes the place of Moses' gift of the law as determinative for Christian

26. This is the view of Harris, *Descent of Christ*, 235–65.

identity and community, and we would be happy to be wrong about dismissing it as the most appropriate reading of the descent.

Each of these interpretations of the descent has its problems, but each also contributes to the task of understanding the story Ephesians tells. The incarnation of Christ, his death on the cross, God's victory over the power of death in the resurrection after Christ had died and entered the realm of the dead, Christ's sovereignty over the powers, even over those spirits imprisoned before the flood according to *1 Enoch*, and the gift of the Spirit—each of these is part of the story. To dismiss any as the least appropriate reading of the descent is not to dismiss the contribution it makes to the reading of Ephesians and of the gospel it tells.

In any case, the emphasis in this parenthesis does not fall on the descent, even if the descent gets most attention from commentators because of the scholarly disputes concerning it. The emphasis falls rather on the ascent, on the victory of Christ, on his having taken our captivity captive, on his giving of gifts to the church, and on the purpose of it all, "that he might fill all things" (4:10).

A Lot of Growing to Do

"The gifts he gave" (4:11) include here the different forms of leadership in the church: apostles, prophets, evangelists, pastors, and teachers (4:11). These leaders are gifts to the church. They are also gifted, of course, but not so that they might boast but so that they might serve. It is not that they are the "gifted" ones and the rest of the church are spiritual clods. "Each" is gifted (4:7), and each is summoned to service. There is no division between the "clergy" and the "laity." Together they are one body. But that unity does not prevent the churches from giving thanks to God for the "gifts" and service of apostles like Paul, and others who provide leadership and service.

These leaders are gifts to the church, but the focus is not on the office itself; the focus is clearly on the purpose of leadership in the church. A long series of purpose clauses begins immediately in 4:12 and crescendos to the end of 4:13. Leaders are given and called "to equip the saints for the work of ministry, for building up the body of

Christ, until all of us come to the unity of the faith and of the knowledge of the Son of God, to maturity, to the measure of the full stature of Christ" (4:12–13).

The calling and purpose of leadership in the church is, first of all, to make the whole church ready (*katartismos*, NRSV "to equip") for the "work of ministry." That is Paul's aim as well, as an apostle, and it is the purpose of Ephesians. The leaders and their gifts are not a substitute for the church; they ready the church for ministry, for service to God's cause in the world. The church's work of ministry includes announcing the gospel, to be sure, but also displaying it even to the principalities and powers by a common life of peaceable difference. Leaders recognize the diversity of gifts in the body; they nurture in the members of this body a readiness to use their own particular gifts for the common good. They do not boast about their own gifts or envy the gifts of others, and they nurture in the church the same attitude. They turn the diversity of gifts toward their common calling and toward ministry to one another in the church.

So the second purpose of leadership is given: to ready the whole church for the work of "building up the body of Christ." The statement mixes metaphors, but to a powerful effect. It calls to mind both the image of the church as the body of Christ (used in Eph. 1:23 and 4:4, and in the Pauline tradition concerning the diversity of gifts) and the image of the church as a building, as a "holy temple," the "dwelling place of God," into which the church must "grow" (Eph. 2:20–22). The church is not ready for the work of ministry or for building up the body of Christ as long as enmity rules. And leadership in the church betrays the giver of gifts if it encourages either division or an oppressive uniformity.

And so another purpose is given. The work of these leaders—and of all the saints—will not be finished until we come to "unity." The church must "grow" into "unity." That unity is characterized, first, as the unity "of the faith," the faith that has been mentioned in the unity creed as "one faith" (4:5), the faith that was their shared confidence in God's promises and common loyalty to God's cause. That unity is characterized, secondly (but equivalently), as the unity of "the knowledge of the Son of God." This knowledge, by the blessing of God, has been made known to the church as knowledge of the

"Son of God" in whom we all are adopted as God's children (1:5). It has been made known as the secret of God's plan to gather up and renew all things in Christ (1:9–10). This is the knowledge for which Paul prayed in his first prayer for the church that they might know fully "what is the hope to which [God] has called you" (1:18).

The purpose clauses have not yet reached their crescendo. The work of these leaders—and of all the saints—will not be completed until the church "grows" "to maturity" (NRSV). "Maturity" fits the image of "growth" (and the subsequent phrase) quite nicely, but it seems a weak translation of *eis andra teleion*, which is literally, "into a perfect man" (4:13). The church must grow into "the perfect man." It must grow into Christ. It is not that the church becomes Christ. It was not the case, after all, that by our adoption as God's children in Christ we became Christ, "the Son of God." The church grows into "the perfect man" by becoming in Christ that new humanity created by Christ (2:15). In that new humanity in Christ there is an end to hostility. In that new humanity there is peace. Christ "is our peace" (2:14).

"Maturity" is nevertheless a well-chosen word, not perhaps to translate *andra teleion*, but to introduce the final and climactic statement of purpose. The work of these leaders—and of all the saints—will not be complete until the church "grows" to "maturity," that is, "to the measure of the full stature of Christ." We prefer a more literal translation also of this phrase. The church must grow "to the measure of the stature of the fullness of Christ [*eis metron ēlikias tou plērōmatos tou Christou*]." The "fullness of Christ" here echoes the first account of the church as the body of Christ in 1:23. There the "immeasurable greatness of [God's] power" (1:19), which was measured by God's raising Jesus from the dead and to sovereignty over

---

An Evangelical Imperative

There is an evangelical imperative for the unity of the church. The world can see something of the reality of God and the truth of Jesus Christ in the quality of human relationships that characterize the church. Or, to put it the other way, the world simply isn't interested in our internal divisions and is bored by our incessant arguing.

—John M. Buchanan

The New Church for a New World (Louisville: Geneva Press, 2008), 64.

the powers (1:19–21), did not leave the church out. There God gave this Christ, as "the head over all things," to the church, which is "his body, the fullness of him who fills all in all," or as we translated it previously, "filled with Christ who fills [or completes] all things completely." Again the gospel that had been announced in the indicative mood is now announced in the imperative. The church *is* Christ's body, filled with Christ. And the church must grow into that body, "to the measure of the stature of the fullness of Christ." By the grace and power and blessing of God, the church is and is called to be an agent in blessing God in words and lives of doxology, in service to God's cause by its proclamation and its display of a new humanity "to the praise of God's glory." That is the final and climactic purpose of the one gift of grace God gave to the church (4:7), of the leaders Christ gave to the church, and of the many diverse gifts of the saints.

The unity of the church, the peace of a new humanity, being filled with Christ, all of it is a gift of God's grace, "according to the measure [*metron*] of the gift of Christ" (4:7), and the gifts and calling of the leaders—and of all the saints—must aim finally at growth to "the measure [*metron*] of the stature of the fullness of Christ." It is not that the gift must be supplemented by the work of the church; the grace of God makes the church an agent in the cause of God. It is by the blessing of God made able to respond to God and so made responsible for a doxological common life, a life worthy of its calling.

Notice how desperately wrong the "church growth movement" gets it! The growth of the church cannot be measured by numbers alone. It is rather that the church is to grow into this new humanity, into peaceable difference. For the sake of increasing numbers, the church growth movement advises evangelism "along socially homogeneous lines," but that is no way to grow toward maturity in Christ. The church in Ephesians was to be normatively inclusive! Because Christ is inclusive! Because all things will be united in Christ! Because Christ created a new humanity! Because he is our peace!

The church has a lot of "growing" to do if it is to attain unity and peaceable difference, if it is to reach "maturity," if it is to grow to the "full stature of Christ." "We must no longer be children" (Eph. 4:14). Changing images suddenly but continuing the point, the author compares the immature children to little boats in a chaotic sea stirred up by parties and schismatics within the church. That is not unity or peaceable difference. That is chaos.

We need teachers and leaders who hold tight to the confession of the unity creed, who hold tight to "the faith and knowledge of the Son of God," who proclaim a gospel of peaceable difference and hold us to it. Those who would divide, who would boast about some little truth they think they know well or some little good that they think they do well, and who for the sake of that little truth or that little good undercut the unity and peace that God intends, are less than faithful leaders and teachers. They are to be regarded as crafty and deceitful schemers (4:14). Our lives and our common life must be shaped by the truth of this one body, one Spirit, one hope, one Lord, one faith, one baptism, and one God and Father of all. Instead of using speech as a weapon against other Christians, instead of engaging in deceit or speaking in ways that destroy the unity of the body, we are to "speak the truth in love" (4:15, *alētheuontes de en agapē*).[27]

FURTHER REFLECTIONS
Speaking the Truth in Love

What are you going to be when you grow up? It is, of course, a question that young people frequently hear from adults—and frequently dread. But it is also a question for the Christian community, and the answer that Ephesians gives goes something like this: "When we grow up, we will be a community capable of living the truth. When we reach maturity, the measure of the full stature of Christ, we will perform the unity of a new humanity." The question presupposes, of course, that there is some growing up still to do. It contains an implicit acknowledgment that one is not yet grown up, not yet mature. That may be the reason young people frequently dread the question. And if we are honest, it may be the reason Christian communities sometimes dread the question too. We are not yet grown up.

27. A more literal translation would be that we are to "truth in love," to perform the truth and not simply speak it, and there is something to be said for that translation, but the context and the parallel in Gal. 4:16 suggest speech.

Ephesians suggests that one way to grow up, one way to become a community capable of living the truth, is to practice speaking the truth in love. To become a grown-up, act like one. But it is hard work. Growing up is not easy. Speaking the truth in love is a tall order for individuals and congregations.

The truth can be difficult to speak and difficult to hear, particularly to and from those one knows well. And it is made more difficult by the presence of some who arrogantly suppose that the truth is their possession, that they possess the truth, the whole truth, and nothing but the truth concerning the faith, or concerning social issues, or concerning themselves. This malady of arrogant certitude is not confined to conservatives, or to liberals, or to moderates. It infects us all. And it is a deadly virus in a world of difference.

The motto of the Reformed tradition may provide a remedy for this disease of arrogance. The prescription is written in Latin: *Ecclesia reformata, semper reformanda* ("The church reformed and always to be reformed"). The reformation is never completed. Reform does and must break out again and again as the Spirit, who reminds us of Jesus, leads us to new and deeper truths about God, the church, the world, and ourselves. So we may and must learn to speak the truth in humility and with the awareness that others may have some truth to share. And so we learn not only to speak the truth but to listen for it from others.

To be a Christian community on its way to maturity does not mean that we will never disagree with one another. There will be disagreements, sometimes profound disagreements. But to be a Christian community on its way to maturity does mean a readiness to engage in honest conversations with one another about those disagreements. Honest conversations are crucial if we are to survive and thrive as a human community. Honest conversations are critical to the tasks of breaking down dividing walls of hostility in the church and society.

Such conversations require respect for those who are different from us and for those whose perspectives differ from our own. They are nurtured by the recognition that God is the author of truth and that every human vision of the truth is seen through a glass dimly

(1 Cor. 13:12). As Ephesians suggests, however, the key to grow-ing into a community capable of such conversations is to practice "speaking the truth in love."

The key is to be guided by the love that we encounter in Christ, and to have our conversations formed and informed by the same love. That love does not insist on its own way (1 Cor. 13:5); that love recognizes in the conversation partner a child of God to be treated with dignity and respect. When people speak and listen to one another in such a spirit, the cultures of enmity lose a little skirmish and the hostility that marks and mars our world retreats a little. Con-versations in such a spirit lead to greater understanding and build up community.

In a world where we have grown accustomed to lies and distor-tions, we grow suspicious of human words and of the human beings who speak them. The cynicism that prevails when we are repeat-edly deceived by people in positions of power leaves us unable to know whom we can trust. Little wonder that there is such a hun-ger for transparency. Transparency requires open communication and accountability for one's words and actions. It seems almost too much to ask, but surely transparency is a minimal requirement in a community called to speak the truth in love. But even such a minimal requirement seems like heavy lifting when we have grown accustomed to secrecy and deception.

Let's be honest. To alter a culture of deceit does require some heavy lifting—and repentance. In the United States we have kept secrets about how we have treated one another, and dividing walls of hostility have been the result. The historian John Hope Franklin has told some of the secrets. The story he has told of the treatment of African Americans by white people does not provide a pretty pic-ture, but he speaks the truth. And the reason for disclosing these secrets and telling these truths is not in order to prove that white people are bad. The reason is rather the realization that unless we face the truth about the past we cannot move toward the reconcili-ation God desires for us.

> Perhaps the very first thing we need to do as a nation and as individual members of society is to confront our past and see

it for what it is. It is a past that is filled with some of the ugli-
est possible examples of racial brutality and degradation in
human history. We need to recognize it for what it was and
is and not explain it away, excuse it, or justify it. Having done
that, we should then make a good-faith effort to turn our history around so that we can see it in front of us, so that we
can avoid doing what we have done for so long. If we do that,
whites will discover that African-Americans possess the same
human qualities that other Americans possess, and African-
Americans will discover that white Americans are capable of
the most sublime expressions of human conduct of which all
human beings are capable.[28]

How often our growth has been stunted because we were
"strangers to the truth." Without the truth we cannot repent, and
without repentance the past is our fate. Without the truth we cannot be free. The reconciliation God desires for us requires a community of truth tellers who speak the truth in love.

Perhaps we can learn from the postapartheid experience in
South Africa. What were the South Africans to do about the injustice
and violence that had marked apartheid? President Nelson Mandela established the Truth and Reconciliation Commission, and he
asked Bishop Desmond Tutu to head the commission. In his book
No Future Without Forgiveness, Bishop Tutu gives an account of the
difficult, painful, and rewarding work of the commission.

Bishop Tutu described the importance of speaking the truth
about injustices: "It is crucial, when a relationship has been dam-
aged or when a potential relationship has been made impossible,
that the perpetrator should acknowledge the truth and be ready
and willing to apologize."[29] Without the truth there can be no honest repentance or any real forgiveness. Without repentance and forgiveness there can be no genuine reconciliation. It is not easy. As
Bishop Tutu went on to say, "We all know just how difficult it is for

---

28. John Hope Franklin, *The Color Line: Legacy for the Twenty-First Century*, Paul Anthony Brick
Lectures (Columbia: University of Missouri Press, 1993), 74–75.
29. Desmond Tutu, *No Future Without Forgiveness* (New York: Image, Doubleday, 2000), 269.

most of us to admit we have been wrong. It is perhaps the most difficult thing in the world—in almost every language the most difficult words are, 'I am sorry.'"[30] Well, perhaps forgiveness of terrible injustices is harder yet. But Bishop Tutu saw that the difficult and painful tasks of truth telling, repentance, and forgiveness were necessary for reconciliation—and that they depended upon some convictions about God and the universe.

> This is a moral universe, which means that, despite all the evidence that seems to be to the contrary, there is no way that evil and injustice and oppression and lies can have the last word. For us who are Christians, the death and resurrection of Jesus Christ is proof positive that love is stronger than hate, that light is stronger than darkness, that laughter and joy, and compassion and gentleness and truth, all these are so much stronger than their ghastly counterparts.[31]

There is hope for our reconciliation with God and with one another where the love of Christ is performed through telling the truth. During the hearings of the Truth and Reconciliation Commission a painful story was told by a man who had been tortured unmercifully. At the end of it Bishop Tutu began to sob uncontrollably. Someone commented afterward, "Healing began to take place through the tears of a man of faith."[32] Telling and hearing the truth in love have the power to enable us to repent and forgive, and to grow up in Christ.

Both truth and love have a claim on our speech. Love has a claim on our speech because of the truth proclaimed in the gospel, and truth has a claim on our speech because love requires mutual encouragement and admonition. "Speaking the truth in love" is shorthand, we think, for being a community "full of goodness, filled with all knowledge, and able to instruct one another" (Rom. 15:14). By "speaking

---

30. Ibid.
31. Ibid., 86.
32. Robert M. Franklin, president of Morehouse College, in an address delivered in Atlanta; cited with the speaker's permission.

God of All Truth

Ours is a seduced world

God of all truth, we give thanks for your faithful utterance of reality.
    In your truthfulness, you have called the world "very good."
    In your truthfulness, you have promised,
      "I have loved you with an everlasting love."
    In your truthfulness, you have assured,
      "This is my beloved Son."
    In your truthfulness, you have voiced, "Fear not, I am with you."
    In your truthfulness, you have guaranteed that
      "Nothing shall separate us from your love
        in Jesus Christ."
    It is by your truthfulness that we love.
    And yet, we love in a world phony down deep
      in which we participate at a slant.
    Ours is a seduced world,
      where we call evil good and good evil,
      where we put darkness for light and light for darkness,
      where we call bitter sweet and sweet bitter (Isa. 5:20),
      where we call war peace and peace war,
    so that we rarely see the truth of the matter.
    Give us courage to depart the pretend world of euphemism,
      to call things by their right name,
      to use things for their right use,
      to love our neighbor as you love us.
    Overwhelm our fearful need to distort,
      that we may fall back into your truth-telling about us,
      that we may be tellers of truth and practitioners of truth.
    We pray in the name of the One whom you have filled
      with "grace and truth." Amen.

                                    —Walter Brueggemann

Awed to Heaven, Rooted in Earth: Prayers of Walter Brueggemann, ed. Edwin Searcy (Minneapolis: Fortress Press, 2003), 129.

the truth in love," by mutual admonition and encouragement, the church can and "must grow up in every way into him who is the head, into Christ" (Eph. 4:15).

It is an important piece of advice. Being tender-hearted does not mean being soft-headed. We must be tender-hearted and tough-minded![33] The gospel requires inclusiveness and peaceable differ-ence, but it does not mean that "anything goes." The thief in W. H. Auden's Christmas oratorio thought that was the appropriate infer-ence: "I like committing crimes. God likes forgiving them. Really the world is admirably arranged."[34] But Ephesians will shortly insist that "thieves must give up stealing" (4:28). The gospel joins to its radical inclusiveness radical claims upon our character and conduct. To be sure, the Jewish Christians in the Lycus Valley were not to condemn all Gentiles as "sinners." And the Gentile Christians were not to despise the Jews as "weak." But this is not a cheap tolerance. That sort of tolerance simply lets the stranger be as long as she is willing to remain a stranger. This is more like hospitality. Indeed, what is required is not the cheap tolerance of strangers but friend-ship with those who are different from us. What is required is the sort of mutual encouragement and mutual admonition that help us to grow and to grow together. What is required is the formation of a community of moral discourse, deliberation, and discernment in memory of this Christ and in hope for God's good future. What is required is "speaking the truth in love" as we learn to build up the one body.

Body Building

"Grow up!" says Paul. It is not that the body should become the head. It is more like the body should "fit" the head. One of our grandchildren had a big head as a child. "Don't worry," we were told, "his body will grow into it." Something like that assurance is given

---

33. See the sermon by Martin Luther King Jr., "A Tough Mind and a Tender Heart," *Strength to Love* (New York: Pocket Books, 1963), 1–9.

34. W. H. Auden, *For the Time Being*, in *The Collected Poetry of W. H. Auden* (New York: Random House, 1945), 459.

in 4:16, except in Ephesians the head is not only the measure of the church's growth but also the source of its life and growth. So it is "from [Christ]" that the whole body grows. Christ is the source of the growth that makes the body "fitting" to its head by being the source of the growth that "fits" the diverse parts of the body to each other. Christ "fits together" and "joins" the parts of the body. The participles are passive, *synarmologoumenon* and *symbibazomenon*; Christ is clearly at work in those participles.

Christ's working, however, does not render the church passive; it renders the church itself an agent, not an independent agent but an agent nevertheless, in its own growth. Christ enables the agency of the church and of its members. He nourishes this body and provides for its own growth by the "working" of each part (*hekastou merous*) properly (*en metroi*) (4:16). Earlier we observed the verbal echo of 4:7 with its claim that to "each [*hekasto*] of us was given grace according to the measure [*metron*] of Christ's gift" in this verse. Notice also the way the "working" [*energeian*] of the members (4:16) echoes the "working" [*energeian*] of God's great power in raising Jesus from the dead (1:20), in the gift of grace to Paul (3:7), and in the church (3:20). God's power is at work in the diversity of gifts Christ gives to each, but it does not render us passive; God's working renders us agents, summoning us to use those gifts for the common good and in service to God's good future, summoning us to our own "working." Christ "promotes the body's growth in building *itself* up in love" (4:16, italics added).

The head is the source of the body's life and of its growth. Surely the church lives by receiving God's one gift of grace (4:7), but it must live in accord with the grace God has given. God has given the gift of grace; therefore, let us live in it and in accord with it. "Therefore . . .," Ephesians said at the beginning of this section. "Therefore," it said, live a common life "worthy of the calling to which you have been called" (4:1). And the thought holds throughout this section. Live a common life worthy of God's grace and gift, worthy of God's promise and plan. Grow up! Build a body fitting to Christ as the head! Love one another!

The Belhar Confession

We believe

—that Christ's work of reconciliation is made manifest in the church as the community of believers who have been reconciled with God and with one another [Eph. 2:11–22];

—that unity is, therefore, both a gift and an obligation for the church of Jesus Christ; that through the workings of God's Spirit it is a binding force, yet simultaneously a reality which must be earnestly pursued and sought: one which the people of God must continually be built up to attain [Eph. 4:1–16];

—that this unity must become visible so that the world may believe that separation, enmity and hatred between people and groups is sin which Christ has already conquered, and accordingly that anything which threatens this unity may have no place in the church and must be resisted [John 17:20–23];

—that this unity of the people of God must be manifested and be active in a variety of ways: in that we love one another; that we experience, practice and pursue community with one another; that we are obligated to give ourselves willingly and joyfully to be of benefit and blessing to one another; that we share one faith, have one calling, are of one soul and one mind; have one God and Father, are filled with one Spirit, are baptized with one baptism, eat of one bread and drink of one cup, confess one name, are obedient to one Lord, work for one cause, and share one hope; together come to know the height and the breadth and the depth of the love of Christ; together are built up to the stature of Christ, the new humanity; together know and bear one another's burdens, thereby fulfilling the law of Christ that we need one another and upbuild one another, admonishing and comforting one another; that we suffer with one another for the sake of righteousness; pray together; together serve God in this world; and together fight against all which may hinder or threaten this unity [Phil. 2:1–5; 1 Cor. 12:4–31; John 13:1–17; 1 Cor. 1:10–13; Eph. 4:1–6; Eph. 3:14–20; 1 Cor. 10:16–17; 1 Cor. 11:17–34; Gal. 6:2; 2 Cor. 1:3–4];

—that this unity can be established only in freedom and not under constraint; that the variety of spiritual gifts, opportunities, backgrounds, convictions, as well as the various languages and cultures, are by virtue of the reconciliation in Christ, opportunities for mutual service and enrichment within the one visible people of God [Rom. 12:3–8; 1 Cor. 12:1–11; Eph. 4:7–13; Gal. 3:27–28; James 2:1–13].

—Confession of Belhar, September 1986

Available at http://gamc.pcusa.org/ministries/theologyandworship/confession.

4:17–5:2

Learning Christ

From the great *berakot* of the first chapter to the prayer for those who read and hear the letter in the third chapter, Paul had emphasized the great secret. In the first chapter he blessed God that God had let the church in on that secret. In the good future of God Christ would be the head of all things, all things would be united and renewed in him. That was the secret, the mystery. That good future of God was *already* established when God raised Jesus from the dead and raised him to sovereignty over the principalities and powers that threaten and divide humanity, those angelic (or demonic) powers that nurture cultures of enmity. That good future, that secret, had been made known *to* the church, and it is made known *in* the church and *by* the church when the church *performs* the secret, when (and if) Jews and Gentiles create an inclusive community in the name of the Jewish Messiah, when (and if) the church displays the "new humanity" established by Christ.

When Paul turned in the fourth chapter to moral exhortation, he began with a great "Therefore" (4:1). And the first section (4:1–16) was a summons to perform the secret, to confess unity and to practice it, to display the peaceable difference of the new humanity created by Christ. It traced in the imperative mood what Paul had announced in the indicative mood in the first three chapters. Paul begged his readers to "lead a life worthy of the calling to which [they] have been called" (4:1), to display in their common life the "unity of the Spirit in the bond of peace" (4:3). He called them to "grow up" and to build up the community (4:15–16), to receive God's grace and to live it.

As Ephesians continues its exhortation in 4:17, the imperative mood is even more pronounced. But there it is again, "Therefore ..." (*oun*, which NRSV translates here as "Now"). This "Therefore" no less than the "Therefore" of 4:1 signals not just a transition from indicative to imperative, from proclamation to exhortation, but also the link between grace and claim, the link between indicative and imperative in the eschatology of the gospel. The subsequent sections are less obviously connected to the themes of unity and inclusiveness, but they do surely display something of the ways the good future of God is to mark their lives and their common life. They do work out something of what it would mean to *perform* the grace by which they have passed from death to life. They do summon the church to radical conformity to Christ.

In ways that are characteristic of the gospel it joins to its vision of an inclusive community some rigorous particular moral instruction.[1] And it does that by making use of moral traditions that are older than the letter itself, traditions that the churches, including the churches of the Lycus Valley, would know. In each of the next three sections of Ephesians, the letter takes up a different identifiable tradition.

The first of them (4:17–5:2), the section examined in this chapter, makes use of a traditional pattern of instruction that admonished Christians to "put off" their old patterns of conduct and character (4:22, 25, 31) and to "put on" a "new self" (4:24). The next section (5:3–20) utilizes a tradition that exhorts Christians to "live as children of light" (5:8). Then, in 5:21–6:9, Ephesians provides its account of a tradition of exhortation concerning the roles and rules of a household.[2]

The use of existing moral traditions does not mean, however, that the exhortations no longer have a basis or context in the gospel that

---

1. Richard A. Burridge (*Imitating Jesus: An Inclusive Approach to New Testament Ethics* [Grand Rapids: Eerdmans, 2007]) makes the case that this combination is characteristic of the New Testament as a whole.

2. See E. G. Selwyn, "On the Inter-relation of I Peter and Other N.T. Epistles," *The First Epistle of St. Peter* (London: Macmillan, 1947), 365–466. He displays and considers the tradition of "putting off" and "putting on" on pp. 393–400 (see especially table VI, pp. 394–95). He treats the tradition of "children of the light" on pp. 375–84 (see table II, pp. 376–78). And he treats the tradition of "be subject," the table of rules for household and community, on pp. 419–39.

has been announced earlier in the letter. They are not permitted to become "a new law" that simply supplements the gospel. Ephesians sets traditional morality in the context of the grace of God, in the context of the gift of Christ to the church, and in the context of the Spirit's work. It links traditional moral instruction to the "growth" of the church that is one body with many members, each of whom is gifted and each of whom is made a responsible agent by the grace of God. The exhortations are no less theological or evangelical because they make use of existing moral traditions. In the following three chapters we will call attention both to the existing moral traditions that were used and to the ways in which the gospel authorizes (and sometimes modifies) the existing moral tradition.

Putting Off and Putting On: A Baptismal Tradition

The moral tradition associated with "putting off" and "putting on," which we find in Ephesians 4:17–5:2 (see especially 4:22, 24, 25), can be identified as a tradition older than Ephesians by the presence of these catchphrases, "put off" and "put on" (or their equivalents), in a number of other letters. The language is found not only in the parallel passage in Colossians 3:5–12 (3:8, 9, 10, 12, 14), but also in 1 Peter 2:1–2; 3:21; 4:1; James 1:21; Romans 13:12, 14; Galatians 3:27; *1 Clement* 13:1; 57:2; *2 Clement* 1:6; and other early texts. There are, moreover, other parallels in these passages besides the language of "putting off" and "putting on." The suggestion of many scholars that this is a baptismal tradition is compelling. The language fits with the disrobing and robing that accompanied baptism in the early church as a symbol of a new identity,[3] and the other parallels fit with the moral instruction that was part of preparation for baptism. Also compelling is the suggestion of many of those scholars that the tradition was especially important to Gentile churches (note, for example, the context both here in Ephesians and in 1 Peter).[4]

---

3. It must be acknowledged, however, that undisputed references to this practice are later than the New Testament.

4. See Philip Carrington, *The Primitive Christian Catechism* (Cambridge: Cambridge University Press, 1940); Selwyn, *First Epistle of St. Peter*, 393–400.

In baptism God gives to people a new moral identity and a new community. Christians are initiated into Christ's death and resurrection in baptism. They pass from death to life in baptism. Because they have been baptized into Christ, they are to regard themselves as dead to sin and as alive to God's righteousness (Rom. 6:1–11). But baptized into Christ, they are baptized into his body. In Christ the baptized are initiated into a new community, a community in which "there is no longer Jew or Greek, . . . no longer slave or free, . . . no longer male and female; for all of you are one in Christ Jesus" (Gal. 3:27–28). Baptism is first of all and fundamentally an act of God. But here again God renders the church an agent of God's work, so it is also an act of the church. The church performs baptism and calls members of the church to perform their baptism in their lives and in their common life. Christians perform their baptism in lives that display the passage from death to life. It is not that baptism works magically to put a stop to old patterns of life and to initiate new ones, but it is the eschatological act of God (and of the community as the agent of God) by which God initiates people into Christ, into his death and resurrection, and into his one body, the church. And God will perfect their baptism at the last day, bringing them safely through the final judgment and giving them life. Until that time the temptations to various sorts of immorality threaten identity theft.

Putting Off the Former Way of Life

It is little wonder, then, that this section begins with a reminder of the "grim picture" of the way of life of Gentiles that was presented in Ephesians 2. There Ephesians had said to the Gentile Christians, "You were dead through the trespasses and sins in which you once lived" (Eph. 2:1–2). There Ephesians had insisted on the "solidarity in sin" of Jew and Gentile (2:3). But there Ephesians also made the glad announcement of the "great love with which [God] loved us" and of the gospel that "even when we were dead through our trespasses" God "made us alive together with Christ" (2:4–5). "[Therefore] . . . you must no longer live as the Gentiles live"(4:17). It is that new life with Christ that must be lived. "[T]he spirit that is now at work among those who are disobedient" (2:2) is still at work. There is still a cosmic conflict between God and the powers that would usurp God's sovereignty. That conflict has been settled, to be sure. God settled it with the resurrection of Christ from the dead and to sovereignty over the powers. God's good future is sure. And those who have been baptized have been made participants with Christ in the passage from death to life and in God's good future. Hence the indicative mood. But the defeated powers still assert their doomed reign, and Christians are summoned to take their part in that cosmic conflict with evil (Eph. 6:12). By the grace of God, and by their baptism, Christians are made responsible agents in that conflict, enlisted on the side of God and of God's Christ. Hence the imperative mood.

So Paul "affirms and insists" that these Gentile Christians should "no longer live as the Gentiles live" (4:17) and that they should "put away [their] former way of life" (4:22). The grace of God does not permit them to act as if nothing has really changed. Everything has changed. They have passed from death to life, and they have no reason to continue to live "as the Gentiles live." Yet, although everything has changed, the cosmic sovereignty of God is not yet everywhere acknowledged. So Paul insists that they acknowledge the sovereignty of God and live a life "to the praise of his glory" (1:14).

Ephesians 4:17–19 is a reminder of the way of life, the death, that they had left behind. The images are no less grim than the earlier picture of Gentile unrighteousness in Ephesians 2. The Gentiles live "in the futility of their minds" (4:17), "darkened in their understanding" (4:18). It is an account familiar to Jewish polemics against Gentile unrighteousness, and it echoes Romans 1:18–21, where Gentile idolatry, their wicked suppression of the truth, their refusal to honor God as God or to give thanks to God, had this result: "they became futile in their thinking and their senseless minds were darkened." The problem in Ephesians (as in Romans) is identified not only as an intellectual problem, not only a problem with their "minds" and their "understanding," but also as a problem with their hearts. The problem was also their hard-hearted refusal to learn the truth and to respond to it by honoring God as God and by giving thanks to God. Ephesians joins this "hardness of heart" to their "ignorance" as reasons for their "alienation from the life of God," from the life God gives

(4:18). The final result of their ignorance and their hard-heartedness, as in Romans, is "every kind of wickedness" (Rom. 1:29).

That wickedness is here characterized, first, as a loss of "sensitivity" (which Calvin takes to be a loss of conscience, a loss of shame[5]); second, as a surrender to "licentiousness"; and finally, as a greedy desire for more and more "impurity" (4:19). That "wickedness" (*kakia*, Rom. 1:29; Eph. 4:31) must be renounced, "put off" (Eph. 4:31). But we are getting ahead of ourselves. That is the conclusion of this section; it is not where Paul turns next.

Learning Christ

He turns next back to the gospel, back to the good news of Christ. The grim picture of their former way of life had been overmatched by the glad announcement that Christ provides passage from death to life. These Gentiles had "heard the word of truth, the gospel of [their] salvation, and had believed in him" (Eph. 1:13). They had been baptized. It had happened through the ministry of those leaders gifted by Christ (4:11) who had proclaimed to them the gospel and taught to them the tradition. So now he contrasts to their former "ignorance and hardness of heart" their new knowledge and love. "That is not the way you learned Christ," he says (4:20).

To "learn Christ" is a curious but powerful phrase. It is obvious in a way. The Christian learns Christ like a good Jew learns Torah. What is learned is Christ. And as a good Jew in learning Torah does not just learn *about* Torah but is initiated into the story it tells, so to learn Christ is not just to learn *about* Christ but to be initiated into his life. Christ is, of course, also the teacher. That is what, it seems to us, Paul says immediately, "for surely you heard him" (4:21; *autōn ēkousate*; NRSV "for surely you have heard about him" is also possible). This is not to suggest that these Christians of the Lycus Valley had been in Galilee or Judea some decades earlier to hear Jesus preach; it is rather to assume that they had heard the Christ who

---

5. Calvin, *Ephesians*, 188. The insensitivity is a moral insensitivity corresponding to the hardness of their heart. They have lost the capacity to lament the moral condition of the world and their own.

"proclaimed peace to you who were far off" (2:17). The other teachers by whom they were taught were "gifted" by Christ to teach them, and when they were taught by these other teachers, they were taught by Christ, they were taught "in Christ" (4:21). Christ is the message but also the medium of this teaching and of this learning. It is grace by which they are taught and grace they learn.

To "learn Christ" is not just to learn some facts about Jesus to which one may adopt any attitude one pleases. One can hardly say "Christ is risen" or "Jesus is Lord" and remain indifferent; such affirmations are self-involving. To "learn Christ" is to be formed by Christ, to have one's character and conduct shaped by this one who was dead and is alive again, this one who is sovereign over the principalities and powers that nurture enmity. To "hear Christ" does not deny the presence or the significance of intermediaries who preached the gospel and handed on the tradition. It is rather to insist that in the preaching and instruction of pastors and teachers the voice of the living Lord can still be heard. Jesus still speaks in the proclamation concerning him as the Christ, still speaks in the summons to live lives and a common life worthy of the gospel.

That is the way they "learned Christ," not by way of their Gentile past but by way of hearing "the word of truth, the gospel of your salvation" (1:13); and when they heard it, they heard not just a pastor or a teacher, they heard Jesus. When they heard it, they heard not just some doctrinal proposition or some moral instruction, they heard the truth about themselves and about their world and about God and the cause of God. That is how they "learned Christ": "as truth is in Jesus" (4:21). Jesus announced God's good future, and as the living Lord he still makes the secret known in the proclamation of the truth about Jesus. Jesus called people to discipleship, and as the living Lord he still summons them to conform to the cross and resurrection into which they have been baptized.

Christ taught them to be faithful to the identity and community into which they had been initiated in baptism. "You were taught to put away your former way of life . . . and to clothe yourselves with the new self" (Eph. 4:22–24). It was Christ who taught them this, even if they learned it through the instructions of others for their baptism. These verses are almost certainly a quotation (or a paraphrase) of

---

A Baptismal Branding

Re-brand Us

You mark us with your water,
You scar us with your name,
You brand us with your vision,
 and we ponder our baptism, your water,
 your name,
 your vision.
While we ponder, we are otherwise branded.
 Our imagination is consumed by other brands,
 —winning with Nike,
 —pausing with Coca-Cola,
 —knowing and controlling with Microsoft.
Re-brand us,
 transform our minds,
 renew our imagination,
 that we may be more fully who we are marked
 and hoped to be,
we pray with candor and courage. Amen.
—Walter Brueggemann

Awed to Heaven, Rooted in Earth: Prayers of Walter Brueggemann, ed. Edwin Searcy (Minneapolis: Fortress Press, 2003), 88.

---

the traditional baptismal instruction (or perhaps even a baptismal liturgy) associated with these key words, "putting off" and "putting on." The tradition is set in the context of having "learned Christ." It was in learning Christ that "you were taught to put away your former way of life, your old self, corrupt and deluded by its lusts, and to be renewed in the spirit of your minds, and to clothe yourselves with the new self, created according to the likeness of God in true righteousness and holiness" (4:22–24).

The meaning of "your former way of life" is clear; it is the way of life already described at the beginning of this section. The "old self" stands in apposition to "your former way of life." When it is described as "corrupt and deluded by lust" that same description of Gentile unrighteousness is echoed. The "old self" must be understood as the self who was marked by that way of life, captive to it and to "the spirit that is now at work among those who are disobedient"

(2:2). It is altogether appropriate to regard this self, as Calvin did,[6] as associated with Adam, who stood at the head of this present evil age. The focus, however, is not on individual persons, not even on Adam; the focus is rather on the eschatological and corporate identity of the self. This "old self" is the self, as Romans put it, who was "conformed to this world," to this present evil age (Rom. 12:2). And the traditional exhortation in Ephesians continues in the same way Romans did, by calling Christians to be transformed, "to be renewed in the spirit of your minds" (Eph. 4:23; cf. Rom. 12:2). Here that renewal is clearly associated with being schooled by Christ, with learning Christ, and it stands in obvious contrast to the "futility of [the] minds [of the Gentiles]" (Eph. 4:17) and the delusions of the old self (4:22).

Learning Christ finally means "to clothe yourselves with the new self" (4:24). But who or what is this "new self"? Relying on the parallel in Galatians 3:27, we might conclude that the "new self" is Christ. There "to be baptized into Christ" is to be "clothed with Christ" (Gal. 3:27). And that reading of "the new self" is surely plausible here as well, and followed by Calvin. But while "the new self" is surely associated with Christ, we do not think it can here simply be identified as Christ. Ephesians had used the phrase used here (*kainon anthrōpon*, "new man"; NRSV "new self") once before, in 2:15. There *kainon anthrōpon* was the one "new humanity" created by Christ. And that is what we think it means here too. Again the focus is not on individual persons, but on an eschatological and corporate identity. The point is not that we become Christ but that, by the renewal of our mind, we become conformed not to this present evil age but to Christ. In baptism we do not become Christ, we become his body, the church, the firstfruits of "the new humanity" created by Christ. It is not Christ who is "created" (in spite of Arius); it is "the new humanity"—"created" to conform to (or "according to") Christ, the image or "likeness of God." The "new humanity" is to display, like Christ, "true righteousness and holiness" (Eph. 4:24). To be baptized is to be identified with Christ and with his body the church, and to *perform* that baptism is to live in ways that honor Christ, that

6. Ibid., 190.

"put on" the new humanity that he created, and that embody "true righteousness and holiness."

"So then . . .," the exhortation continues (4:25). In what follows Ephesians develops this tradition of "putting off" and "putting on" with several examples of the sort of conduct and character that are to be "put off" with the "old self" and, by way of contrast, examples of the sort of acts and attitudes appropriate to "the new humanity." The several examples all follow the same pattern. There is first a prohibition, a renunciation, followed by a prescription, a positive exhortation, and concluded by a reference to a basis and motive for the appropriate action.[7] Only in the last and climactic example is Christ explicitly mentioned, although the whole clearly belongs to an account of what it means to "learn Christ."

Put Away Falsehood; Speak the Truth

Pride of place among these examples belongs to truth telling. Little wonder, since the transition from "learning Christ" to moral exhortation was marked by the affirmation that "truth is in Jesus." The first renunciation utilizes the language of the tradition, "Put off the lie!" (4:25; NRSV "putting off falsehood"; but the participle can function as an imperative and quite clearly does so here). The corresponding positive exhortation is, "Speak the truth to your neighbors!" And the somewhat surprising motive for truth telling is that "we are members of one another" (4:25). One might have expected the affirmation that "truth is in Jesus" to be repeated here and the motive to be loyalty and conformity to the one who is truth. Perhaps its proximity makes it unnecessary to repeat here. Instead Ephesians provides as a motive this "truth" that we know "in Jesus," that we are members one of another. Truth is owed to the neighbors because of our social solidarity with them. It is also a bit surprising that the text does not say that we are members of the "body." The "body" is not mentioned. Perhaps it is also too obvious to mention. But perhaps the reference to the "body" is left out because "the neighbors" to whom we are

7. Barth, *Ephesians 4–6*, 545–47.

to "speak the truth" evidently include those who are not members of the body, not members of the church. The exhortation was not simply that we should tell the truth "to one another." Truthfulness is not just owed to other members of the church, but to any and all "neighbors." The "truth" in Jesus of our social solidarity, that "we are members of one another," points beyond the church to the universal community that is God's plan. It may be a "secret" too well kept that we are members of one another in a universal community, but it *is* the truth in Jesus. The church as the body of Christ is the firstfruits of a "new humanity," and it is called to make the "secret" known also (if simply) by speaking the truth to the neighbor. Deception belongs to the old way of life, to the old associations and communities; it is to be renounced. But Christians do not renounce those still bound by the old way of life, the members of those old communities. In memory of the Messiah's work and of God's work and in hope for God's good future, Christians perform the gospel and anticipate God's future by "speaking the truth to our neighbors."

The motive clause that "we are members of one another" marks the obligation as a social obligation. All ethics are social ethics, and so is the prohibition of deception. No genuine community can be built on deception. It must be built on the truth. This community, the church, is to be built on the truth, "as truth is in Jesus" (4:21), and it is to be marked by truthfulness. The intimate connection of truth telling and community works both ways: truth telling nurtures genuine community, and genuine community nurtures truth telling. And it works both ways in Ephesians. Here community is the basis of the command to "speak the truth to our neighbors"; earlier "speaking the truth in love" promoted the growth of the body in unity (4:15).

William C. Placher observed that churches are too frequently not such communities. They too often retreat from the risks of honest community, playing it safe, keeping up the pretenses of respectability.[8] The churches, Placher insisted, should know better. They are,

---

8. William C. Placher, *Narratives of a Vulnerable God: Christ, Theology, and Scripture* (Louisville: Westminster John Knox Press, 1994), 151. The quotations within this paragraph are also from p. 151.

Telling the Truth and Making Community

They are sitting in the basement of a church. . . . Fluorescent lights buzz overhead. There is an urn of coffee. There is a basket which is passed around at some point which everybody who can afford to puts a dollar in to help pay for the coffee and the rent of the room. In one sense they are strangers who know each other only by their first names and almost nothing else about each other. In another sense they are best friends who little by little come to know each other from the inside out instead of the other way round, which is the way we usually do it. . . .

They could hardly be a more ill-assorted lot. Some are educated, and some never finished grade school. Some are on welfare, and some of them have hit the jackpot. Some are straight, and some are gay. There are senior citizens among them and also twenty-year-olds. Some groups are composed of alcoholics and some, like the ones I found my way to, of people who have no alcoholic problems themselves but come from families who did. The one thing they have in common can be easily stated. It is just that they all believe that they cannot live fully human lives without each other and without what they call their Higher Power. . . . What they all do believe in, or are searching for, is a power higher than their own which will make them well.

—Frederick Buechner

Telling Secrets: A Memoir (San Francisco: HarperSanFrancisco, 1991), 89–91.

after all, communities of people who recognize that they are sinners and that they along with other sinners have been accepted by God. "People will find a place where they are free to tell the truth," he said, and he pointed to "all the people flooding the church basement for meetings of twelve-step groups as the size of the regular congregation declines."

The motive clause assumes what 4:15 had made explicit, that we are to "speak the truth in love." What we said in that context remains true, that love requires truth telling and that the truth in Jesus requires love. But sometimes in this sad world, truth and love can come into conflict. Ephesians is not interested in casuistry here, in asking, for example, whether the midwives of Exodus 1 sinned in their deception, or whether those who hid the Jews from the Nazis should have told the truth to any who inquired. Issues of casuistry may be left to the discernment of the body as a community of moral discourse in memory of Christ. But that community is formed by its renunciation of "the lie," and it will hardly delight in any lie.

Put Away Sinful Anger

The second example concerns reconciliation with an enemy. It is not that anger is repudiated, but that sin is. "Be angry but do not sin" (4:26). Anger at injustice is permitted. Indeed, an injustice not only prompts anger; it requires it. When we see the poor oppressed, we should get angry. When the "other" is demeaned or insulted, we should get angry. But anger can be an occasion for sin, for seeking revenge instead of justice, for holding a grudge instead of seeking reconciliation. It is sin that is renounced. "Put off sin! When you are angry, even when your anger is righteous, do not sin!" The positive exhortation here is framed in the negative, "do not let the sun go down on your anger" (4:26), but the positive meaning is clear, "seek to be reconciled before the sun goes down, before the day is up." The basis for this exhortation is again somewhat surprising, "lest you give the devil an opening" (4:27; NRSV "do not make room for the devil"). One might have expected again some reference to the Christ here, to the Christ who is our "peace," to the Christ who reconciles, but again Christ is not explicitly mentioned. Perhaps the author thought it obvious, not requiring mention. There is, instead, a reference to the devil, the *diabolos*. The *diabolos* is the "accuser," the "slanderer," the "spirit now at work" (2:2) to nurture hostility. The *diabolos* can do some awful things with a little anger, and we are here, no less than in 6:11–12, summoned to "stand against the wiles of the devil" in the strength of the Lord.

We are not to give the devil "an opening" (4:27; *topos*), but we are to "leave room [*topos*] for the wrath of God" (Rom. 12:19). That is the antidote for the malignant tendency of anger toward violence and enmity. "Never avenge yourselves," Romans says, but "if your enemies are hungry, feed them; if they are thirsty, give them something to drink" (Rom. 12:19–20). The eagerness for reconciliation overwhelms the anger, even the legitimate anger, when injustice is done to one's self. Indeed, the "wrath of God" may be the model here, for in Isaiah this is the word of God, "In overflowing wrath for a moment I hid my face from you, but with everlasting love I will have compassion on you" (54:8).

But what if injustice is done to another? Genuine community requires justice no less than truth telling. Indeed, peace itself requires justice. A peace without justice looks too much like the Pax Romana, a peace secured by violence and serving Roman self-interest. Peaceable difference does not mean indifference to the injustice that hurts or harms another. In this sad world justice and peace do not always embrace. Ephesians is not interested in the casuistry that would negotiate the claims of justice and of peace on this side of the eschaton any more than in the casuistry concerning whether deception is ever required or permitted to protect a neighbor. That may be left to the discourse and discernment of the community. It will not necessarily be an easy conversation. Different communities and traditions have different languages for "justice." Surely the Jews and the Gentiles of the Lycus Valley would not understand justice in precisely the same way. There have been different languages—and different conceptions of justice—since the tower of Babel. But that curse too, that confusion, has been answered by the blessing of God, by Pentecost and the gift of the Spirit. The discourse and discernment that are necessary are possible in this community by the Spirit. They will listen to each other, silencing neither the other nor the Spirit of God. They will discern the claims of justice and of peace in the conviction that in God's good future justice and peace shall indeed embrace and "kiss" (Ps. 85:10). They will not use justice as an excuse to exclude. They will set the claims of justice in the context of God's cause to embrace and to renew "all things" and all people.

Put Away Stealing

The third example concerns money. "Thieves" are told to renounce "stealing" (Eph. 4:28). The commandment echoes here, and like the commandment this verse is sometimes celebrated by the wealthy both for the authorization it seems to afford to their possessions and for the protection it evidently provides against any who would take them away—including (and especially) the poor. But there are many different kinds of theft, as Scripture makes clear. There is the sort of theft to which the poor and powerless are tempted, but there are also the subtle forms of stealing that tempt the rich and powerful. It is a kind of theft when the rich get richer at the expense of a decent wage for laborers or by taking advantage of slaves. It is a kind of theft when merchants "make the ephah small and the shekel great" (Amos 8:5). It is a kind of theft when a judge takes a bribe. And it is a kind of theft when the wealthy do not recognize that what they call "their own" is really God's and an opportunity to practice justice and generosity. It is a kind of theft when the rich ignore and dismiss the legitimate claims of the poor upon them, when they do not share

---

To Give Up Stealing

Q. What does God forbid in the eighth commandment?

A. He forbids not only outright theft and robbery, punishable by law. But in God's sight theft also includes cheating and swindling our neighbor by schemes made to appear legitimate, such as: inaccurate measurements of weight, size, or volume; fraudulent merchandising; counterfeit money; excessive interest; or any other means forbidden by God. In addition, he forbids all greed and pointless squandering of his gifts.

Q. What does God require of you in this commandment?

A. That I do whatever I can for my neighbor's good, that I treat others as I would like them to treat me, and that I work faithfully so that I may share with those in need.

—Heidelberg Catechism, Q & A 110, 111

[S]ince all men are born for the sake of each other, human society is not properly maintained except by an interchange of good offices. Wherefore, that we may not defraud our neighbours, and so be accounted thieves in God's sight, let us learn . . . to be kind to those who need our help, for liberality is a part of righteousness, so that he must be deservedly held to be unrighteous who does not relieve the necessities of his brethren when he can. . . . [T]hose who have abundance do not enjoy their possessions as they ought, unless they communicate them to the poor for the relief of their poverty.

—John Calvin

Commentary on the Four Last Books of Moses, trans. Charles William Bingham (Grand Rapids: Eerdmans, 1950), 3:126.

with the needy what is due them by God's justice. It is likely that the latter sorts of theft are in view here in Ephesians rather than the first. Then one need not suppose that there were a lot of petty thieves and shoplifters in the churches of the Lycus Valley.

The positive exhortation here is, "Do an honest day's work with your own hands!" The advice commends work without glorifying it. Work itself is a good thing, but it is not God. Some of us are tempted to make it a god, making it the center and foundation of our lives, staking our identity upon it. And some of us are tempted to make ourselves gods in our work, as if we were the Messiah and our work messianic. Against such temptations it is important to say that there is a God, and our job is not it, that there is a Messiah, and we are not him. Work, whether religious work or secular work, can be "sacred" not because work is God but because work can participate in the calling to serve God's cause in the world.

Work is not God, but it can be good. Some of us are tempted to regard it as evil, as a necessary evil, perhaps, if we are to earn a living, but as an evil nonetheless. Work, in this view, is something we endure in order to have enough money to escape from work, to do something, anything, else. For reasons that are understandable and that we should work to correct, this is the view of some who work under brutalizing conditions for an insufficient wage. But it is shared by many more in our culture. Some teachers seem to regard their time with students as something to be endured in order to make enough money to get away from work. Some doctors seem to regard their patients as consumers and the weaknesses of those patients as opportunities for profit; they too want to escape from work. Against this temptation, it is important to be reminded that work can be good, that it can engage and express our creativity, our energy, and our vocation to serve God and the neighbor.

When we regard work as an evil, even if a necessary evil, we leave ourselves no way to judge good work except on the basis of its commercial success. The successful entrepreneur is the one who can retire at forty. The good book is the bestseller. The rich and famous are admired and envied because they can live in leisure. Such judgments are in accord with the view of work as something to be endured in order to make enough to quit and with the yuppie axiom that money equals value. Most of us, however, know better than that. Most of us have had some experience that has taught us how much we depend on those people who regard the integrity of their work as more important than the fact that they get paid enough to escape it. There was that teacher who took extra time and effort with our child when he needed it. There was that mechanic who fixed the car for a few dollars when we were five hundred miles from home and thought there was a major problem.

Still, some work is not good. Ephesians used what was already evidently a time-worn expression, "honest work," exhorting the Ephesians to "work honestly with their own hands" (4:28). Christian discernment will hardly claim that, to be good or "honest," work must be done with one's hands rather than with one's brain, but neither will it regard intellectual work as somehow better than work with one's hands. Any academics tempted to boast about their work should remember just how much the honest work of many others, including maintenance people and secretaries, contributes to the efficiency and pleasure of their work. All work takes some effort, all work takes place in community, and all work should be oriented toward some service to others.

In the discourse and discernment of the Christian community, members of the body will caution one another against certain kinds of work and against some practices of some work that are incoherent with the gospel and with God's cause and calling. They will admonish people, as Ephesians put it, to "give up stealing." They will counsel young people (and everyone) to look for work consistent with God's cause and the neighbor's good, to find work in which and through which they can exercise their fundamental calling to be disciples. They will counsel those who have found work to conduct themselves in their work as responsible not only to their employer but also to their craft, to their neighbors, and to God.

The motive here, the motive to do an honest day's work, is not simply to earn a living for oneself and one's family, honest enough motives, to be sure. The motive is surely not to accumulate enough possessions to pretend one has achieved by oneself and for oneself security and an identity. The motive, rather, is simply "to have something to share with the needy" (4:28). That will include those who do not have work. Again, there is no explicit mention of Christ in the grounds for this renunciation and exhortation, but the claims of the needy upon us surely belong to what it is to "learn Christ." And the theological grounding is obvious. Our money is not simply our own; it is finally God's. It is to be earned honestly, not by various forms of theft, surely not in ways that take advantage of the needy and "trample on the poor" (Amos 5:11). And it is to be shared generously. How else shall we respond to God's great gift if not by being generous ourselves (Eph. 4:7; cf. 2 Cor. 8:8–15)? The idea that one's life is secured by "the abundance of possessions" (Luke 12:15) belongs to the "old self," not to the "new humanity."

Again, as in the first motive clause, "we are members of one another" (4:25), the motive clause has a moral horizon that reaches beyond the church. We need not ask to see the church membership papers of "the needy" before we share with them. And again, Ephesians is not interested in casuistry here, in the weighing of conflicting needs and goods in the context of scarce resources. That may be entrusted to the church as a community of discourse faithful to its calling, but this community, formed by having learned Christ, will hardly be content to let any need of any neighbor go unmet.

Put Away Evil Talk

The next example returns to the topic of our "talk." "Evil talk" is renounced. The focus here is not on truth telling, although evil talk might include deception. If our talk is to be "speaking the truth in love," then it is not just talk that violates truth that we must renounce but also any talk that violates love. Moreover, there is a "truth which is of Satan," a speech that may not strictly violate the standards of truth telling but that is nevertheless hurtful, tearing down persons and destroying community.[9] "Let no [such] evil talk come out of your mouths" (4:29).

9. Dietrich Bonhoeffer, *Ethics*, ed. Eberhard Bethge, trans. Neville Horton Smith (New York: Macmillan, 1955), 366.

> **Gossip**
>
> We delight in a certain poisoned sweetness experienced in ferreting out and in disclosing the evils of others. And let us not think it an adequate excuse if in many instances we are not lying. For [God] who does not allow a brother's name to be sullied by falsehood also wishes it to be kept unblemished as far as truth permits.
>
> —Calvin
>
> *Institutes* 2.8.48.

The positive exhortation summons us to talk that "builds up" persons and the community rather than tearing them down, that encourages conversations that are constructive rather than destructive. The qualification "as there is need" (4:29) suggests that there was indeed a need. There are people who simply need a kind word now and then. And in these churches it was not enough simply to renounce the insults that Jew and Gentile could hurl at one another; such talk created a need for conversations that "build up" the one who is different from the one talking and "build up" the community that includes both Jew and Gentile as members of one body.

The ground and motive is found in the closing line, "so that your words may give grace to those who hear" (4:29). Our talk should bear a resemblance to the grace God gave and gives (3:2, 7; 4:7), to Christ. That grace should make us bold to speak, but also careful to talk in ways that build up the neighbor and the community. We are made agents by the grace of God, and by God's gift and grace our own words "may give grace to those who hear." They may not be rhetorically powerful words, but they must be "gracious words." We may and must serve God's cause by talking with one another in ways that "build up" a community that can display and serve God's cause in the world. Every time we open our mouths to speak, there is something like a cosmic conflict at work, and every time we greet and bless the neighbor with God's peace, there is a little beachhead for God's good future. But every time we insult or curse the neighbor, God's cause loses a little ground. James made the point quite elegantly after calling attention to the difficulty of taming the tongue. "With it," he said, "we bless the Lord and Father, and with it we curse those who are made in the likeness of God. From the same mouth come blessing and cursing. My brothers and sisters, this ought not to be so" (Jas. 3:9–10).

Do Not Make the Spirit Sad

After these examples—and before a final and climactic example—is set an initial summary, "And do not grieve the Holy Spirit of God, with whom you were marked with a seal for the day of redemption" (4:30). It is formulated as a prohibition, "Do not make the Spirit sad!" but it provides a positive grounding for and motive for a life worthy of the "truth in Christ," a life fitting to the work and grace and plan of God. The description of the Spirit here echoes the description given the first time the Spirit was mentioned in Ephesians. In 1:13–14 those Gentiles who had "heard the word of truth, the gospel of [their] salvation, and had believed in Christ," "were marked with the seal of the promised Holy Spirit," and that Spirit was the "pledge," the guarantee, the down payment on our inheritance. Marked by this gift, the Gentiles were given a destiny as well, "redemption as God's own people." That destiny did not destroy or deny their agency; on the contrary the blessing of that destiny made them agents, able to respond to God's gift, able to bless God, and responsible for living "to the praise of his glory." We make the Spirit sad when we do not live "to the praise of his glory," when we do not serve God's cause in the world, when we do not make "the secret" known by putting "the new humanity" created by Christ on display. We make the Spirit sad when we lie and when we nurse a grudge or insult a neighbor, when we do not share with the needy, when our talk is destructive to persons or to the community (4:25–29). We make the Spirit sad whenever we are conformed to this present evil age rather than transformed by a vision of God's good future and by a devotion to God's cause. This is no "passionless" God. When we sin, the Spirit grieves.

This verse serves to mark the moral instruction of this section of Ephesians, and indeed the whole of the moral exhortation as a "Spiritual ethic." But linked to what has gone before, this Spiritual ethic is not disembodied or individualistic. Precisely because it is a Spiritual ethic, it is embodied and communal. The Spirit does not work like magic; it works in and through the body, making peace and maintaining community. We had been reminded that we are "members of one another" (4:25), members of the social body. Here different members, different parts, of individual bodies have been enlisted in the Spirit's work: our hearts, to be sure, but also our "hands" (4:28) and our "mouths" (4:29). The conflict of this Spirit with "the devil" here reaches into stuff as mundane as everyday anger and reconciliation, as material as work and a loaf of bread shared with "the needy," as commonplace as gossip.

Put Away Community-Destroying Vices; Put On Kindness

Finally, a climactic example is offered, more like an epitome and summary than another example. Nevertheless, the same pattern is found. It begins with a renunciation, "Put away from you all bitterness and wrath and anger and wrangling and slander, together with all malice" (4:31; the word translated by the NRSV as "put away" [*arthētō*] is a passive, but it is probably simply a stylistic variation, "these things are to be put away").

The new identity and the new community in Christ require the renunciation, the "putting off," of an assortment of vices. The little catalogue here repeats the list found in Colossians 3:8, adding "bitterness" and "wrangling." Perhaps that connection to Colossians is enough to explain the presence of "anger" here when it had been permitted in 4:26, but the better explanation is that "anger" here is a vice, a settled disposition, a readiness to react angrily to any little offense, whereas the anger permitted earlier was a response to genuine injustice and was joined to a settled disposition to seek reconciliation. All of these vices make community difficult; to renounce them serves peaceable difference. "Bitterness" (*pikria*), for example, is a character trait that nurses a grudge, nurtures resentment, and refuses reconciliation. "Wrath" (*thymos*) is to be given to fits of rage when one does not get one's own way. "Anger" (*orgē*), similarly, is that vice that makes us quick to lose our temper at any little offense. "Wrangling" (*kraugē*) is the readiness to argue and quarrel; a more literal translation of this word is to "shout"; it is to shout down an opponent rather than to listen to the reasons given by another, and to shout louder when one's own argument is weaker. "Slander" (*blasphēmia*) is to curse or insult another (cf. again Jas. 3:9–10).

"All" of them are to be renounced, and more besides. That is the force of the concluding item in this catalogue of vices: renounce "wickedness" (*kakia*, Eph. 4:31, our trans.; see also 1 Pet. 2:1; Jas. 1:21; Col. 3:8). "Wickedness" (*kakia*) is a very general term. It is almost as if Ephesians added "and so forth." In the NRSV, however, *kakia* is translated as "malice" (Eph. 4:31). That may sacrifice the summarizing character of this phrase (and the verbal link with other passages related to this tradition of "putting off"), but it is nevertheless a commendable translation, for it captures the way in which Ephesians has quite creatively and deliberately turned this tradition to the issue of a Christian response to cultures of enmity. All of the vices listed are violations of the "peace" that Christ is and gives, violations of the peaceable difference that belongs to this community and to the "new humanity."

This general renunciation is followed, as the pattern would seem to require, by a positive exhortation, "be kind to one another, tenderhearted, forgiving one another," and by a clause providing a basis and motive, "as God in Christ has forgiven you" (4:32). Here, however, that positive exhortation and motive clause are paired with another and even more climactic exhortation and motive clause: "Therefore, be imitators of God, as beloved children, and live in love, as Christ loved us and gave himself up for us, a fragrant offering and sacrifice to God" (5:1–2).

"To clothe yourself with the new self" (4:24) is to "put on" kindness (*chrēstoi*), compassion (*eusplangchnoi*), and forgiveness (*charizomenoi*). Each of these is characteristic of God's grace in Christ, and when we are instructed next to be "imitators of God," these virtues are surely included.

The kindness of God had already been celebrated in 2:7. In a sense Ephesians simply follows the lead of the psalmist, "O give thanks to the LORD, for he is good [LXX *chrēstos*]; for his steadfast love endures forever" (Ps. 106:1; cf. also, e.g., 107:1; 136:1). But here Ephesians also—and more closely—follows the lead of Jesus. Jesus too had called attention to the kindness of God, and he had used that kindness to call his disciples to love their enemies, to do good, and to lend, expecting nothing in return. In such behavior, he said, they will display that they are "children of the Most High, for he is kind to the ungrateful and the wicked. Be merciful, just as your Father is merciful" (Luke 6:35–36). He calls them to be "imitators of God, as beloved children" (Eph. 5:1).

That Ephesians makes creative use of a baptismal tradition in this section may be confirmed by what may be regarded as another parallel, this one evidently also a baptismal tradition, Titus 3:4–8a. It makes no mention of "putting off" and "putting on," but it too calls attention to the kindness of God: "when the goodness [*chrēstotēs*] and loving kindness of God our Savior appeared, [God] saved us . . . through the waters of rebirth and renewal by the Holy Spirit." We are brought safely through the judgment by God's mercy, but we are also made new by baptism and the Spirit. They summon us to kindness.

Compassion (*eusplangchnos*; NRSV "tenderhearted") is the second in this triad of virtues. Compassion is a visceral response to the suffering of another. It is to share the suffering, to "suffer with" (*com-passion*) another. Compassion will seek to relieve the suffering of another, even if the only way to relieve it is to be present to it, present to the sufferer, lest the sufferer be abandoned to the desolating loneliness of suffering. Compassion motivated the Good Samaritan to tend to the needs of the one left "half-dead" by the side of the road (Luke 10:33). By that attention he became a paradigm of compassion, and the parable concludes with the call to "go and do likewise." But the still richer paradigm of compassion is Christ himself. His "com-passion," his readiness to "suffer with" others, prompted him to make human flesh his own and finally to make the human cry of lament his own cry (Mark 15:34; Matt. 27:46; cf. Ps. 22:1). And Christ only follows the pattern of God's own self-giving love, God's own mercy and grace (Pss. 103:8; 111:4; 145:8; Joel 2:13; Jonah 4:2; etc.), God's own "compassion."[10] Indeed, like the psalmist, Jesus relied on that compassion, and God "did not despise or abhor the affliction of the afflicted" (Ps. 22:24). God heard that cry and answered it. God raised Jesus from the dead and set him at his right hand, making him the "new humanity" (Eph. 1:20–22). In solidarity

10. See Oliver Davies, *A Theology of Compassion: Metaphysics of Difference and the Renewal of Tradition* (Grand Rapids: Eerdmans, 2001), 232–53.

with that Christ, we hope for the day of resurrection, the day when death will be no more, when there will be no more suffering. But meanwhile we share in Christ's death. And if we share in that death in baptism and the Supper, then to refuse to share the suffering of another is quite unfitting, quite unworthy of our new identity and community. Meanwhile we are "aching visionaries."[11] We have been let in on the secret of God's good future, and we ache for its coming. We ache whenever that good future is challenged and contradicted in the present by death and suffering, by injustice and enmity.

Our eyes have caught a vision of the good future of God, but our eyes fill with tears whenever it is so clearly not yet that future, still sadly not yet that future. So, learning from Christ, we weep with those who weep, we share the suffering of others, we "mourn" (Matt. 5:4). In Christ and in our baptism we are formed to be compassionate.[12]

Finally, the third item in this triad of virtues is the readiness to forgive. It is surely characteristic of God in the Old Testament. Any reading of Hosea should make that clear (see, e.g., not just the relation of Hosea to Gomer but also Hos. 11:1–9). It was the assumption in the practice of the rituals of Yom Kippur, the Day of Atonement (see Lev. 16:29–34). On that day with a sacrificial atonement for the sins of the people, their sins are forgiven. God's readiness to forgive does not, of course, render particular injustices or the infidelities in the common life of Israel a matter of indifference to God. Sin is condemned, but condemnation is neither the first nor the

> **The Compassion of the Lord**
>
> In the *Testament of Naphtali* 4:5 the Messiah is identified as "the compassion of the Lord":
>
> > "and the Lord will disperse them over the face of the whole earth until the compassion of the Lord comes, a man who effects righteousness, and he will have compassion on all who are far and near."
>
> —James H. Charlesworth, ed.
>
> *The Old Testament Pseudepigrapha*, vol. 1, *Apocalyptic Literature and Testaments*, ed. James H. Charlesworth (London: Darton, Longman & Todd, 1983), 812, quoted in Oliver Davies, *A Theology of Compassion: Metaphysics of Difference and the Renewal of Tradition* (Grand Rapids: Eerdmans, 2001), 245.

---

11. Nicholas Wolterstorff, *Lament for a Son* (Grand Rapids: Eerdmans, 1987), 86.
12. This compassion stands in contrast to the Gentile "insensitivity" of 4:19.

last word even in the Old Testament. God's readiness to forgive is God's readiness to embrace Israel in spite of their infidelities, God's readiness to embrace the sinner, the readiness to let go God's (righteous) indignation prompted by an injury or an insult for the sake of the renewal of a relationship. God's readiness to forgive means that forgiveness—and a renewed relationship with God—is possible for Israel and for anyone who turns to the Lord in repentance (e.g., Ezek. 18:25–32). That repentance required restitution for injustices against another human being (e.g., Lev. 6:1–7); it required seeking their forgiveness and righting the wrong. One more point should be made about God's readiness to forgive in the Old Testament: there grows a hope for an eschatological forgiveness, for the renewal of covenant identity and community by the mercy and forgiveness of God, for a renewed relationship with God (e.g., Jer. 31:31–34; Isa. 65:17–25).

It is that hope that provides the context for Jesus' announcement that God's good future is at hand and for his performance of that future also in his readiness to forgive. Again Christ simply follows the pattern of the Father in his readiness to forgive. In this case, however, Jesus makes already real and present God's eschatological forgiveness. He still calls for repentance, to be sure (e.g., Mark 1:15), but to repent is to welcome that good future and to be formed by it. The focus falls not on sackcloth and ashes, not even so much on restitution (which is, however, not forgotten), but on the joyful renewal of broken relationships between God and the people and between members of this community. God's good future makes its power felt in the ways Jesus performs forgiveness, in his friendship with sinners, in his healing the sick, in his fellowship with those whom the "righteous" had forced to the margins of the community, and in his refusal to participate in the human cycles of vengeance and violence. That last performance finds climactic expression on the cross and in the words of forgiveness Jesus managed to speak from it, "Father, forgive them . . ." (Luke 23:34). The cycle of vengeance is broken there, on that cross that Christians share in their baptism. Forgiveness is accompanied by restored relationships, in which the hold that sin has on each and all of us in this present evil age is acknowledged and broken.

This is no "straight-line dues-paying morality."[13] This is a common life formed by the grace of God. And it was to be performed also in the character and community of these Christians of the Lycus Valley and of all those who "learn Christ" and are baptized. Let it be said again, however, that neither God's readiness to forgive nor this virtue of forgiveness among Christians denies the claims of justice. Indeed, forgiveness affirms justice in the very act of forgoing the claims that we might rightly make against a neighbor. Forgiveness does not render sin a matter of indifference to either God or to the community. If all of the items in the list of examples were a matter of indifference to God, God would not have to forgive sins but could simply ignore them. And the community is called to forgiveness, not to ignore sin or injustice. The readiness to forgive sins, the eagerness for renewed relationships, provides the context for communal discipline, not a substitute for it. (See Matt. 18, which sets communal discipline in the context of the charge to protect "the little ones" and the duty to forgive.) It will require considerable discernment to know when the readiness to forgive and the eagerness to renew broken relationships is best performed by insisting on an apology and/ or restitution, but when a kind neighbor suggests to a parent that his child should apologize for some foolish prank, the wise parent will not suppose that the neighbor lacks a readiness to forgive nor that an apology is inappropriate, because God forgives.

The virtue of forgiveness is the readiness to embrace the one who did you wrong, to let go the (righteous?) indignation one feels after an injury or an insult. That indignation, righteous or not, is sometimes as much at fault for the brokenness of a relationship as the injury or insult that prompted it. The readiness to forgive has its basis and its motive in God's forgiveness. The practice of forgiveness in the church ("Whenever you stand praying, forgive"; Mark 11:25) makes that obvious. But it is precisely what the motive clause says, "as God in Christ has forgiven you" (Eph. 4:32).

Once again, at the end of this little list of virtues, indicative and imperative are joined together. And again, it is not that the gospel

13. Lewis Smedes, *Forgive and Forget: Healing the Hurts We Don't Deserve* (San Francisco: HarperSanFrancisco, 1996), 124.

stops when the prohibitions and prescriptions begin; it is the gospel that comes to us in both the indicative mood and the imperative mood. As in Matthew's parable of the Unforgiving Servant (Matt. 18:23–35), God's forgiveness is both gracious and demanding. To receive grace is to be enabled and permitted to live in accord with it. It is not that we earn forgiveness by being forgiving ourselves; it is no calculating "works righteousness"; it is rather that we are made new, made a part of new humanity in which kindness, compassion, forgiveness, and mutual love are the rule. That is good news indeed.

FURTHER REFLECTIONS
The Rustenburg Declaration

Peter Storey is a retired bishop in the Methodist Church in South Africa. He worked with Nelson Mandela and Desmond Tutu in the struggle against apartheid in South Africa. This is his account (from personal correspondence) of an extraordinary meeting after the fall of apartheid.

The Dutch Reformed Church had been for years the church most closely associated with the state and with apartheid. Many of those who had resisted apartheid had had nothing to do with them for years, and they had wanted nothing to do with us. Now everything they stood for had crumbled. It seemed right that we should reach out to them and say to them, "You are our sisters and brothers. Let us talk together and see what can be healed."

Invitations were also issued to the churches that had hidden their heads in the sand, the Pentecostals and evangelicals. Under the auspices of the South African Council of Churches and an evangelical body called Africa Enterprise, we all came together in a little town called Rustenburg, about seventy miles from Johannesburg, in November 1990.

Like many of my colleagues, I did not want to be there. I had little stomach for meeting people I felt had betrayed the gospel. As far as I was concerned, they were part of the whole nasty problem that we had been living with all these years. But I went, and a couple of days later found myself sitting with some of them in the wee small hours of the morning, drafting an amazing statement that came to be known as the *Rustenburg Declaration*.

At first the meeting was tense. We watched one another very suspiciously. But sometime during the afternoon, a professor from Stellenbosch University, the cream of the Dutch Reformed seminaries and the cradle of apartheid's ideology, came to the podium. His name was Willie Jonker, and these were his words:

> I confess before you and the Lord, not only my own sin and guilt, and my personal responsibility for the political, social, economic, and structural wrongs that have been done to many of you, the results of which you and our whole country are still suffering from. But vicariously I dare to do that in the name of the Dutch Reformed Church, of which I am a member.

For a while there was a stunned silence; you could have heard a pin drop. Then Archbishop Desmond Tutu stood up, went up to the platform, and he looked at us all, and said, "My faith tells that when somebody confesses, I have no choice, I must forgive them." This was a moment of breakthrough, and from then on a new spirit moved among us. It was the spirit of confession. Later, a Pentecostal leader spoke. "We sinned. We preached individual salvation, without social transformation. We were neutral, and therefore we collaborated with apartheid."

Well, once they had confessed, it left the people who had led the struggle (or so we thought). What would "the good guys" say? In the final declaration we too made a confession: "Some of us were bold in denouncing apartheid, but timid in resisting it. We failed to give support to courageous individuals at the forefront of the protest. We spoke for justice, but our own church structures continued to oppress."

Imitating God

The phrase, "forgiving one another, as God in Christ has forgiven you" (Eph. 4:32), might also be translated, "be gracious to one another, as God in Christ has been gracious to you." (The word used in this verse, both to name the virtue and to name the act of God, is *charizomai*, a word that may include forgiveness but might also be translated more broadly as "to be gracious." The aorist tense for God's act suggests an action in the past, an action once for all, and the present tense for the participle used to name the virtue suggests a continuing activity.) The broader meaning would surely provide a fitting penultimate summary to this section (and it would echo the motive clause in 4:29 that our words should "give grace to those who hear"). Most translations, however, use the narrower meaning, "forgive." It is suggested by the parallel in Colossians 3:13, and it is also appropriate in this context.

Nevertheless, the broader meaning should not be neglected here. Both God's forgiveness and the practice of forgiveness within the church are, after all, works of grace. Moreover, kindness, compassion, and forgiveness—and the whole set of renunciations and exhortations in this section—find their final motive and basis in the grace of God made known in Christ. Forgiveness, surely, but also kindness and compassion, follow upon this affirmation of the gospel, that "God in Christ has been gracious to you."

The broader meaning is not neglected in the final and climactic exhortation and motive clause that follow and sum up what it means to "put on" the new identity and community given by Christ, the new humanity. "Therefore," it says, "be imitators of God." This is the only place where this particular exhortation is found in the New Testament, but the meaning is clear from both what precedes it and what follows it. We are to imitate God by practicing kindness, compassion, and forgiveness "as God in Christ has forgiven us" (Eph. 4:32). We are to imitate God "as beloved children" (5:1). Every parent knows (to their shame, sometimes) how children learn to speak and to act by imitating a parent. God's actions and dispositions are a model for God's beloved children to follow. And to be "beloved" by God is to have a model for love of the neighbor. We are to imitate God, as the climactic conclusion of this section states, by "living in love," by a way of life and a common life that is marked by love.

Love is the mark of God's own life, both in the relations of the Trinity and in God's creative and redemptive relationship with God's creation. But here, no less than in John's epistle, "we know love by this, that he laid down his life for us" (1 John 3:16). We are to imitate God by living in accord with Christ's love. We imitate God by following Christ; we are to "walk [*peripateite*] in love, as Christ loved us and gave himself up for us, a fragrant offering and sacrifice to God" (Eph. 5:2). Here, no less than in John's epistle, the implication is that "we ought to lay down our lives for one another" (1 John 3:16). That imitation of God, that following of Christ, may mean first, as in 1 John, something as mundane and commonplace as helping the needy in the community (Eph. 4:28; cf. 1 John 3:17).

When Jesus' death is here described as "a fragrant offering and sacrifice to God" (Eph. 5:2), we may be reminded of the reference in 2:13 to "the blood of Christ." There we suggested that as Moses sealed the covenant between God and Israel at Sinai by sacrificing oxen as a *zebach shelamim*, or peace offering, to God (Lev. 3:1–17), so God has brought the Gentiles into his covenant and its promises "by the blood of Christ." Christ is the peace offering that seals the new covenant and creates the new community, which includes the Gentiles. Christ's sacrifice (cf. Eph. 2:13) brought those "near" who "once were far off." That peace offering was pleasing to God, "a fragrant offering and sacrifice."

There is no repeating the sacrifice of Christ, of course, but it is no stretch to infer that our imitation extends to sacrifice. In Romans 12:1 Paul had instructed the Jewish and Gentile Christians of those churches, "by the mercies of God, to present your bodies as a living sacrifice." And Paul had commended the church at Philippi for its self-giving love for him with the very phrase of Ephesians 5:2; he had received the gifts they sent with Epaphroditus, and he called it "a fragrant offering, a sacrifice acceptable and pleasing to God" (Phil. 4:19). We cannot—and we need not—repeat the sacrifice of Christ, but because of that peace offering, we may and must imitate it.

We do not seal the new covenant by our little sacrifices, but we celebrate it by living in love, by kindness, by compassion, by forgiveness, by speaking the truth, by reconciling with our enemies, by sharing with the needy, and by words that are gracious. Such words and deeds, by the mercies of God, will also be a "fragrant offering." We do not create the new community or "the new humanity" by our little sacrifices, but we perform it and display it when we live in peaceable difference, putting off the cultures of enmity and the "bitterness and wrath and anger and wrangling and slander, together with all malice" (Eph. 4:31) that they sponsor. To imitate God, to live in love, to perform the unity of Jews and Gentiles, is to live to "the praise of God's glory"; it is to "lead a life worthy of the calling to which you have been called." In contrast to the acts and attitudes that make the Spirit sad, such lives will make God happy. God will delight in them and in the praise offered up in the lives of his people and in their common life. To name Christ's death as "a fragrant offering and sacrifice to God" is not simply a rhetorical flourish at the end of the section. And it is not a cryptic reference to some doctrine of substitutionary atonement. It is to affirm once more that Christ is our peace offering. "He is our peace."

5:3–20

Children of the Light

Christians are not only to "put off" their old patterns of conduct and character (4:22, 25, 31) and to "put on" a "new humanity" (4:24). They are also to "live as children of the light" (5:8). As we said in the last chapter, the language of "putting off" and of "putting on" was a traditional mode of moral instruction in the early church, very likely associated with baptism, and used creatively by Ephesians. In this section of Ephesians (5:3–20) another tradition of the moral instruction in the early church is adopted and adapted, a tradition that centers around that exhortation to "live as children of the light."

The moral tradition associated with this section can also be found in 1 Thessalonians 5:1–9, Romans 13:11–13, and throughout 1 Peter. There is frequently some variation on the language of "children of the light" (Eph. 5:8; cf. John 12:36; 1 Thess. 5:5; 1 Pet. 1:14, "obedient children") prompting the exhortation that Christians should conduct themselves in ways befitting that characterization. The tradition emphasized the eschatological contrast between light and darkness (Eph. 5:8; cf. Rom. 13:12; 1 Thess. 5:4–5; 1 Pet. 2:9; cf. also Acts 26:18). The exhortations that belonged to the tradition evidently included exhortations to watchfulness and sobriety (Eph. 5:15–18; cf. Rom. 13:11–13; 1 Thess. 5:6–8; 1 Pet. 1:13; 4:7; 5:8; the letters of Ignatius to Smyrna, 9:1; and to Polycarp, 1:3; 2:3; 2 *Clement* 13:1; cf. also Matt. 25:13; Mark 13:35, 37).

This Christian tradition, too, may be related to baptismal instruction or to a baptismal liturgy.[1] It is perhaps indebted to Jewish modes of moral instruction; in the community at Qumran, for example, the idiom of "children of light" and the contrast between the light and the darkness were already commonplace. Of course, the contrast of light and darkness in moral or religious instruction is common in many other traditions as well. Whatever the sources of the Christian tradition, they were utilized and modified in the light of Christian convictions. "The sun of righteousness [had risen], with healing in its wings" (Mal. 4:2). Christ, "the light of all people," had been made manifest, and that "light shines in the darkness, and the darkness did not overcome it" (John 1:4, 5).

The tradition itself and the use of it in Ephesians is moral exhortation, to be sure, but moral exhortation that is linked to the good news of God's grace, to the announcement that the light has come. This passage of Ephesians is heavy with imperatives, but it is not merely a list of demands. It is an invitation to live in the light, an invitation to give thanks for the gift of God's grace, for the triumphant power of the light, for the deliverance from darkness. It is an invitation to joy. But God and God's grace intend a new humanity, a renewed creation. God and God's grace intend that the lives and the common life of the Christians of the Lycus Valley—and of First Presbyterian in Durham and of every community—will be filled with Christ and with the Spirit. Therefore, the announcement of the gospel requires the imperative mood, and not as a mere supplement or appendage to the indicative mood. This passage, with its imperatives, is one more invitation to live "to the praise of [God's] glory."

Christians are to live as "children of the light." They are to live "enlightened" lives and lives that "enlighten" by reflecting Christ. There is no triumphalism here. The darkness continues, and it will continue until that day when "there will be no more night" (Rev. 22:5) in the city where the leaves of the trees are "for the healing of the nations" (Rev. 22:2). Until that day to be "children of the light" will require vigilance and judgment. Where the light shines

---

1. So E. G. Selwyn claimed at least; see Selwyn, *First Epistle of St. Peter*, 379, 382. It should be observed that Selwyn thought that the commands to be watchful and sober belonged to a tradition formed in response to persecution; see p. 454.

brightest, the shadows are darkest. Little wonder, then, that where the light shines there is judgment and that judgment begins within the community (1 Pet. 4:17). Where the light shines, darkness and evil are exposed to judgment. With "the eyes of [the] heart enlightened" (Eph. 1:18), we can see and then set aside the self-deception and the lies that made malice and wickedness seem reasonable. The dawning of the sun of righteousness enables discernment and requires judgment, and that judgment must begin with the church.

Two Little Catalogues of Sins

This section of Ephesians begins, prosaically enough, with two little catalogues of sins, each with three items in the list. The first of these triads mentions "fornication," "impurity," and "greed." The same three words had been used in 4:19 to characterize the way Gentiles live (except that there "licentiousness" was used and here "fornication" is used). In 4:17 Paul had insisted that the Gentile Christians should "no longer live as the Gentiles live." There it was already clear that the problem was not just an intellectual problem but also a problem of their "hardness of heart" (4:18), their hard-hearted refusal to learn the truth and to respond to it by honoring God as God and by giving thanks to God. The final result of their ignorance and their hard-heartedness was a way of life characterized as a surrender to "licentiousness" and as a greedy desire for more and more "impurity" (4:19). Here Paul insists that such things "must not even be mentioned among you" (5:3). It is an odd rule if taken literally, violated in the very listing (and mentioning) of the things not to be mentioned. The point is rather something like this: your behavior should be such that no one would even think of accusing you of such things. That is not the sort of behavior that is "proper" or "fitting" to the lives of the saints.

The second little catalogue focuses once again on talk. There is to be no "obscene, silly, and vulgar talk" (5:4). Such talk is "out of place," not fitting to the lives of saints. It seems, frankly, a little too rigorous. One should, of course, renounce "obscene talk" (*aischrotēs*), and one should, we suppose, be a little suspicious of "silly talk" (*mōrologia*), although grandchildren seem to enjoy it, but *eutralpelia* (NRSV "vulgar talk") was often used by the Greeks in a good sense, as "wittiness." We might acknowledge, as Calvin does, that "it is exceedingly hard to be witty without becoming biting,"[2] but it still seems a little too rigorous. The earlier advice of Ephesians concerning "talk," renouncing "evil talk" and prescribing talk that "is useful for building up" and that "gives grace to those who hear" (4:29), should control our interpretation (and performance) of this text. Sometimes a little "silly talk" or a "witty" joke can be "useful" to the care of a grandchild or a friend and capable of "giving grace." Perhaps the NRSV, with its prohibition of "vulgar talk," points in the right direction. We should reject any talk that demeans others, including those jokes that demean others, ethnic jokes, and filthy jokes.

The terms "proper" (*prepei*) (5:3) and "out of place" (*anēken*) (5:4) are themselves instructive concerning the morality of Ephesians. They suggest that moral judgment is not simply a matter of determining what acts are obedient to some code nor simply a matter of determining which acts might be effective in achieving some ideal. They suggest that moral judgment, like aesthetic judgment, is more a matter of determining what is "fitting" to the rest of the picture, what is appropriate to the circumstances and to the agent, and above all what is worthy of the story that reveals God's character and cause. H. Richard Niebuhr seems to have captured this in his notion of "the responsible self." When he suggested how the image of "the responsible self" was itself "fitting" to Scripture, he said that "at critical junctures in the history of Israel and of the early Christian community the decisive question [people] raised was not 'What is the goal?' nor yet 'What is the law?' but 'What is happening?'"[3] In Ephesians what is happening is that God in Christ is renewing all things, bringing all things under Christ. And what is happening in Ephesians is that we are being summoned to respond to God in all things, even in our sexual lives, even in our talk. We are being called to lives and a common life worthy of the gospel, fitting to the power of God that is at work among us.

---

2. Calvin, *Ephesians*, p. 197.
3. H. Richard Niebuhr, *The Responsible Self: An Essay in Christian Moral Philosophy* (New York: Harper & Row, 1963), 67.

After these two little catalogues of sins, there is an abrupt shift to a single positive instruction, "Instead, let there be thanksgiving" (5:4). It seems a strange contrast to the evil talk just renounced, and perhaps Calvin is right to translate *eucharistia* here as "grace."[4] Instead of "evil talk," let your talk "give grace" to those who hear (cf. 4:29). But because this section concludes (5:20) with the same instruction to give thanks (*eucharistountes*), it seems best to us to read Ephesians as setting the words and practices of "thanksgiving" in contrast to these two little lists of sins. Surely "gratitude" is characteristic of the Christian life; as Paul had said, thankfulness is "the will of God in Christ Jesus for you" (1 Thess. 5:18). Indeed, great thanksgiving in words and deeds is "proper" and "fitting" to the saints. It is a fitting response to God's great gifts of grace—and inconsistent with a life of sin.

The passage then shifts just as suddenly back to an announcement of God's judgment upon the first triad of sins. "You had better remember this," Paul says, introducing what Ernst Käsemann might call "a sentence of holy law."[5] The form is usually a conditional sentence with the protasis stating some violation and the apodosis rendering the divine (and eschatological) judgment. For example, in 1 Corinthians 3:17 Paul states, "If anyone destroys God's temple, God will destroy that person." In such "sentences of holy law" the

---

4. Calvin, *Ephesians*, p. 197.

5. Ernst Käsemann, "Sentences of Holy Law in the New Testament," *New Testament Questions of Today*, trans. W. J. Montague, New Testament Library (Philadelphia: Fortress Press, 1969), 66–81. The category of "law" might suggest a challenge to the observation just made that the morality of Ephesians does not provide a code or a law that must be obeyed. Käsemann uses the category because the protasis uses some "casuistic legal expression" and because the apodosis seems to be modeled on the jus talionis, "an eye for an eye." But the category of law is misleading if we expect the "sentences of holy law" to provide a basis for casuistry. These "sentences of holy law" may have originated, as Käsemann says, in the utterances of early Christian prophets, but the form is closer to certain sayings of Jesus than to OT case law. Consider, for example, the saying of Jesus in Mark 8:38, "Those who are ashamed of me and of my words in this adulterous and sinful generation, of them the Son of Man will also be ashamed when he comes in the glory of his Father with the holy angels" (also Matt. 5:19; 6:14–15; 10:32, 41–42, etc.). The future judgment is already announced, but the attention to the future judgment puts merely external observance of the law in crisis. Even in Matthew, where the law holds, the announcement of the future calls for a "righteousness" that goes beyond the law. The announcement of God's coming judgment makes total claims and cannot be reduced to case law. They are not used by the community as if they added rules to a developing code but as a constant call to turn again, to reform their lives, and to reformulate the rules in ways that are faithful to God's future. Incidentally, Käsemann does not mention Eph. 5:5 among his examples.

eschatological judgment of God is already announced in the present. Here the form is not strictly conditional, but the condition is easily supplied: "If anyone is a fornicator or impure or greedy, that person is cut out of the inheritance of the kingdom of Christ and of God" (Eph. 5:5). The same trio of sins is used here as in 5:3 and 4:19, but here they are (or at least greed is) characterized as "idolatry." Idolatry was among the root sins of "Gentile unrighteousness" according to Romans 1:23 and the standard Jewish polemic. And here those sins are not merely prohibited; here God's verdict against such sinners is already made effective. Christians are warned in the strongest possible terms against such immorality.

In 1 Corinthians 5:1–5 Paul had "pronounced judgment in the name of the Lord Jesus on the man" who was evidently sexually involved with "his father's wife." In that instance Paul instructed the Corinthian church to exclude the man, "to hand him over to Satan," in the hope that such discipline would lead to his repentance and his salvation. The announcement of God's verdict here in Ephesians 5:5 does not seem to be an excommunication of a specific individual, but it does call the churches of the Lycus Valley to take seriously the communal task of mutual encouragement and admonition, to undertake faithfully a practice of church discipline, in order to attend to the moral character of the community and to care for an erring brother or sister, even when that grace must be severe.

Hard on the heels of this sentence of holy law, the community is warned, "Let no one deceive you with empty words, for because of these things the wrath of God comes on those who are disobedient" (5:6). The "empty words" may be words uttered by those outside the church belittling the concern for morality in the Christian communities. But it is more likely that they are words uttered from within the community by those who would trivialize righteousness. They may have been words that echoed the words of the Corinthian enthusiasts, "All things are lawful for me" (1 Cor. 6:12) and "What I do with my body is a matter of spiritual indifference" (cf. 1 Cor. 6:18).[6] Or they may have echoed the "empty words" of the libertines who

---

6. We understand 1 Cor. 6:18 (NRSV: "Every sin that a person commits is outside the body") to be another slogan of the Corinthian enthusiasts.

read grace as license, "Let us continue to sin in order that grace may abound and in order to display that we are not under the law" (cf. Rom. 6:1, 15). There were those who had drawn libertine inferences from the gospel, but Paul had no sympathy for such an inference. He consistently corrected such reasoning. Here Ephesians describes such talk as "empty words," insisting, as Calvin says, "that we must guard against that sophistry by which consciences are ensnared to their ruin."[7]

There remain Christians skilled in the arts of rationalization, of course. Sometimes (as Phyllis Verhey has claimed) they are even called "ethicists." But Christians know something of the cause of God, the good future of God, and they know that that cause does not include immorality. God does not cease being righteous by being gracious, and the cause of God does not cease being "true righteousness and holiness" (4:24) by being inclusive. To be the recipient of God's blessing is to be made an agent in blessing God, not in blaspheming God by libertine words and deeds. To scorn the cause of God is to scorn the grace of God, to reject the sovereignty of Christ, and to grieve the Spirit. God's very kindness requires God's severity within the church, "for the time has come for judgment to begin with the household of God" (1 Pet. 4:17).

The warning had reminded them of God's "wrath," of God's judgment against sin. It is a reminder that God does not take sin lightly; God hates sin. From that warning Ephesians concludes that the members of the church should "not be associated with [the disobedient]" (5:7). It can hardly be the case, however, that Ephesians is warning Christians against having any association with non-Christians. In 1 Corinthians 5:9–13 Paul had clarified what must have been a similar instruction in an earlier letter to the Corinthians.

> I wrote to you in my letter not to associate with sexually immoral persons—not at all meaning the immoral of this world, or the greedy and robbers, or idolaters, since you would then need to go out of the world. But now I am writing to you not to associate with anyone who bears the name of brother

---

7. Calvin, *Ephesians*, 198. The warning against such "empty talk" may echo the earlier warning against being misled "by people's trickery, by their craftiness in deceitful scheming" (4:14).

or sister who is sexually immoral or greedy, or is an idolater, reviler, drunkard, or robber. Do not even eat with such a one. For what have I to do with judging those outside? Is it not those who are inside that you are to judge? God will judge those outside.

The Ephesian churches are "to judge," but they are to judge only those "who bear the name of brother or sister," not "those outside." And they should be prepared not to associate with one who bears the name of brother or sister who continues in such sins, ignoring the encouragement and admonition of the community, still "alienated from the life of God because of their . . . hardness of heart" (4:18) in spite of having "learned Christ" (4:20). For the sake of the faithfulness of the church, for the sake of the truth that they learned when they "learned Christ" (4:20), and for the sake of the one liable to God's wrath, the church must take seriously its task of discipline, its calling to mutual admonition and encouragement.

The Light

The alternative to libertinism is, however, not legalism but the light. The mutual admonition and encouragement does not treat Torah as a moral code, does not reinstate Torah as the final authority. The alternative is rather the light, the Lord—and the life and discourse of a community "enlightened" by the Lord. The alternative to the "empty words" of the libertines is the sort of talk he has already recommended, "speaking the truth in love" (4:15, 25), talk that "is useful for building up" (4:29). They are to be a community of mutual encouragement and exhortation, a community of moral discourse, deliberation, and discernment. They are to be "children of light" (5:8), not "children of wrath" (2:3). That is the context within which Ephesians sets the tradition of moral exhortation identified above. Allowing the light of Christ to shine, that is the method of mutual admonition and discipline. This light is gracious and life-giving, but it also "exposes" all works of darkness (5:11).

The transition from the former way of life to a new way is once again emphasized. But complementing the transition from death to life (2:1–10) here we have a transition from darkness to light. As they have passed from death to life in Christ, so in Christ they have passed from darkness into the light; as 5:8 says, "Once you were darkness, but now in the Lord you are light." There is no place here for boasting, only for thanksgiving. But to be thankful for the light is to let it shine. Therefore (again the link between the gospel in the indicative and the gospel in the imperative), "live as children of light" (5:8).

The light is fruitful, not barren (cf. 5:11). It bears "children of the light," and like the Spirit (Gal. 5:22), it bears fruit. Since "the fruit of the light is found in all that is good and right and true" (Eph. 5:9), to "live as children of light" is to live lives and a common life that are full of goodness, justice, and truthfulness. This light and its fruits provide the basis for communal discernment and discipline. Full of goodness, justice, and truth, they are able and commanded to "find out [or 'discern,' *dokimazontes*] what is pleasing to the Lord" (5:10; cf. Rom. 12:2).[8] Full of goodness, justice, and truth, they are able to instruct one another (cf. Rom. 15:14). This is neither legalism nor license—it is the light casting light on discernment in the Christian community.

They are to have nothing to do with the "unfruitful works of darkness" that bring God's wrath (Eph. 5:11). Earlier we read the instruction that they should "not be associated with them" in the light of Paul's clarification in 1 Corinthians; the instruction was not that they should not be associated with Gentiles but rather that they should not be associated with one "who bears the name of brother or sister" and engages in gross immorality. Here Ephesians clarifies the point still more. It is not that they are to have nothing whatsoever to do with the erring brother or sister but that they are to have nothing to do with their "works of darkness."

---

8. The NRSV's "Try to find out what is pleasing to the Lord" is a wonderfully subtle acknowledgment that it is not always easy, but the participle seems to function as a simple imperative, and to translate it as "try to discern" is not required.

The "works of darkness" are "unfruitful," in contrast to the light with its fruits. A similar contrast is made in Galatians 5:22, where the "fruit of the Spirit" stands opposed to the "works of the flesh" (5:19). That is not to say that the "works of darkness" are without consequences. The "wages of sin is death" (Rom. 6:23), after all. They were "dead" (Eph. 2:1), but by the grace of God they were brought from death to life (2:5). The old self was "rotting" (4:22, *phtheiromenon*; NRSV "corrupt"); it had the stench of death about it. There is no reason to return to that death, to revisit that darkness. The community owes it to the erring brother or sister to say as much, to allow the light to "expose" the darkness and to "expose" sins as the works of darkness (5:11, 13). The verb *elengchō*, here appropriately translated "expose" because of the reference to the light, also means "convict" or "correct." The light—and the community living as children of the light—are the means by which the sinner is corrected. "The night has no shame," to use the proverb Calvin used to capture the sense of 5:12.[9] When darkness rules, there is no light to see one's wickedness, but when the light comes, when light illumines, then our eyes can see wickedness for what it is. "Everything exposed by the light becomes visible" (5:13). Sin becomes manifest as sin.

Then the good news: Darkness is powerless against the light. "The darkness did not overcome [the light]" (John 1:5). The "light" and the "darkness" denote conflicting ways of life, conflicting attitudes and actions. And the conflict calls for decision; it does not permit neutrality. But the good news is that the conflict has been settled. The good news is the sovereignty of light over darkness. Darkness can never finally prevail in conflict with the light. However powerful and frightening darkness seems, the good news is that wherever the light shines darkness surrenders. So in this remarkably brief announcement in Ephesians 5:14a the cosmic extent of the triumph of the light is reported, "Everything that becomes visible is light." Christ, who is "the light of all people" (John 1:4), shines in the darkness, and the darkness cannot put it out. Instead, the darkness is finally put out. The light makes light; it makes a community of the children of light; it exposes the darkness and saves what was

9. Calvin, *Ephesians*, 210.

captive to the darkness. It brings light to all, not just illuminating all, but transforming all, renewing all things according to God's plan, all things, even the erring brother or sister, all things, even us. Therefore, there is hope for the erring brother or sister, and hope also for us. There is hope not by trivializing or privatizing the darkness but by letting the light shine.

"Therefore it says, 'Sleeper, awake! Rise from the dead, and Christ will shine on you'" (5:14b). Here the announcement of the gospel comes again, comes even to the erring brother or sister, and even to us. It comes as an imperative. "It is time to wake up!" Ephesians cites what is probably an early Christian hymn (and cites it as if it were Scripture) that seems at home again in the baptismal traditions of the early church. It is a delicious mix of metaphors, waking from sleep, rising from the dead, and feeling the sunshine. It summons us to wake up, but it points to the possibility of that in the resurrection and to the promise of that in the blessing of the light. "Rise from the dead"—with Christ, of course—already in baptism and again in God's good future, but also *now*. It is the good news of Easter.

> **The Message of Easter**
>
> The message of Easter, then, is neither that God once did a spectacular miracle but then decided not to do many others nor that there is a blissful life after death to look forward to. The message of Easter is that God's new world has been unveiled in Jesus Christ and that you're now invited to belong to it.
>
> —N. T. Wright
>
> *Surprised by Hope: Rethinking Heaven, the Resurrection, and the Mission of the Church* (New York: HarperOne, 2008), 252–53.

Now, while the powers of death and darkness assert their doomed reign, now there is hope in God's grace and greater power. So, "Sleeper, awake! Rise from the dead." Perform your baptism by renouncing those forms of death that would enslave you again. Now, as once in baptism and as surely again in God's good future, "Christ will shine on you." It is time to wake up from your slumber, to rise up from your death, in memory of Jesus' resurrection and in anticipation of that great "gettin' up mornin.'"

The Discipline (and Joy) of Watchfulness

Until that morning, in the meantime, life in the light requires moral vigilance and discernment. It requires that we "be careful then how [we] live" (5:15). It requires wisdom. It requires that we "live, not as unwise people, but as wise" (5:15).

<table>
<tr><td>

Not as Fools

We must learn to live together as brothers or perish together as fools.

    —Martin Luther King Jr.

From a speech in St. Louis, Missouri, March 22, 1964.

</td></tr>
</table>

Life in the light requires that we use our time wisely (5:16). It requires watchfulness and sobriety in contrast to sleep, sloth, and drunkenness (5:18). There are a number of parallel passages to this call to watchfulness and sobriety (e.g., 1 Thess. 5:6–8; cf. Rom. 13:11–13; 1 Cor. 15:34; 16:13; 1 Pet. 5:8; 4:7; Ignatius, *To the Smyrnaeans* 9:1; *To Polycarp* 1:3;

2:3; *2 Clement* 13:1). But a member of the Sunday school class we taught reported that she was reminded of the story of the ten virgins in Matthew 25:1–13. The five foolish bridesmaids, so the story goes, made no preparation for the possible delay of the bridegroom (and the bride, according to some manuscripts) on his way to the wedding banquet; the foolish bridesmaids did not bring more oil for their lamps. The story ends, as she observed, with the instruction to "stay awake, for you know neither the day nor the hour."

It was a good story to be reminded of in this context. To live as children of light is to "stay awake," to persist in faith and hope in spite of the darkness. Christ may come when the night seems to have overcome the light, when "the days are evil," but the "children of light" stay awake and, in the meanwhile, they give light to the darkness.

It was also a good story to be reminded of because the bridesmaids did not fear the time of his coming. They hoped for it. They were eager for it. They looked forward to a party, to a good time, to laughter and joy. The church looks forward to God's good future in the same way. We do not know "the day or the hour," but we know it will be good. It will be a time of hilarious grace, of blessing and delight, of love and peace, a good time. To be prepared for such a time requires watchfulness and sobriety, but it also permits delight in the promise of such a future. It permits—and requires—an anticipation of that joy and blessing upon the whole world, a little merry-making already. To be prepared for God's good future is not simply to live for this moment, but to live each moment in anticipation of God's good future. That is what the cryptic instruction in 5:16, "making the most of the time," means, we suggest—to turn each moment into an opportunity, a *kairos*, for the display of God's cause.

Such anticipation of God's good future is evident in the turn Ephesians makes from drunkenness to being "filled with the Spirit" (5:18), from sober warning to the happy invitation to "sing psalms and hymns and spiritual songs among yourselves, singing and making melody to the Lord in your hearts" (5:19). It is an invitation to make merry in watchfulness, to taste already the delights of that future banquet, to display already the joy of a new humanity, renewed and reconciled "among yourselves."

Singing

We will not keep silent

We are people who must sing you,
  for the sake of our very lives.
You are a God who must be sung by us,
  for the sake of your majesty and honor.
And so we thank you,
  for the lyrics that push us past our reasons,
  for melodies that break open our givens,
  for cadences that locate us home,
    beyond all our safe places,
  for tones and tunes that open our lives beyond control
We thank you for the long parade of mothers and fathers
  who have sung you deep and true;
We thank you for the good company
  of artists, poets, musicians, cantors, and instruments
  that sing for us and with us, toward you.
We are witnesses to your mercy and splendor;
  We will not keep silent . . . ever again. Amen.
                    —Walter Brueggemann

Awed to Heaven, Rooted in Earth: Prayers of Walter Brueggemann, ed. Edwin Searcy (Minneapolis: Fortress Press, 2003), 133.

Included in this invitation is "giving thanks to God the Father at all times and for everything in the name of our Lord Jesus Christ" (5:20). Earlier we noted this verse and worried a little that it seemed to allow no space for lament (see pp. 54–56, in "Further Reflections: Toward a Prayerful Ethic," pp. 49–57). One of the things we are thankful for, we said there, is that we do not always have to give thanks, but this verse seems on the face of it to insist that we always give thanks "and for everything." It seems a little extravagant, a numbing requirement to give thanks, for example, when a child is killed by a drunk driver. It should be clear from the context, however, that this thankfulness does not deny the reality of evil or call evil good. It does not deny the awful reality of a world not yet God's good future. It invites us to live in anticipation of that future. Then we may lament that it is not yet, still sadly not yet that future, and still give thanks that that future is sure to be. Lament itself, as we have seen, turns toward the faithfulness of God. The pattern is not the pattern of the dirge, remembered glories and present misery, but its reversal, the honest acknowledgment of present misery and the hope for, the certainty of, a hearing, the hope for, the certainty of, God's making good on God's promises and plan. So give thanks in the midst of lament. Give thanks for the promises of God, for the cause of God, for the good future that will make things right, for the renewal and restoration of all things. Mourn, but give thanks that the mourners "will be comforted" (Matt. 5:4). Lament the debilitating consequences of poverty and hunger on soul and body, but give thanks that the poor and hungry "will be filled" (Luke 6:20–21). Weep with those who weep now, but give thanks that they "will laugh" (Luke 6:21). In response to God and in anticipation of God's future, we may always and in all circumstances give thanks. That thankfulness "at all times and for everything" will often have—and must often have—an "in spite of" attached. In spite of the darkness, we give thanks for the light. In spite of that death of a child, we give thanks for the promise of life. In spite of the enmities that still mark our culture, we give thanks for a new humanity. In spite of the evil that still asserts its power, we give thanks for the greater power of God that raised Jesus from the dead in triumph over death, darkness, and division. And if that is so, then thankfulness can adopt no other posture toward the evil, toward enmity, toward the death of a child, than to stand in spite of such things with confidence in God. And that surely means that there is a place for lament, for the cry to heaven to make things right. Such lament is a form of attention to God, a form of anticipation of God's good future while it is still sadly not yet, a form of thankfulness for the promises and cause of God in spite of evil and enmity.

5:21–6:9

Being Subject and Being One

In Ephesians 5:21–6:9 we come to a *haustafel*, or a table of rules for the household, for the relations of wives and husbands, children and parents, slaves and masters.

Another Early Christian Tradition

The first thing to observe here is that once again the author of Ephesians is making use of an existing moral tradition. And once again we can identify the tradition by a key instruction, "Be subject." (Parallels may be found in Col. 3:18–4:1; 1 Tim. 2:1–15; 6:1, 2; 1 Pet. 2:13–3:8, and in other early Christian literature.) The tradition emphasizes role responsibilities, the responsibilities of wife and husband, child and parent, slave and master. The moral life is in no small measure a matter of fulfilling role responsibilities.

This tradition is older than the Christian church itself. The emphasis on role responsibilities had been part of the Greek moral tradition for centuries. Aristotle had emphasized role responsibilities and tied roles to "nature." It was the nature of some to rule and the nature of others to be ruled, to be subject. According to Aristotle, for example, some were born to be slaves. The Stoics too had emphasized role responsibilities and had traced these responsibilities to "nature." It was part of the received moral tradition among any who spoke Greek in the first century, including Greek-speaking Jews. Each of these three traditions, the Aristotelian, the Stoic, and Hellenistic Judaism, has been regarded as the source of the early

Christian teaching concerning the household.[1] Scholars may have quarreled about the immediate source of the Christian tradition, but there was widespread agreement that the Christian community adopted what was regarded as conventional moral wisdom. To be sure, a few dissenters insisted that these rules for the household were a Christian creation, but most acknowledged some borrowing and some adapting of a tradition older than the Christian church.[2]

That agreement, however, was accompanied by considerable disagreement about why the church adopted and adapted such a tradition. Some scholars (e.g., Martin Dibelius)[3] argued that when Jesus did not return as soon as expected, when the church was faced with the task of establishing settled communities in a continuing world, then they were forced to abandon the radical ethic of Jesus and to adopt the common and conventional morality of their neighbors.

1. Initial research into the background of this tradition identified Stoicism as the source for this tradition (K. Weidinger, *Die Haustafeln* [Leipzig: Hinrichs, 1928]). That was the prevailing opinion for a generation of scholars, but it was challenged by the view put forth by James E. Crouch (*The Origin and Intention of the Colossian Haustafel*, Forschungen zur Religion und Literatur des Alten und Neuen Testaments 109 [Göttingen: Vandenhoeck & Ruprecht, 1972]) and others that the early Christian church had adopted it from Hellenistic Judaism, where it could be found in Philo and Josephus among others. That became the new consensus—until David Balch and others argued convincingly that the source was rather the Aristotelian tradition of managing the household, a tradition that was still lively in first-century philosophy. See, for example, David L. Balch, *Let Wives Be Submissive: The Domestic Code in 1 Peter*, Society of Biblical Literature Monograph Series 26 (Chico, CA: Scholars Press, 1981). The Aristotelian tradition emphasized authority and obedience and treated the relationship of master and slave, husband and wife, and father and children as part of the larger topic of the politics of the *polis* (see Aristotle, *Politics* 1253b ff.).
2. One of these "dissenters" was John Howard Yoder, *The Politics of Jesus* (Grand Rapids: Eerdmans, 1972). His dissent, he acknowledged (p. 165 n. 2), was indebted to the "dissenting" work of David Schroeder, "Die Haustafeln des Neuen Testaments" (diss., Evangelical Theological Faculty of the University of Hamburg, 1959). Our own treatment of the *haustafeln* is much indebted to Yoder's chapter on "Revolutionary Subordination" (pp. 163–92), but we think his refusal to admit the "borrowing" and "Christianizing" of non-Christian traditions tendentious. Heinz-Dietrich Wendland ("Zur Sozial ethischen Bedeutung der neutestamentlichen Haustafeln," in Otto Michel and Ulrich Mann, eds., *Die Leibhaftigkeit des Wortes: Festgabe Adolf Köberle* [Hamburg: Furche Verlag, 1958], 34–56) came to many of the same conclusions as Yoder did (and as we do) not by denying the borrowing of non-Christian moral traditions but by attending to the Christian communities' adaptations of them. We admit, however, that it is impossible to reconstruct the "original" tradition that stands behind the Ephesians material. In the second edition of *The Politics of Jesus* (Grand Rapids: Eerdmans, 1994), Yoder acknowledges the possibility of "borrowing" from other sources, but claims it "does not matter much. . . . What matters is how those borrowed materials were transformed as they were taken into the witness of the apostles" (p. 189 n. 55).
3. M. Dibelius and H. Greeven, *An die Kolosser, Epheser an Philemon*, 3rd ed., Handbuch zum Neuen Testament 12 (Tübingen: J. C. Mohr, 1953).

Others (e.g., Crouch)[4] have said that the enthusiastic performance of the equality expressed in baptism (Gal. 3:28) without sufficient attention to the common good had disrupted Christian communities and prompted the adoption of such household and community rules. Some (e.g., Balch)[5] have suggested that hostility from critics outside the church prompted the development of traditions that reflected continuity with accepted social patterns. Elisabeth Schüssler Fiorenza combined these three positions, arguing that because early efforts to enact a community of equals in radical discipleship had sometimes been accompanied by ecstatic excess and had drawn hostility to the church, church leaders surrendered the social implications of the preaching of Jesus and returned to patriarchal structures.[6] It may be as difficult to retrieve the early church's motivation for adopting such a tradition as it is to recover the "original" tradition of the *haustafel*.

We do think, however, that there was a moral tradition older than the church that the churches adopted and adapted. And we do think that the churches—and Ephesians—did not simply surrender the Christian and baptismal vision of mutuality and equality when they adopted and adapted this emphasis on role responsibilities. The memory of Jesus and the hope for God's good future were not forgotten or neglected but brought to bear on the traditions of the culture in which they lived. But let us put off developing such an alternative account in order to make a couple of other observations.

The second thing to be noted here is that this tradition has done some mischief in the continuing Christian moral tradition. We have sometimes read the *haustafeln* as if they provided timeless moral rules, as if some kinship system had dropped out of the heavens to be forever the rules to guide our lives. As a result this passage and others like it have been used to defend patriarchy, slavery, and abuse.

And that prompts a third observation. This tradition, on the face of it at least, does not seem to fit well with the understanding of the Christian ethic that we have seen in Ephesians so far. Can this really

---

4. Crouch, *Origin and Intention of the Colossian Haustafel.*
5. Balch, *Let Wives Be Submissive.*
6. Elisabeth Schüssler Fiorenza, *In Memory of Her: A Feminist Reconstruction of Christian Origins* (New York: Crossroads, 1984), 251–84.

be what it means to lead "a life worthy of the calling to which you have been called"? Well, perhaps, but only if we reduced "calling" to a role in society, to the role expectations of wife or husband, child or parent, slave or master, in the first century. We have seen, however, that the "calling" to which they were called was related to the hope that they had been given, to the hope established when God raised Jesus from the dead, to God's good future. That is the "hope to which [God] has called you" (1:18), not some conventional morality for the relations of Jew and Gentile or husbands and wives and other members of a household.

Or consider baptism: We have suggested that the earlier two sections of Ephesians are related to baptismal traditions. But consider another baptismal tradition: Galatians 3:26–28. It was already a traditional baptismal declaration when Paul reminded the Galatians of it.[7]

When people were baptized in the early church, they were initiated into Christ and into the body of Christ. They were baptized "into Christ Jesus" (Rom. 6:3), into his death and resurrection. Baptism was an act of God; God brought the believer both into judgment (together with Christ) and safely through it (together with Christ) into "newness of life" (Rom. 6:4), into a "new creation" (Gal. 6:15), into a new community in which "there is no longer Jew or Greek, . . . slave or free, . . . male and female" (Gal. 3:28). God brought them into "a new humanity," and this baptismal declaration of Galatians 3:28 is the "Magna Carta of the New Humanity."[8]

Baptism was also an act of the church, an act in memory of Jesus and in hope for God's good future, an act of faith, an act of receiving the grace of God and the promise of God by welcoming those who were different into a community of mutuality and equality.

The ones being baptized acted too, of course. They "put off" their old patterns of conduct, and they "put on" Christ. They clothed themselves with Christ, "with the new self, created according to the likeness of God in true righteousness and holiness" (Eph. 4:24; cf.

---

7. Richard Longenecker, *New Testament Social Ethics for Today* (Grand Rapids: Eerdmans, 1984), 31–34.
8. Ibid., 30.

Col. 3:9). In baptism they "put on Christ" (Gal. 3:27 RSV), and in Christ "there is no longer Jew or Greek, . . . slave or free, . . . male and female; for all of you are one in Christ Jesus" (Gal. 3:28). They put on the new humanity (Eph. 4:24). A new identity and a new community were owned in baptism, and a new world was envisioned— an identity, a community, and a world in which sexual hierarchies along with ethnic and class hierarchies were radically subordinated to community and equality in Christ. That identity does not seem to fit this passage very well. So what gives? How shall we understand— and perform—this passage?

This brings us to the fourth point. This passage and others like it did not just adopt an existing moral tradition about roles; they adapted it. They *transformed* that tradition as well. In spite of baptism there remained Jew and Gentile, male and female, and slave and free. The social and sexual world in which these people lived did not suddenly and simply vanish. The early church could not snap its fingers and create ex nihilo new role relations and social structures. Nevertheless, in memory of Jesus and their baptism they struggled against the enmity, the patriarchy, and the classism of that world, and that struggle left its mark both on them and on this passage in Ephesians. Jesus had provided no social program, no alternative kinship system, but because they remembered Jesus, they envisioned a different world, a world of God's unchallenged cosmic sovereignty, a world with Jesus at the right hand of God, a world in which there "is no longer Jew or Greek, . . . slave or free, . . . male and female" (Gal. 3:28). They struggled to bring the world in which they lived into conformity to the world they envisioned, and the struggle was the critical thing.[9]

9. The model here is the religious transformation of social interactions or, more modestly, the religious qualification of existing structures and relationships. This is the model Elisabeth Schüssler Fiorenza adopts in *In Memory of Her* as well. She presumes, however, that the historical choices open to the churches can be adequately described by simply juxtaposing patriarchy and a community of coequal disciples. These ideal types are simply played off against each other and, in her account, one of them is swallowed up and nearly destroyed in the course of early church history. It is not unlike (or unrelated to) the overly simple contrast between charismatic and institutional authoritarian accounts of the early church's history. That overly simple contrast was challenged by Bengt Holmberg, *Paul and Power: The Structure of Authority in the Primitive Church as Reflected in the Pauline Epistles* (Philadelphia: Fortress Press, 1980); he concluded that in the Pauline churches one can see not only the authority of "charisma" but also the authority of "office." Moreover, he concluded that the person with

To be sure, there is always some distance between their vision and the historical realization of their vision. Both the distance and the struggle are on display in the household code of Ephesians. Nevertheless, the critical thing in our view is that the early churches continued to envision a community of mutuality and equality and struggled to give that vision some communal embodiment, some fleshly consequence.

And this is the point: In this household code Ephesians nudged conventional morality toward something a little more fitting to God's good future.

As we have said, the household codes articulate a moral tradition that was not native to the church. The church borrowed these rules for behavior in the household from the Greek philosophical tradition. There was in the first century a retrieval of the Aristotelian position that the relation of ruler and ruled in the household was "natural."[10] The "natural" role for free men in a household was to rule, and the "natural" role for slaves and children and women was to be ruled, to obey. The Christian church entered the social world of the first century. The memory of Jesus and the hope for a community in which there is "no longer . . . male and female" did not (and could not) magically provide new gender roles and household structures; the churches did not (and could not) create ex nihilo a new social world. The church adopted the commonplace rules, but they also *adapted* them. They assimilated the moral traditions important in the wider culture to reflection about these rules, but they also *transformed* them. Perhaps we must put it more modestly:

---

charismatic authority is as likely to be the initiator of institutional authority as its victim, and that persons with institutional authority are likely still to recognize (and claim) charismatic authority. Charismatic authority seeks institutional realization; institutional authority seeks to retain charism. The real choice for the early church was not either charismatic authority or institutional authority but how to shape and reshape authority in the church both to preserve freedom and to provide a different kind of freedom, freedom from an unstructured common life. Similarly, in our view, the real choice for the early church was not simply between a community of coequal discipleship and patriarchy; the real choice was how to shape and reshape a common life that was both historically realizable and faithful to its new vision of equality and mutuality. It is not simply that an ideal is provided toward which we must strive but which we must always be ready to compromise in reality. It is rather that a reality has been established in the resurrection of Jesus, the good future of God, a reality to which we always and already respond, even while it is not yet that future.

10. On this see especially Balch, *Let Wives Be Submissive.*

they also qualified them; they nudged them in the direction of God's good future.

To be sure, the effect of that adoption was taken by many simply to authorize and legitimate the moral commonplaces of the culture within the church. But neither the early church nor Ephesians simply baptized the Hellenistic moral commonplaces as God's law, and they surely did not absolutize them. It is our view that the adaptation is more significant than the adoption, that the church should not absolutize the *haustafel* as a timeless moral code but rather attend to the direction in which it nudged the received tradition.

Nudging Leaves Marks

There can be no doubt that the tradition of the household codes represented an historical achievement that left the church at some distance from the future it envisioned. There can be no doubt that the household codes have been used to put (and to keep) women and slaves at the margins of society. But there can also be no doubt that the church's memory and vision left its marks on the conventional morality of the first century and nudged it in the direction of God's good future.

It left its mark, first of all and fundamentally, on the *justification* for "Be subject": the justification is no longer "nature" but Christ. The justification is no longer that ruling and being ruled are "natural," simply the way things are, or in accord with some cosmic patriarchal Reason. The justification is not that by our willing participation in the "nature" or the "reason" at work in the way things are we can transcend our passions. And where the Christ is the justification and the pattern for submission, there the one who would rule is also called to serve. Where the story of the cross is remembered, the model is not that we should be passionless but that we should make Christ's passion our own. Where the humility of Christ is remembered, the pattern is that we should not make the claims that are ours to make but humbly serve. Where the resurrection of Christ is remembered, the way things are is not confused with the way things are to be. Where Christ, in whom "there is no longer slave or free, there is no longer male and female," is remembered, there is justification not only for the household code as an accommodation to the social world in which they lived but also for continuing the struggle against inequalities and against sexism and divisions of class.[11] Where Christ is remembered, his solidarity with those who do not count for much as the world counts may not be neglected or forgotten. The point is this: to appeal to Christ to authorize these rules for the household is also to provide for the qualification and limitation of the application of these rules.

The church receives also its own tradition, including its biblical traditions, including the household codes, as tested by the story of Jesus and as requiring continuing discernment. It continues to assess the tradition and performances of the tradition in the light of its memory of Jesus. The tradition of submission represented by the household codes is justified by the memory of Jesus, but it also must be continually tested and qualified by that memory. Where it is used in the service of sexism or the defense of slavery, we may and must in memory of Jesus put a limit to it and reorient it, nudge it a little closer to our hope and calling.

That justification qualified the way these conventional Greek commonplaces were received in the church and reiterated in the household codes; the different justification created other differences. A second mark left on the tradition of the household codes is simply that the woman, the slave, and the child are addressed. They are addressed as moral agents in their own right. The grace of God renders them agents too. This stands in contrast to the philosophical account of role responsibilities that typically addressed only the free noble man as a moral agent. And if the *agency* of the woman and the

---

11. Justifications are like that: they not only authorize rules, they guide and limit the application of the rules. For example, if one were to justify the rule that one should tell the truth by saying that truth telling serves the greatest good for the greatest number, then that justification would also guide *how* the truth is told and limit the duty to tell the truth. It would require us, for example, sometimes not to tell the truth if the greatest good for the greatest number were served by deception. On the other hand, if one were to justify truth telling by saying that telling the truth is a rational necessity, then the rule will be applied differently and deception will not be justified simply by its utility. Still other reasons for telling the truth might be given, and each justification would not only authorize the rule to tell the truth but also affect the way the rule is applied and limited.

slave and the child is addressed, their submission is to be *voluntary*, not simply conscripted.

A third mark left on the tradition is that submission is *mutual*. Ephesians 5:21 says it best in its preface to its household code: "Be subject *to one another* out of reverence for Christ" (italics added). It is not just women and slaves and children who are called to be subject. "Out of reverence for Christ" free fathers and husbands are called to be subject too. "All of you must clothe yourselves with humility in your dealings with one another" (1 Pet. 5:5). Men "put on Christ" when they clothe themselves with humility, when they are ready not to make the claims that some "natural" order of ruler and ruled would license. They may not conscript the submission of the relatively less well situated in society if they are unwilling to be submissive themselves—and submissive to the ones relatively less well situated. The emphasis on role responsibilities in the tradition is hardly innovative or surprising, but the emphasis on *mutuality* signals a new chapter in the story of our world of gender. It displays something of the vision born in the resurrection and in baptism. Related to this mutuality is the observation that the duties are *reciprocal*.

There is a fourth mark left on the household codes, an even more surprising one: the biblical codes recognize *equality*. The masters of slaves, for example, are reminded that both slave and master "have the same Master in heaven, and with him there is no partiality" (Eph. 6:9; cf. Col. 4:1). And husbands are reminded that both wife and husband have the same Christ, the same bridegroom of the church, that men are members of the bride, the church, and that their wives are members of the body of Christ, the Lord (Eph. 5:25–30). Neither sexism nor slavery can finally endure the recognition of *equality* that marks not only the baptismal vision of the church but also this *haustafel*.

Finally, the memory of Christ left a fifth mark on this tradition, a fifth transformation. The biblical codes do not call attention to the self, to the natural nobility of the free husband and father; they call attention instead to the *neighbor*—and to the neighbor *as one who is to be loved* (e.g., Eph. 5:28, 33). Moreover, this duty to love the neighbor is not construed according to the conceit of philanthropy; it is not motivated by a self-serving sense of one's own goodness in nobly granting kindness to those "naturally" under one. It is rather under-stood as our response to Christ, as a self-forgetful sense of gratitude to this ruler of all who was (and is) among us as one who serves.

The distance between the vision and the historical realization of that vision in the household codes remains—and it remains trou-bling. But the struggle is the crucial thing. And there is much to be learned from the marks which that struggle left on the household codes as the church continues its pilgrimage toward the good future of God that is still on the horizon, a good future in which the remem-bered Jesus rules.

These five marks left by nudging the received tradition in the direction of God's good future allow this conclusion: we perform this passage well not when we regard it as a timeless code, as an eter-nal set of rules, but when our lives (and our roles) are marked by Christ, by the recognition and affirmation of the agency of the other, by mutuality, by equality, and by love of the neighbor (including the neighbor who is our wife or husband).

The church may never be content with the distance, and it may not today simply repeat this first-century code as the timeless word of God. That would be to allow the tradition to fossilize and to pet-rify; it would be to permit the struggle to be forgotten and neglected; and it would put a stop to our pilgrimage. A pilgrim's progress still comes by remembering and by envisioning the future born in memory. The memory of Jesus still does not enable us to create ex nihilo new social structures nor permit us to suppose that, even if we could, these structures would eliminate the distance between our creation and the reign of this Jesus. Nevertheless, we are enabled to talk together and pray together and exercise discernment together about the "household traditions" we still receive and assimilate. The memory of Jesus must continue to qualify the way these biblical texts—and the moral commonplaces of our own social world—are received and handed down. And we are required in memory of Jesus to continue to struggle to put on Christ within them, to struggle against the patriarchy and racism and classism within them and within us. So we think about our choices together in the community Christ still makes and still marks by mutuality and equality and a self-forgetful love of the neighbor.

There is no remembering Jesus that does not censure oppression, that does not struggle for some fleshly consequence of the vision of a world in that there is "no longer Jew and Gentile, slave and free, male nor female." To remember the story is not simply to follow a set of rules as though a normative kinship system has dropped from heaven either into first-century Scripture or into post-Enlightenment political philosophy. To remember the story is rather to nurture and cherish a continuing tradition of liberation in the moral discourse and deliberation and discernment of the church. Let our choices be in memory of Jesus. Let our choices be a recognition and celebration of the full and equal participation of women in the life of the churches. Let our choices nudge our communities in the direction of mutuality and equality.

Mutual Submission and Reverence for Christ

"Be subject to one another out of reverence for Christ" (5:21). In this heading for the whole section we find already three of the marks we have just surveyed: the appeal to Christ, mutuality, and an address to all members of the community as moral agents. But both "Be subject" and "fear" (*phobos*; NRSV "reverence") can still give us pause.

Consider first the key word of the Christian tradition, "Be subject" (*hypotassomai*). It is an unusual term for the tradition of role responsibilities. It differs, for example, from Aristotle's insistence that: "The strength of man is shown in commanding, of women in obeying" (*Politics* 1260a). The call to "be subject" is not identical to a call to "obey," although it can include obedience (Eph. 6:1, 5). It is surely not a call to adopt an attitude of servile or obsequious obedience. We get closer to its meaning, we think, by remembering not Aristotle but the list of virtues in 4:2–3, "humility and gentleness, ... patience, bearing with one another in love, making every effort to maintain the unity of the Spirit in the bond of peace." And we get closer to its meaning by remembering 1 Peter 5:5, "All of you must clothe yourself with humility in your dealings with one another."

We also get closer to its meaning by remembering Jesus. He came announcing the good future of God with axioms of a great reversal, "Many who are first will be last, and the last will be first" (Mark 10:31; cf. Matt. 20:16; Mark 9:35; Luke 13:30), and "All who exalt themselves will be humbled, and all who humble themselves will be exalted" (Matt. 23:12; cf. Matt. 18:4; Luke 14:11; 18:14). Jesus not only announced such a great reversal; he performed it. He put those on the margins of Israel's common life at the center of his ministry. He blessed the poor, healed the lepers, ate with "sinners," taught women, and ministered to Samaritans and Gentiles. He made the last first. And those who exalted themselves—for example, the scribes who insisted on the best seats in the synagogue (Mark 12:38–40) and the Gentile rulers who "lord it over" their subjects (Mark 10:42)—did not count for much with Jesus. Jesus performed the great reversal he announced also by his presence among the disciples "as one who serves" (Luke 22:27; cf. Matt. 20:28; Mark 10:45; John 13:2–17). And the only fitting response to this good future of God and to this Jesus who makes it known was captured in his command to "be last of all and the servant of all" (Mark 9:35; cf. Matt. 20:26–7; 23:11; Mark 10:43–44; Luke 22:26; John 13:12–17). To "be subject" is to "subordinate yourselves," to "be last of all and the servant of all."

When, in Philippians, Paul remembered Jesus, he wanted "the same mind" to be in the community "that was in Christ Jesus, who . . . did not regard equality with God as something to be exploited, but emptied himself, . . . humbled himself" (Phil. 2:5–8). The good future of God was displayed when God exalted that Jesus (2:9). Meanwhile the "mind" of Christ is expressed in the community by mutual subjection, by the "humility" that regards others as "better than yourselves," by each looking "not to your own interests, but to the interests of others" (2:3–4).

This call to "be subject to one another" sets the context for the household code. It is true that in what follows what were the "natural" hierarchies to Aristotle and to the culture of the first century seem to be affirmed. Wives are to "be subject"; children and slaves are to "obey." But there is a world of difference between enforced subordination and voluntary subordination. In the "mind of Christ" the assumption is not that there is a natural hierarchy but rather that there is both a fundamental equality and a readiness for the sake of others not to make the claims that are ours to make. The call to "be subject" is not an attempt to break the will of any of the members of these communities; on the contrary, it recognizes and appeals to them as agents, agents by God's grace and blessing. And Christ is not just the source of their agency but the pattern for it, and not just for their agency but for the agency of those free adult males who naturally think of themselves as "first." In the grip of the mind of Christ, those who are "first" are in no position to enforce subordination, to conscript submission while refusing themselves to "be subject," and to humbly serve and to love those whom the culture regards as "last."

Such mutual submission finds its pattern and motive in Christ; it is undertaken "out of reverence for Christ." As we have noted, however, "reverence" is a weak translation of *phobos*. But to take *phobos* more seriously, to suggest that the "fear of Christ" provides a motive and justification, seems curious at best. Paul himself had insisted to the Roman churches that "you did not receive a spirit of slavery to fall back into fear, but you have received a spirit of adoption" (Rom. 8:15). We are, as Ephesians itself has insisted, "beloved children" of God (5:1). Christ shows the kindness of God, the tenderheartedness of God, the forgiveness of God (cf. 4:32). What have we to fear? Still, there it is: "out of fear [*phobos*] of Christ."

It is not only here, of course. Paul had instructed the Philippians to "work out your own salvation with fear and trembling; for it is God who is at work in you, enabling you both to will and to work for his good pleasure" (2:12–13). God makes us agents in God's own cause, but it is God who is God, not us. We do not claim to understand exactly what Ephesians had in mind with this reference to the "fear of Christ," but two points seem important.

The first is simply to insist that fearing God is not antithetical to loving God. (Indeed, in Deuteronomy they are nearly synonymous.) It is more like the implication of the love of God *as God*, as the one upon whose mercy we utterly depend, as the one to whom we are ultimately accountable, as the holy one before whom we shudder in the recognition of our sins, as the numinous one before whom we tremble, as the one whose works of power prompt awe. This fear joined to love Calvin named "piety."[12] It is not that we stand in terror

---

12. Calvin, *Institutes* 1.2.1.

before God or Christ. The love of God in Christ evokes from us an answering love, but that love is not empty of the recognition that it is God who is God and not us, that it is Christ who is Lord and not us.

The second point is to set the fear of Christ in contrast to the fear of the "powers." Puah and Shiphrah, the midwives of Exodus 1 who stood guard over the cradle of Israel, did not kill the new-born Hebrew boys as Pharaoh had commanded. They did not fear Pharaoh; they "feared God" (Exod. 1:17). In Ephesians it is clear that we need not fear the principalities and powers. The powers were regarded as intimately involved with political and social realities. They were active in the structures of human life and of the cosmos, in government and gravity, but also in received social institutions, in the "natural" arrangements of marriage and family and economy. We need not fear the powers. They have been stripped of their claims to ultimacy. They have been unmasked; the deceptions by which they nurture enmity and division have been revealed. They are not gods, but there is one! They do not rule, but Christ does! They have been made subject to Christ. So we can be subject to the governments and to social institutions but reject their claims to ultimacy and the enmity they nurture. We can be subject to so-called natural arrangements but qualify and adapt them and transform them into something a little more worthy of Christ's sovereignty over them. It is not the authority of the "powers" or of some "natural" order (not even some "creation order"), not the authority of a husband or parent or master, that we must respect and fear. But there is an authority, Jesus Christ, who made himself a servant, and his authority both wife and husband, both child and parent, both slave and master, must respect and "fear."

Christ and the Church—and Marriage

Hard on the heels of this call to mutual submission comes an account of the role responsibilities of husband and wife. The wives are addressed first, addressed as agents, capable of making their own decisions. They are instructed to "be subject to your husbands" (5:22), not to all men but to their husbands. Actually, "be subject" is not in the best manuscripts of verse 22; it is supplied from verse 21, which should make clear that we are dealing with an example of that *mutual* submission.[13]

Still, wives are clearly encouraged to "be subject." "Just as the church is subject to Christ, so also wives ought to be, in everything, to their husbands" (5:24). The relation of Christ to the church is invoked throughout this account of the role responsibilities of wife and husband (5:22–33). It provides the pattern, the analogy, by which we are invited to understand the relationship. But the limits of the analogy are not to be forgotten. Both wife and husband are members of the same church, the same bride of Christ. Both have the same head, Christ. That equality is fundamental, but it does not license a self-serving autonomy for either husband or wife.

Husbands are not told again to "be subject." But they are also not told to "rule" their wives. The husband is only told to "love" his wife. Again the relation of Christ and the church provides the analogy. He is to love her "just as Christ loved the church and gave himself up for her" (5:25). Christ is head of the church, but the husband is not told to "be the head" of his wife, just to love her. He is given no other command in this passage than to "love her." But that command is a refrain here: "Love her. . . . Love her. . . . Love her . . ." (cf. 5:25, 28, 33). It is learned from Christ's love for the church, not from some "natural" order of things à la Aristotle. If the husband is to be regarded as head in this relationship, he is only to be head after the pattern of Christ who "gave himself up" for his bride (5:25). That self-giving love is the normative pattern for husbands. Christ's "humility," Christ's readiness to be a servant, is the model. Like Christ, the husband seeks the well-being of his bride (5:26). He "cares" for her "as Christ does for the church" (5:29). The husband's love invites an answering love from his bride, invites an embrace that is faithful and exclusive.

Ephesians cites Genesis 2:24, "For this reason a man will leave his father and mother and be joined to his wife, and the two will become one flesh" (5:31), but the point is not to invoke some "creation order" as another and independent justification of marriage or

13. See Barth, *Ephesians 4–6*, 610. He attempts to capture this by his translation, "e.g., wives to husbands."

The Church's One Foundation

The Church's one foundation is Jesus Christ her Lord;
she is his new creation by water and the Word;
from heav'n he came and sought her to be his holy bride;
with his own blood be bought her, and for her life he died.

Elect from every nation, yet one o'er all the earth,
her charter of salvation, "One Lord, one faith, one birth!"
One holy name she blesses, partakes one holy food,
and to one hope she presses with ev'ry grace endued.

Though with a scornful wonder we see her sore oppress'd,
by schisms rent asunder, by heresies distress'd,
yet saints their watch are keeping, their cry goes up, "How long?"
And soon the night of weeping shall be the morn of song.

'Mid toil and tribulation, and tumult of her war,
she waits the consummation of peace forevermore,
till with the vision glorious her longing eyes are blest,
and the great church victorious shall be the church at rest.
　　　　　　—Samuel John Stone, "The Church's One Foundation"

In *Rejoice in the Lord*, ed. Erik Routley (Grand Rapids: Eerdmans, 1985), no. 394.

of role relationships within it. Rather this verse and marriage itself are taken to point to "a great mystery" (5:32), and the great "mystery" in Ephesians remains "the secret," the plan of God to renew all things, to restore the creation and humanity. That good future has been accomplished in Christ, who is our peace, and the firstfruits of that future may be found in the unity of the church, in the peaceable difference that marks its life, in a common life marked by the praise of God and love for one another. But marriage too can be and should be marked by that unity, peace, and love; and when it is, then it too is a small token of that good future. In the "one flesh" union of two who remain different but seek the welfare of the other we may see a reflection of the great mystery, the secret. That is the way God intended marriage, but it is discovered not in some natural authority structure but in the pattern of Christ's love for the church.

Similarly, when the command to love your neighbor as yourself was alluded to (5:28; cf. Lev. 19:18), it was not to invoke the law as another and independent justification for the husband's love or the husband's authority. The law too is read and understood in the light of the "mystery," in the light of God's plan of unity in Christ. The wife is a "neighbor," to be sure, and the husband's attention is directed toward her rather than to his own noble status as "head." But the "one flesh" union of marriage and the paradigm of Christ's care for his body, the church, entail a special status for his wife among his neighbors. The law itself is fulfilled in faithful and self-giving love. In the new covenant the law is written on the heart. Merely external observance of a statute is not enough. The self-giving love of Christ creates a new covenant, a new humanity of Jew and Gentile, and a new paradigm also for marriage.

The advice came first to wives, and then to husbands, but it is noteworthy that at the end of this advice it is the husband's self-giving love that provides a context for the wife's "respect" (Eph. 5:33). There is a kind of dance, a giving love and receiving love, a preceding love and a following love, a hearing love and an answering love.

The "respect" asked of wives is, however, once again *phobos*, "fear." It provides an echo of 5:21, "Be subject to one another out of reverence [*phobos*] for Christ." The echo serves to remind us of the opening command of "mutual submission," but once again this reference to fear should give us pause. We said earlier that the "fear of God" was not antithetical to the "love of God." It was to love God *as God*. We said that because of God's love, because we are God's "beloved children," we have no need to stand in terror of an arbitrary and despotic temper. Analogous remarks may be made in this context. To "fear" the husband is not antithetical to loving the husband. It is to love the husband *as husband*. And because of the husband's love, because the wife is his "beloved bride," she need not stand in terror of an arbitrary and despotic temper. Nevertheless, these analogous remarks have a bizarre and perverse ring when, in this sad world, a husband abuses his wife. A wife's fear of her husband can be a sign of the curse, of patriarchy (Gen. 3:16). When those in authority, whether ruler or husband, "lord it over" those who are subject to them, it is the way of the Gentiles, not the way of Christ (Mark 10:42–45), not the way of peace. This reference to the wife's "fear" is a reminder that patriarchy was—and is—deeply embedded in the culture, deeply embedded in the received tradition of rules for household management. It is a reminder that the Christian adaptation of that tradition did not yet eliminate patriarchy, even if it nudged the tradition in a different direction.

As we have said before, we will not perform this passage well if we take it to be a timeless code. We will not perform this passage well if we take it to be a permanent authorization for patriarchy or for patriarchal marriages. If we have read well the way this passage nudges the tradition in the direction of God's good future, then it neither requires nor permits us simply to adopt the role relations that were commonplace in the first century. But having said that, we must also say that the passage will hardly permit us to adopt without qualification and transformation the commonplaces of our own culture, which reduces marriage to a contract between independent and self-interested individuals. This passage points us in a different direction, toward a celebration and performance of marriage as an effect and sign of Christ's work in making the two one, of creating unity, peaceable difference, a relationship of mutuality and equality, of love and "mutual submission." Husband and wife are one and different. Their unity does not require an oppressive uniformity, but it does require a commitment of each to seek the well-being of the other. And their equality does not require a nitpicking calculation of this and that responsibility according to the measure of some abstract egalitarianism. The measure is rather Christ's love and humility.

Marriage is not simply a contract between independent and self-interested individuals. It is a covenant that establishes a new identity. The one who says, "I do," is never the same one again. It is a covenant that establishes a new community, a unity of peaceable difference, a "one flesh" union. It is a covenant that can, by God's grace, be a sign of God's intention to bring together all things under Christ.[14]

14. We do not regard marriage as a sacrament. Perhaps it is just that we have been formed by the Reformed tradition on this question. (See Calvin, *Institutes* 4.19.35, 37.) Ephesians 5:32 played a significant role in the definition and celebration of marriage as a sacrament in the Roman Catholic tradition, especially since most Latin translations, including the Vulgate, translated *mystērion* as *sacramentum*. We have read *mystērion* as consistent with the earlier uses of the "mystery" or the "secret" in Ephesians and not as a reference to an ecclesiastical rite. Indeed, the Vulgate uses *sacramentum* consistently to translate *mystērion*, which suggests that Jerome and the other translators were not thinking primarily of an ecclesiastical rite with this word. Even so, we acknowledge that there can be something sacramental about marriage. (See Calvin, *Institutes*, 4.19.36.)

Children and Parents

Ephesians turns next to the role relationships of children and parents. Again those who find themselves in the subordinate role are addressed first. The children are addressed as moral agents, not as independent moral agents but as possessing developing capacities for discernment and choice. Those developing capacities, as the advice to fathers will make clear, are to be respected and nurtured by parents.

Even so, children are simply told to "obey [their] parents" (6:1). The first and fundamental justification for that advice is given immediately, "obey your parents in the Lord." That justification may also serve as a qualification and limitation on the obedience due to parents, but no qualifications or limitations are explicitly stated. Once again, perhaps, hard cases may be left to the discernment of the community that welcomes little children as their own.

Other justifications are given as well: it is simply "right" (6:1). It is commanded by God (Exod. 20:12; Deut. 5:16), and joined to a promise of well-being (Deut. 5:16). Children are to obey their parents.

It is to "fathers," however, rather than to "parents," that the reciprocal advice is addressed (Eph. 6:4). It is another indication that patriarchy was deeply embedded in the culture and not eliminated from the *haustafel*. Indeed, in Roman law the legal power of the father, the so-called *patria potestas*, was widely recognized and almost absolute, extending to the right to put his children to death. In Jewish law too the death penalty was authorized for dishonoring parents (Lev. 20:9; Deut. 21:18–21), and Hellenistic Judaism could call attention to that authorization.[15] Surely the legal authorization to kill one's child could be joined to practices of affection and patience in both Greek and Jewish families. Even so, the advice given here to "fathers," that they should "not provoke [their] children to anger" (Eph. 6:4), seems to us to be a pretty strong nudge away from the patriarchy of the received culture. There were obvious reasons in the culture for children not to provoke their fathers to anger; it could cost them

---

15. For example, Philo, *On the Special Laws* 2.232; and Josephus, *Against Apion* 2.206.

their lives. But here that advice comes to fathers. Here that advice is made reciprocal. And the reason can only be that the heading, "Be subject to one another out of reverence for Christ" (5:21), has not been forgotten. Fathers are not here reminded of their great authority, of their *patria potestas*; they are reminded of the heading (and the head) under which (and under whom) their authority stands. They are to be attentive not to their own status but to their children.

Indeed, fathers are to be attentive to their children as those who have just been addressed as agents. Their children have developing capacities for moral agency themselves, and fathers should not run roughshod and tyrannically over those capacities. Rather, they should nurture those capacities. That is what Ephesians goes on to say to fathers, "bring them up in the discipline and instruction of the Lord" (6:4). Bring them up, bring them toward that "maturity" that is measured by the stature of Christ (4:13). Give them an identity, not just as the son of so-and-so, but as a beloved child of God (cf. 5:1). Give them a community, not just as a member of the family of so-and-so, but as a member of the church. Baptize them, and then with the help of the community correct them and train them as "children of light" (5:8).

We admit that the Christian adaptation of the received cultural tradition did not yet eliminate patriarchy, but it nudged that tradition in a different direction. Again, we will not perform this passage well if we take it to be a timeless code or a permanent authorization for something like *patria potestas*. In this sad world sometimes children need to be protected from their fathers. Again the hard cases seem left to the discourse and discernment of the community. But having said all of that, let it also be said again that this passage will hardly permit us to adopt without qualification and transformation the commonplaces of our own culture. Our culture's emphasis on autonomy, including the autonomy of the child, sometimes rejects not only parental discipline and correction but also the parental responsibility to give the child an identity and a community. Fathers (and mothers) may not run roughshod over the developing capacities for moral discernment in their children. They may and must engage those capacities. But freedom is not to be found in some pretense of neutrality.

If we are tempted by our own culture to think that we are all independent and autonomous creatures who create a community by entering into voluntary contracts, the relation of children and parents should be enough to dispel such a notion. All of us start life as babies, dependent creatures. None of us get to choose our parents. A relationship with them is not a matter of our choosing. And parents may choose to have children or not, but they do not really choose the children they get. But they are properly expected to care for them; that is a given, not a choice.[16] And to care for them means to provide for them an identity and a community, not for the sake of an oppressive uniformity but for the sake of peaceable difference, a peace that can celebrate the different gifts also of our children.

Slaves and Masters

Finally, this *haustafel* turns to the roles of slaves and masters (6:5–9). Again, those without cultural authority are addressed first and addressed as moral agents. Slaves are agents. A slave is not just, as Aristotle had said, "a piece of property" and "a living tool."[17] Their submission is to be voluntary, but it is clearly submission to which they are called. "Slaves, obey your earthly masters with fear and trembling, in singleness of heart, as you obey Christ" (6:5).

The advice to slaves to be subject seems to leave unchanged and unchallenged the institution of slavery. Still, in the advice to slaves and masters the community was nudged toward attitudes that would eventually find slavery intolerable. The justification here is not, as in Aristotle, for example, that some are "naturally" slaves;

---

16. To be sure, the responsibility of parents to care for their children is sometimes unfulfilled. Children were—and are—sometimes abandoned by their parents, and tragedies of one sort or another can make it too difficult or impossible to fulfill that responsibility. Then we thank God for adoptive parents. But one reason to praise those who undertake such responsibilities by adoption is that they are under no prior obligation, no natural obligation, to care for children. Natural parents assent to an existing obligation. Adoptive parents graciously undertake obligations that did not previously exist for them. The grace of adoptive parents is to be praised as a display of God's own grace when God adopted us as God's "beloved children" (cf. 1:5).

17. Aristotle, *Nicomachean Ethics*, trans. Martin Ostwald (New York: Bobbs-Merrill, 1962), 5.8 1134b10; 8.6, 1161b4.

the justification is the reverence due Christ. The heading remains mutual submission out of reverence for Christ (5:21). The slaves are reminded that they are first and fundamentally "slaves of Christ" (6:6), an honorable title that Paul can use of himself (e.g., Rom. 1:1, *doulos* [NRSV "servant"]) and of the free (1 Cor. 7:22, in a passage where the distinction between slave and free is clearly relativized, "For whoever was called in the Lord as a slave is a freed person belonging to the Lord, just as whoever was free when called is a slave of Christ"). Slaves are reminded not only of their own dignity by being addressed as agents but also of the dignity of their work and service, of the "good [they] do" (Eph. 6:8). They are reminded of Christ in each of the four verses inviting their voluntary submission.

The justification in the reverence due Christ seems to leave slavery unchallenged in the advice to slaves, but it put the lie not only to the assumptions Aristotle and the culture made about slaves as "chattel" and as "living tools" but also to other assumptions that Aristotle and the culture made. Aristotle had said that there could be "nothing common" to slave and master, and therefore that there could be no "friendship" and no "justice."[18] But in the reverence due Christ, there is something "common" to slaves and masters, as the advice to the masters will make clear; they "have the same Master in heaven" (6:9). If they have Christ in common, then there is "friendship," the unity of peaceable difference. And if they have Christ in common, the Master with whom "there is no partiality" (6:9), then there is the promise also of "justice."

Masters are told to "do the same to them" (6:9). It must have seemed shocking advice to masters. It could only mean that they were expected to "be subject" to their slaves "out of reverence for Christ" (5:21). It could only mean that they too should think of themselves as "slaves of Christ." It could only mean that there was equality in Christ and before God. That equality, moreover, could not be a disembodied and "spiritual" reality; it had to have some

---

18. Aristotle, *Nicomachean Ethics* 8.6 1161a32–b5. Aristotle does, however, recognize that the slave is still a human being, and he does admit that friendship with a slave as a human being is possible (1161b6–8).

"fleshly" consequences (cf. Phlm. 16, where Onesimus is to be welcomed as "a beloved brother . . . both in the flesh and in the Lord").

Here the consequences are at once the extraordinarily expansive "do the same to them" and the minimal requirement, "Stop threatening them" (Eph. 6:9). But the church needed to keep thinking about the consequences of this equality, and it needed to give some better performance of those "fleshly consequences." Too often it was content to read this passage as an authorization for slavery, but sometimes it performed this passage well by nudging the received tradition in the direction of God's good future, in the direction of the recognition of the dignity of each, of equality before God. The "fleshly" consequences of that dignity and equality required finally that slavery itself be challenged and ended.

The abolitionists were in the right against those who read the *haustafel* as a timeless authorization for slavery. To free the slaves was an historic achievement, but it did not achieve the "one new humanity" created and promised in Christ. It did not free us from our own cultures of enmity. When white power and privilege were preserved by racist policies of segregation, the "white church" was too often formed by the culture, too submissive to the principalities and powers. Ephesians challenges the very notion of the "white church," but it went unchallenged by far too many congregations. And when calls for integration came, they sometimes masked an oppressive hegemony of one culture over another. Ephesians still announces the victory of God over the principalities and the powers, still invites us to be formed not by our own cultures of enmity but by the hope to which God has called us. It still calls us to lives and a common life "to the praise of [God's] glory" (1:12, 14). It still calls us to break down the walls of hostility. It stills calls us to peaceable difference, to "one new humanity." But it never said it would be easy. It only promised that there is strength "in the Lord" (6:10).

And to that strength Ephesians will now turn again in its description of the Christian's armor.

Walking Humbly

The Reverend Jin S. Kim, a Korean American and pastor of Church of All Nations in Minneapolis, Minnesota, preached a sermon at the 218th General Assembly of the Presbyterian Church (U.S.A.) on June 24, 2008, that identified racism as a powerful force in America and repented of the churches' complicity in it. This is part of what he said:

> There is a powerful myth at work in America—the myth of the white man as the good guy.
>
> It's not that there is a deliberate attempt to distort history. It's that there is such a powerful need in America to maintain a parallel myth of the white man as the hero that it overwhelms actual history and prevents white people from speaking honestly about the past, and therefore taking responsibility for the present. . . .
>
> So here's the deal we middle-colored people made with the white power structure of this nation. . . . "No, we're not as white as the Europeans, but at least we're not black." And so we Asian immigrants used the same strategy as every immigrant group before us, stepping on the backs of black people to enter into white privilege. . . .
>
> . . . On behalf of all Korean immigrants in this country, I apologize to you, my African American sisters and brothers, and ask your forgiveness. . . . Please forgive me and my people, by the grace of God.
>
> —Jin S. Kim

"Walking Humbly," *Journal for Preachers* 32, no. 2 (2009): 47–50.

6:10–24

Enlisted in the Battle for Peace

The Strength of God's Power

"Finally, be strong in the Lord and in the strength of [God's] power" (6:10). We know what power this is. The same phrase was used once before, in 1:19. There in the author's prayer for his readers/hearers, he prayed that we would know the hope to which God has called us, our inheritance, God's good future. That hope and future were, he said, in accord with the workings of the strength of his power. There the NRSV translated the phrase as "his great power," here it translates it as "the strength of his power," but it is the same Greek phrase.

It is worth reminding ourselves of that passage. There *and here* "the strength of his power" was at work when God raised Jesus *from* the dead, raised Jesus *to* sovereignty over the principalities and powers, including the political powers that nurtured cultures of enmity. The strength of God's power was and is at work in the creation of a "new humanity." We saw the reference to Psalm 8 in that passage. Psalm 8 is a song of praise, beginning and ending with "O LORD, our Sovereign, how majestic is your name in all the earth" (Ps. 8:1, 9). The psalmist looked to the heavens, which prompted both a sense of God's glory and a sense of the insignificance of humanity. It prompted the question, "What are human beings that you are mindful of them?" (8:4). The psalmist answered his own question by calling attention to the place of humanity in God's creation: "Yet you have made them a little lower than God" (8:5). And again, "You have given them dominion over the works of your hands; you have put all

248

things under their feet" (8:6). What a magnificent creature a human being is! And how majestic the Creator! But the psalmist's response to his own question may prompt a question of our own. Is it true? It may have been true at the creation (Gen. 1:26), but is it still true? Human beings seem to have forfeited the magnificence of their creation. A dash of realism seems to be called for. As the author of Hebrews said in quoting this same psalm, "As it is, we do not yet see everything in subjection to them" (Heb. 2:8). Then he said, "But we do see Jesus, who for a little while was made lower than the angels, now crowned with glory and honor" (Heb. 2:9). In Ephesians Paul made the same move. He read Psalm 8:6 in reference to Christ without leaving behind its meaning with reference to humanity. We may still ask whether it is true of humanity, but the answer is clear when we are let in on the secret, the mystery. It is true of Jesus, the Son of Man, and because it is true of Jesus, we may know it is God's plan that it will be true of humanity as well. Humanity may have forfeited its magnificence, but in Jesus the Messiah it is restored. The angelic beings, the principalities and the powers, may for a time lord it over humanity, pressing human beings into their service and nurturing their alienation from God, from each other, and from the good creation. "But we do see Jesus," the one who reveals both God and our own true humanity, our glorious destiny as well as our good creation. We do see Jesus, the new humanity!

In that first chapter of Ephesians the author went on to emphasize the solidarity of Christ with the church, the blessing upon the church and the mission of the church—to be his body, to be the way a new humanity is present here and the way God's good future is to be already displayed. "[God] has given him [that is, Christ], the head of all things, to the church, which is his body, filled by the one who completes all things completely." It is all "the working of his great power" (1:19).

Here it is again, now in the form of an imperative. "Be strong in the Lord and in the strength of his power." The "in the Lord" signals the solidarity with the Lord, and "in the strength of his power" displays that we have been made alive together with him (2:5). We have been raised with him; we are seated with him above the principalities and powers (2:6). It is not our own strength upon which we rely; it is God's strength. But we must live in it! We must perform our baptism, our being raised with Christ, our being united not only to Christ but to those who are different from us, to those the culture of enmity has trained us to despise (cf. 3:6 and the unity of Jew and Gentile).

"Finally," it says, as if marking the last extended exhortation to those who hear or read this letter. But *tou loipou* may also be read as having temporal force, as "from now on" (Gal. 6:17) or "in the time remaining." We are unsure of the best translation, but we are quite sure that in the eschatology of Ephesians we live in the interim between the triumph of God in raising Jesus from the dead (1:20–23) and the final triumph for which we hope (e.g., 1:14; 4:13, 30). Even if this *tou loipou* is not translated "in the time remaining," the advice given is given for life in the interim, for life in memory of God's triumph in Christ and in anticipation of God's final victory over all that demeans and destroys the creation and humanity.

The Armor of God for the Cosmic Conflict

How shall we strengthen ourselves in this interim? How shall we strengthen ourselves "in the Lord" (6:10)? By putting on the "armor of God" (6:11).

If, as we suggested may be the case (without, however, any great certainty), Ephesians was written at (or near) the time of the war of 66–73, this reference to armor and to the tools of warfare would be altogether appropriate. It would also be quite spectacularly counter-cultural. To be sure, it uses the language of warfare, but this is not a war against Jews or Gentiles. This is a war against "the devil" (6:11). It is resistance to the "wiles of the devil," holding our own against "the dirty tricks of the devil" (*methodeias* may be better translated as "dirty tricks" than as "wiles," as in NRSV; see 4:14). This is a battle not against human enemies ("enemies of blood and flesh," 6:12), but against angelic (or demonic) powers, "against the rulers, against the authorities, against the cosmic powers of this present darkness, against the spiritual forces of evil in the heavenly places" (6:12). This is a cosmic conflict that is as old as sin. To be sure, it is a battle that is fought on the turf of every soul. A battle rages between "the old self" and "the new self," a battle between our inclination to hate and despise and our participation in the peaceable difference of our creation and renewal. From the beginning the vision in Ephesians has been cosmic in scope and social and political in its implications. Here it would enlist us in a battle not only for our own souls but especially for the renewal of the cosmos and humanity.

There are sovereignties in conflict, and we are enlisted on the side of God and of God's Christ. We are called to resist the resistance to God's cause, to "stand against . . . the devil" (6:11) and "the cosmic powers of this present darkness" (6:12), all the powers and "rulers" and "authorities" that have grown corrupt, the structures of our life in society and culture that have claimed ultimacy and nurtured enmity. (See pp. 65–71, "Further Reflections: The Powers.")

The famous metaphor of Oscar Cullmann seems apt for Ephesians.[1] The decisive battle has been already fought and won; when God raised Jesus from the dead, that was D-day. God has already raised Jesus to sovereignty over the principalities and the powers. The light has triumphed over the darkness. The powers of death and doom had done their damnedest, but God would not let sin or death or evil have the last word in God's world. Now we wait and watch and pray and work for V-day, for that day on which the enemy forces of enmity and death will finally lay down their arms and admit defeat. It is not yet that day, still sadly not yet that day. While we wait for it, there are little battles to be fought, battles that can be fought with courage and confidence because we remember the great triumph wrought by the strength of God's might and because we know the secret of God's good future. The final struggle is not ours to win; that is already sure and in God's hands. But in the interim we are to resist the resistance to God's cause. We are not called to defend God, not even called exactly to defend our own souls; we are called to defend the beachheads God's cause has made, the displays here and there of a renewed creation and a new humanity, the places and times that bear the promise of God's good future.

1. See Oscar Cullmann, *Christ and Time*, trans. Floyd V. Filson, rev. ed. (Philadelphia: Westminster Press, 1964), 84.

Although the final victory is assured, the cosmic conflict contin-ues, and we had better display not only courage but prudence. We had better arm ourselves with the armor of God. "Put on" (6:11) is the same word we noted in 4:24, where we called attention to the baptismal tradition of disrobing and robing. It is in baptism, in union with Christ and with his cross and resurrection, that we "put on" a new humanity, "created according to the likeness of God in true righteousness and holiness" (4:24). And it is in baptism that we are equipped for the struggle "in the time remaining," putting on the armor of God.

Lord Sabaoth His Name

A mighty fortress is our God, a bulwark never failing;
our helper he amid the flood of mortal ills prevailing.
For still our ancient foe doth seek to work us woe;
his craft and power are great;
and, armed with cruel hate,
on earth is not his equal.

Did we in our own strength confide, our striving would be losing;
were not the right man on our side, the man of God's own choosing.
Dost ask who that may be? Christ Jesus, it is he;
Lord Sabaoth his name,
from age to age the same,
and he must win the battle.

And though this world, with devils filled, should threaten to undo us,
we will not fear, for God hath willed his truth to triumph through us.
The prince of darkness grim, we tremble not for him;
his rage we can endure,
for lo! His doom is sure;
one little word shall fell him.

That word above all earthly powers, no thanks to them, abideth;
the Spirit and the gifts are ours through him who with us sideth;
let goods and kindred go, this mortal life also;
the body they may kill;
God's truth abideth still;
his kingdom is forever.

—Martin Luther

"A Mighty Fortress Is Our God," trans. F. H. Hedge, in *Rejoice in the Lord*, ed. Erik Routley (Grand Rapids: Eerdmans, 1985), no. 179.

To resist the "rulers," the "authorities," the "cosmic powers of this present darkness," the "spiritual forces of evil in the heavenly places" (6:12), to withstand their power, even on that "evil day" when the battle seems lost (6:13), to "stand firm," we must be prepared with the armor of God. Enlisted on the side of God and of God's Christ in this cosmic conflict, we are, like good soldiers, equipped with armor.

A soldier wore a belt around the waist to hold loose garments tight to the body and to allow quick movement. Sometimes a special belt would designate an officer. Our "belt" is "truth" (6:14, *alētheia*). In Isaiah 11:5 the Messiah wears a belt, "Righteousness shall be the belt around his waist, and faithfulness [LXX *alētheia*] the belt around his loins." The belt is a sign of his office. Here is the Jewish Messiah, the "branch" from the roots of "the stump of Jesse" (Isa. 11:1), who defends the poor and the meek (11:4) and brings peace to the cosmos (11:6–9). Because of him the "earth will be full of the knowledge of the LORD" (11:9). His belt is "righteousness" and "faithfulness." The belt of the Christian is "truth," that is, truthfulness, or loyalty to God and to the cause of God, righteousness and faithfulness.

A soldier wore a breastplate made of leather or metal covering his breast (and sometimes his back). The breastplate for the Christian is "righteousness" (Eph. 6:14; cf. Isa. 11:5). It is the righteousness, the justice, of the Messiah who defends the poor and the meek and in whose judgment there is peace; it is the righteousness of the new humanity (Eph. 4:24) that is the work of the Messiah.

It is worth observing that when Isaiah 59:17 talks about God's armor and about righteousness as God's breastplate, it also talks about God's "garments of vengeance" and "fury." Such offensive weapons are absent here. "Vengeance" and "fury" are not part of the Christian's equipment. They are not to be "put on" but left to God (cf. Rom. 12:19).

Soldiers know they better pay attention to their shoes. Shoes are important to preparation for battle. And the shoes provided for Christians provide a firm footing in the "gospel of peace" (Eph. 6:15). It was the Messiah who "came and proclaimed peace to [those] who were far off and peace to those who were near" (2:17). It is the Messiah who "is our peace" (2:14). It is that Messiah and the peace he made and proclaims that gives us a firm footing for the struggle against the powers that nurture violence and enmity. Put on the gospel of peace; then you will have firm footing. Then you will be able to "stand firm" (6:13), ready to do whatever makes for peace, ready to speak and to perform "the gospel of peace" (6:15).[2] There is another allusion to Isaiah here: "How beautiful upon the mountains are the feet of the messenger who announces peace, who brings good news, who announces salvation, who says to Zion, "'Your God reigns'" (Isa. 52:7).

In addition to these pieces of equipment, a soldier better have a shield. Ancient shields were of different sorts and sizes, but one kind of shield was large enough to protect the whole body, made of wood and covered with leather. The leather could be soaked with water before battle so that it would extinguish burning arrows (cf. Eph. 6:16). Our shield is "faith" (6:16). This faith is not to be reduced to the acceptance of certain propositions as true; it includes that, to be sure, but it is more. It is faith that unites us to Christ, to his death and resurrection, and to his body, composed of Jew and Gentile and all those divided by the walls of hostility. It is trust in God and loyalty to the cause of God; it is faithfulness. If faith is, as Luther defined it, "a lively reckless confidence in the grace of God,"[3] then our best protection is ironically a certain nonchalance about our own protection.

A helmet is a good thing for a soldier, and we are given one. "Receive the helmet of salvation" (6:17 our trans.; "receive" is a better translation of *dexasthe* than the NRSV "take"). In Isaiah 59:17 God's helmet is salvation. Our helmet, God's salvation, is a gift of God. It is God's good future, already ours in hope while we wait and watch and pray and struggle for it.

Finally, with all these defensive weapons, a soldier better have a sword. That too is a gift of God. "Receive . . . the sword of the Spirit, which is the word of God" (6:17). With all the allusions to Isaiah

---

2. There is considerable controversy about the proper translation of *en hetoimasia* (6:15; NRSV: "whatever will make you ready"). We are unable to settle the controversy and have attempted to honor both the sense of "steadfastness" (or "firm footing") suggested by some scholars and the sense of "readiness" that is followed by the NRSV.

3. Cited in Robert McAfee Brown, *The Spirit of Protestantism* (New York: Oxford University Press, 1965), 61.

in this list of armor, we suggest one more. When the prophet gave an account of his mission, the mission of God's servant, he said that God had "made [his] mouth like a sharp sword" (Isa. 49:2). When he complained that he had "labored in vain" (49:4), God assured him that his mission would "raise up the tribes of Jacob" (49:6), and more than that, "I will give you as a light to the nations, that my salvation may reach to the end of the earth" (49:6). And this is the word of assurance to Isaiah, "Kings shall see and stand up, princes, and they shall prostrate themselves, because of the LORD, who is faithful, the Holy One of Israel, who has chosen you" (49:7).

The Spirit's sword is not simply identical with Scripture, at least not as an artifact that we can hold in our hand. It is rather the powerful and creative Word of God. It is the word that said, "Let there be light," and there was light. It is the word that called Jesus from the tomb. It is the word of salvation that does not return void to God. It is the word that makes the "peace" that it proclaims (cf. Eph. 2:17). It is "the word of truth" that even these Gentiles of the Lycus Valley had "heard," "the gospel of salvation" that they had "believed" and because of which they were "marked with the seal of the promised Holy Spirit, . . . the pledge of our inheritance" (Eph. 1:13–14). That word, the Spirit's sword, is given to the church in her mission of peace. When it looks to us, as it looked to Isaiah, that our work is "in vain," the promise of the Spirit is still that by that word God will "raise up" the people of God to be "a light to the nations, that [God's] salvation may reach to the end of the earth." Principalities and powers are not as strong as this word. The "prince of darkness grim" is not as powerful as this word; "one little word shall fell him" because the Lord is faithful, because the Holy One of Israel has chosen you and equipped you with his word (cf. Isa. 49:7).

Compared to the armor of the Zealots and the Roman soldiers, this list of items—truthfulness and righteousness and the proclamation of the gospel of peace, faithfulness and the gifts of salvation and the word—is deeply countercultural. There is no confidence in the ordinary weapons of war; there is confidence in God. It is as deeply countercultural as peace and unity in the midst of the cultures of enmity that marked the life of the first century.

Judith Mason, *The Man Who Sang and the Woman Who Kept Silent 2*, 1995, mixed media, c221 x 70 x 45 cm. Credits: Photo by Gisele Wulfsohn; image courtesy David Krut Publishing and the Constitutional Court of South Africa

Woman in a Blue Dress

Phila Ndwandwe was shot by the security police after being kept naked for weeks in an attempt to make her inform on her comrades. She preserved her dignity by making panties out of a blue plastic bag. This garment was found wrapped around her pelvis when she was exhumed. "She simply would not talk," one of the policemen involved in her death testified. "God . . . she was brave."

I wept when I heard Phila's story, saying to myself, "I wish I could make you a *dress*." Acting on this childlike response, I collected discarded blue plastic bags that I sewed into a dress. On its skirt I painted this letter:

> Sister, a plastic bag may not be the whole armour of God, but you were wrestling with flesh and blood, and against powers, against the rulers of darkness, against spiritual wickedness in sordid places. Your weapons were your silence and a piece of rubbish. Finding that bag and wearing it until you were disinterred is such a frugal, commonsensical, house-wifely thing to do, an ordinary act. . . . At some level you shamed your captors, and they did not compound their abuse of you by stripping you a second time. Yet they killed you. We only know your story because a sniggering man remembered how brave you were. Memorials to your courage are everywhere; they blow about in the streets and drift on the tide and cling to thorn-bushes. This dress is made from some of them. *Hamba kahle. Umkhonto.*

—Judith Mason, the artist

"The Man Who Sang and the Woman Who Kept Silent," in *Art and Justice: The Art of the Constitutional Court of South Africa*, ed. Ben Law-Viljoen (Johannesburg: David Krut Publishing, 2008), 123.

Still Praying

"Pray in the Spirit at all times in every prayer and supplication. To that end keep alert and always persevere in supplication for all the saints." This next verse in Ephesians (6:18) is in the NRSV a new paragraph, but in the Greek it is not even a new sentence. It is a participial construction. The participles, "praying" and "keeping alert," may reach all the way back to verse 14, to the beginning of this list of the armor of God, and to the exhortation there to "stand." It is plausible to consider prayer one more piece of armor for the struggle against evil, and we surely have no quarrel with those commentators who regard it as such or those members of the church who regard themselves as "prayer warriors." It is also plausible to read this verse as an exhortation to "put on" all these pieces of armor (in vv. 14–17) with prayer. Nevertheless, because verses 17 and 18 are one sentence, we think it best to connect this verse most closely to verse 17. We are to receive the gifts of God, the salvation of God and the word of God, "praying" and "staying alert."

The Spirit and the powerful and creative word of God prompt our prayers, our praise, our petition, our blessing upon God (*berakot*), our thanksgiving to God. We are to be constantly and persistently praying. And the gift of God's salvation prompts watchfulness. We are to "keep alert," to "watch" and "pray." It is what the disciples failed to do (three times) in Gethesemane (Mark 14:32–42). It is what Jesus had called them all to do (three times) at the end of his remarks concerning the signs of the times (Mark 13:33–37). From Ephesians the call, "Sleeper, awake!" (5:14), finds an echo here. The call to "live as children of light" (5:8), to "expose" the darkness (5:11), to "make the most of the time, because the days are evil" (5:16), all help to understand what it would mean in this time remaining to "stay alert."

We are always to make supplication "for the saints" (6:18). But watchfulness prays most persistently and most urgently that God's future may be made present, that God's kingdom will come, that God's cause will be accomplished, that God's will be done, on earth as it is in heaven. That is the prayer of the saints, and it is the prayer also "for the saints," for such is their "inheritance" (1:14, 18).

Paul asks them then to pray for him (6:19). He wants them to pray for his mission, to pray that he may speak boldly so that he can "make known . . . the mystery [or the secret] of the gospel" (6:19; cf. 3:9). That "secret," of course, is God's plan for the fullness of time (1:10), God's good future, one new humanity, the unity of Jew and Gentile in peaceable difference. As he had once before (3:1–13), he uses his own mission to remind these churches of their mission. As if to remind them of that passage, he states that he is "an ambassador in chains" (6:20; cf. 3:1, "a prisoner for Christ Jesus"). And, without having to say so, it is one more subtle invitation to perform that unity and to make the secret known, "so that through the church the wisdom of God in it rich variety might now be made known to the rulers and authorities in the heavenly places" (3:10), to "the powers."

We have noted several times the significance of prayer to this letter. (See pp. 49–57, "Further Reflections: Toward a Prayerful Ethic.") We are not surprised to find that the last word of the exhortation is an exhortation to pray. Prayer here, finally, is a form of watchfulness, of waiting and hoping for God's good future. It is a way to "stay alert." But here too this form of attention to God, this waiting and hoping, is not simply passivity. Attentive to God, we are attentive to the one who makes us agents in God's cause, the one who invites us to bless God, the one who invites our lives and our common life to be doxology, to be for "the praise of [God's] glory" (1:12, 14).

Tychicus

Paul cannot bring the letter to these churches himself or visit them just now. He is tied up, "a prisoner for Christ Jesus" (3:1), "an ambassador in chains" (6:20). So he has sent Tychicus as his own ambassador, authorized him to read this letter to the churches of the Lycus Valley, to let them know how Paul is and what he is doing (6:21), and to encourage them (6:22). Paul commends Tychicus warmly as "a dear brother and a faithful minister in the Lord" (6:21).

"*Peace . . . and Grace*"

A benediction closes the letter. It is two benedictions really, two wishes at least. The first wish is for the "peace" of the community. Anyone who had paid attention to the letter as it was read will know that this "peace" is the peace of Christ, the peace Christ made when he created in himself one new humanity in place of the two (2:15). Anyone who had paid attention would not be surprised that the wish for peace is joined to a wish for "love with faithfulness [NRSV faith]." The peace Christ made, the peace Christ *is*, has put an end to the hostility between Jew and Gentile and called for them to "live in love" (5:2) and to be faithful to the identity and the community, the peace, that Christ gave and gives. It was faith that would protect them in the time remaining against the attacks of the evil one (6:16) and all his allies in the cosmic struggle. And anyone who had paid any attention at all would know that this wish is not just wishful thinking. This wish is sure to be, for the source of peace is "God the Father and the Lord Jesus Christ" (6:23; cf. 1:2).

The second wish is for "grace." "Grace be with all who have . . . love for our Lord Jesus Christ" (6:24). It is not surprising that grace is wished. This wish too is not just wishful thinking; it is sure to be, for God is gracious. The grace of God had been present from the beginning and in all that God and the Messiah of God had done. It was "by grace" that they had been saved (2:5, 8). It was "by grace" that a new social reality of peaceable difference had been established. And it was grace that put an end to boasting and despising.

It is at first a little surprising, however, that the recipients of this grace in the church are called those who "love the Lord." We have heard much in Ephesians of God's love and much of love of one another in the community. We have observed that the church had been called to be subject to one another "out of reverence [or fear] for Christ" (5:21), and we said then that "fear" was a kind of love for God as God, a love for Christ as the Christ. But nowhere else was to be found this description of the church as those "who love our Lord Jesus Christ." Still, the church is the bride of Christ (5:25–32), after all, and at the end the bride answers the affection of her husband with an answering love.

The Benediction

When the Reverend Joanna M. Adams was pastor of the North Decatur Presbyterian Church in Decatur, Georgia, a member of her congregation stopped by her office for a visit. The woman told Joanna that worship was essential in her life. "Your sermons are excellent, and I love singing the hymns. But I will tell you what is the most important part of the service. It is the benediction. When you raise your arms and assure us that God will go with us as we leave the sanctuary to go out into the world where we face trial and tribulation, I need to hear your assurances that God goes with us to bless us and keep us. Joanna, it is the benediction that enables me to make it through another week."

—Joanna Adams (personal conversation)

As the letter had begun with "grace . . . and peace," now it ends with "peace . . . and grace" (6:23, 24). Together they create a kind of envelope for this message of God's blessing and our calling, for this account of the peace wrought by Christ and the peace to be performed in the church, for this proclamation in both indicative and imperative of a grace that triumphs over the cultures of enmity. The triumph of God's peace and grace is certain, even if the cultures of enmity still threaten. Even while they threaten, Ephesians promises peace and grace. And because they still threaten, Ephesians calls the church to resist the cultures of enmity, to "be strong in the Lord," and to perform God's peace and grace.

FURTHER REFLECTIONS
A Sample Sermon on Ephesians

As we said in the introduction, one way that Ephesians is performed is in the sermon. It is not the only way or even the most important way, but it is a way in which congregations may be moved to perform Ephesians in other ways and in more important ways. So we thought it good to bring this theological commentary to a close by providing a sample sermon that one of us has preached. The text was Ephesians 2:14–18.

Imagine a place in the Lycus Valley where these words might first have been heard. Let me introduce you to Jacob—not Esau's brother, not the old patriarch of Genesis, a different Jacob. Our Jacob lives in Miletus, along the Lycus River, a city of many ethnic groups and many gods. Jacob has no use for many gods. He is a Jew—a Jew who believes in one God, "the God of Jacob," as he likes to say, and a Jew who has learned to call Jesus the Christ.

There are other Jews in Miletus—and other Christians, some Jewish like Jacob, and some Gentiles. All the Jews are a little worried right now. The news from Judah isn't good. The Roman procurators there are ever more corrupt and oppressive. And the Zealots among the Jews call for revolt ever more belligerently. If the revolution comes, Jacob and his Jewish friends know that the soldiers will not simply and politely reassert Roman authority. They know it will be a bloodbath. And they know it will spill over to other cities. Already there is a report of Jews being killed in Alexandria. They fear the violence may come to Miletus. God knows there is no shortage of enmity here.

It has not been easy for Jacob. Oh, he's still glad to have learned of Jesus, but the little congregation of Christians to which he belongs seems to be falling apart. Last Sunday the love feast disintegrated into name-calling. Those miserable Gentiles called Jacob and the other Jews "weaklings" and "wimps-in-the-faith" and worse things. Jacob felt like joining some of his friends in returning the insults, calling those upstarts "sinners" and "pigs" and "the uncircumcision." But he didn't. He just went home and wondered about ever returning.

It was all Paul's fault really, and those ministers of the gospel in the Lycus Valley who looked to Paul, Jacob said to himself. Why had Paul insisted on one congregation of Jew and Gentile as though the truth of the gospel were at stake? Paul was not stupid. He should have known of the enmity between Jew and Gentile. He should have known that one community of Jew and Gentile could never work.

Surprisingly, it had worked for a while, Jacob admitted to himself. Jacob and his family had even gotten quite friendly with the Gentiles

Julius and Julia and their children. There had been times of awkward and anguished silence, of course, like the first time they were invited to eat Gentile food. Hardly anything had been kosher! Still, the vegetables were good, and the awkward moments seemed a price worth paying for the adventure of friendship with such strange people. Or so Jacob had thought at least, until recently when the world just seemed to ooze enmity, and until last week when he thought he heard Julius's voice among those throwing insults.

Jacob was feeling weak just now—not weak in the sense that the Gentiles meant it, not weak in the sense of being unable to break the law—he didn't want to do that. But he felt weak against the world, weak against "reality." Jews and Gentiles are different, and they just don't get along. That's just the way things are. That's what the world says. And the world seems to be shouting it right now. There was news of racial conflict in Alexandria and Antioch and Caesarea. There were rumors of violence in Palestine and of Jewish revolutionaries winning support. If enmity is just the way things are in the world, who am I to fight it, Jacob thought, and with what?

Jacob was feeling weak just now—and not just against the world but weak against his own anger and spite. He wanted to throw an insult back into the face of Julius or, better yet, his fist. He wanted to show his kids he wasn't weak, that Jews aren't weak. "We'll go one more time," he said to his wife, "but if those pigs so much as make a joke about our food or our law or even my nose, I'm going to smash something—or someone—and never go back."

So they went—and Tychicus was there with a letter that he said was from Paul, and that he read to the congregation. Evidently Paul knew the world was at risk of racial conflict. In the world there is enmity. Paul knew that. And he evidently also knew that there were tensions within the churches of the Lycus Valley. But in Christ, Paul said, there is a new humanity and peace!

Tychicus read from the letter: "He is our peace. Jesus has made us both one. He has broken down the dividing wall, that is, the hostility that divides us. . . . He has created in himself one new humanity of Jew and Gentile, so making peace. He has reconciled us both to God in one body through the cross, putting hostility to death."

A silence came over the congregation as Tychicus read those words, a guilty silence, for some remembered last Sunday, and a submissive silence, a silence ready to do God's will.

It dawned on Jacob then that this was the promise of God to Abraham long ago, that all the nations would be blessed. This was God's project from the beginning when he called Abraham and Sarah to leave Ur of the Chaldees and to begin a journey that had as its destination a blessing on all the nations.

It dawned on Jacob then—and on Julius and on Julia—that the problem in the world—and in the church—is not difference. The wall that divides us, as Paul said, is not difference but enmity, "the hostility between us." And the solution is not that everybody should be the same. The solution is not the imposition of uniformity, because the problem is not difference. Neither the imposition of Julius's Gentile "freedom" nor the enforcing of Jacob's Jewish law will put hostility to death.

But Jesus did put hostility to death. He reconciled both Jews and Gentiles to God. And so he reconciled them to each other. He made them "one body," his body. He put hostility to death—"through the cross," as Paul said. Hostility was put to death by the self-giving love of the cross. Peace comes "by the blood." We are made "one body"— with many different members—"through the cross." The differences remain, but the hostility is "put to death" through the cross. The cross did not eliminate difference, but it did, so Paul claimed anyway, put hostility to death. Lives formed by the cross, then, must be marked by love. And a common life formed by sharing the story—and the blood—of Christ must be marked by peaceable difference. That's what Tychicus—or Paul—went on to say, "I beg you to lead a life worthy of your calling."

It dawned on Jacob—and on Julius and on Julia—that Christian identity is a calling to love in a world of hostility, a vocation to care for the stranger, a task of making peace. That calling demands our simplest gifts and our best—but it always also demands something like the self-giving love of the cross.

Jacob blushed at his readiness to insult and curse Julius, when the letter talked of humility and gentleness and patience, of forbearance and love, and of an eagerness to maintain the unity of the Spirit in the bond of peace. But he didn't feel weak anymore.

"Enmity and animosity may rule the world and threaten war, but I am part of a new humanity," he said, "I am in Christ, a member of the body of Christ, and in that body, in Christ, there is no Jew or Gentile. Enmity and hate may still assert their power over me, but so does the blood of Christ, and the blood of Christ has put hostility to death. God's good future is sure to be."

Jacob felt strong—not proud. He knew that he had a long way to go to reach maturity in Christ. And he knew that the church had a long way to go too. But he felt strong just the same, strong in the gospel, strong in the power of God that raised Jesus from the dead and set him far above the principalities and powers.

The whole community was strengthened that day, strengthened to wrestle against the powers, to fight against the enmities and animosities that seemed to rule the world, strengthened to stake a claim in the world of hostility to God's good future of peaceable difference, to an identity as one new humanity, and strengthened for the adventure of faithfulness to it while we wait and watch for that future.

There was no name-calling that day. There was a handshake with Julius that grew into a hug. There was forgiveness and healing and renewal. The love feast was genuine. They grew up a little, knit together into one body by the love of Christ, and they acknowledged together that they had some way to go.

Jacob was still a Jew, of course, and Julius, still a Gentile, but each was also by the grace of God "a new creation." Jacob was not just a Jew. Julius was not just a Gentile. They were Christians, and therefore brothers in Christ.

There were two things that the work of Christ accomplished long ago and on that Sunday in Ephesus. The first thing was this: The blood of Christ, the grace of God, had made *a space* for each to receive the other, to welcome the other, and to be enriched by difference. They learned in the Spirit that they needed each other to be properly themselves, to live a life worthy of their calling in memory of Jesus and in anticipation of God's good future.

And the second thing was no less important: The blood of Christ, the grace of God, created for Jacob and for Julius enough *distance* from their own cultures to be self-critical, to exercise judgment and discernment. Jacob was not just a Jew. He could see now—and condemn—the self-righteousness that boasted about being Jewish. Julius was not just a Gentile. He could see now—and condemn—the presumptuous readiness of the empire to regard Jewishness as a pestilence.

Jacob still had his Jewish blood, and Julius still had his Gentile blood, but they *shared* the blood of Christ—in the cup at the Supper—and that bound them together. The blood of Christ gave them life—and gave them a common life. The body of Christ made them one body and nourished them. The blood of Christ was more precious than the blood that separated them. Their common participation in the body of Christ was more important to who they were and to who they hoped to become than their different cultures, customs, language, political allegiances, and economic interests.

The Letter to the Ephesians was God's word to people like Jacob and Julius, Jews and Gentiles in the Lycus Valley in the first century. And this letter is God's word to us in a different place and a different century. Lots of years and lots of miles separate us from Jacob's story. But some things have not changed.

One thing that has not changed is this: The power of hate is still too strong. The problem with our world too is not difference but enmity. And the solution is still not to eliminate difference or to enforce uniformity but to find in the body and blood of Christ the space to receive the other and enough distance from our own cultures to be self-critical.

The intervening centuries have seen lots of idols raised in the name of blood: blue blood, Anglo-Saxon blood, white blood. Ethnic cleansing continues into the twenty-first century, and we feel weak sometimes. But this word from Paul is still the gospel. Christ is our peace. He has put hostility to death.

And that gospel still demands that we reject as false doctrine the idea that Christians (or churches) should regard allegiances to the culture or nation or class they inhabit as more important than their allegiance to brothers and sisters in Christ of other cultures, other races, or other nations.

That gospel still commands that we "lead a life worthy of the calling to which [we] have been called." In situations of hostility and conflict we Christians too often find it difficult to distance ourselves from our cultures and political allegiances, and so we simply echo their reigning opinions.

If we are to keep Paul's vision alive, if we are to live lives worthy of the gospel, we will need to make a place for those who are different, we will need to listen to those Christians who are in another place and culture. We need them to be most properly ourselves.

To live lives worthy of this gospel, worthy of this calling, is still to undertake an adventure of *love*—in a world of *hostility*, of *forgiveness*—in a world of holding a grudge, of *faithfulness*—in a world of treachery, of *speaking the truth*—in a world of spin and propaganda, of *hospitality* to those the culture shuns and neglects, of *making peace* and *doing justice*—in a culture of racism and nationalism.

And oh, one more thing has not changed: It will not be easy. There will be some awkward moments, and probably some suffering. No real adventure is altogether free from such risks—and the story of a cross surely does not promise that we will be protected from them. It won't be easy! It wasn't easy for Jacob. And it won't be easy for us. But then, it wasn't easy for Jesus either. The new humanity was purchased with his blood. And because of his blood and by the resurrection of his body, God's good future is sure to be. Amen.

Benediction: Ephesians 3:20–21: "Now to him who by the power at work within us is able to accomplish abundantly far more than all we can ask or imagine, to him be glory in the church and in Christ Jesus to all generations, forever and ever. Amen."

An Unconcluding Postscript

Our work on the Letter to the Ephesians has come to an end, but the work of performing this epistle is an ongoing task for the churches. There will be a variety of performances reflecting the various circumstances in which communities find themselves, the challenges they face, and the work of the Holy Spirit among them. There is no such thing as the one authentic way to let this text shape our common life.

That having been said, we believe that Ephesians can help us live more faithfully as the church of Jesus Christ in the twenty-first century. It can help us resist the danger of becoming a victim of identity theft.

In Judith Guest's novel *Ordinary People,* Calvin is a man struggling to discover his identity. "*I'm the kind of man who*—he has heard this phrase a million times, at parties, in bars, in the course of normal conversation, *I'm the kind of man who*—instinctively he listens; tries to apply any familiar terms to himself, but without success. . . . *I'm the kind of man who—hasn't the least idea what kind of man I am.*"[1]

The church sometimes resembles that Calvin more than Calvin the reformer. It seems sometimes sadly to echo that Calvin, "We are the kind of church that . . . hasn't the least idea what the church is called to be and to do."

"We are the kind of church that. . . ." The culture has always wanted to complete the identity sentence for us and is continually defining the church using its own narratives. One narrative tells the

---

1. Judith Guest, *Ordinary People* (New York: Penguin Books, 1982), 48–51.

church that its members are consumers in a religious marketplace: "You should be the kind of church that competes for its share of the religion market." Then our mission is to provide what consumers want and to make sure it does not cost too much. People want to associate with people like themselves; their "beloved community" does not include strangers. Another narrative tells the church that its members are self-made men and women who work hard for what they get. They enter associations by contract and leave when such associations no longer serve their self-interest, voiding the contract: "You should be the kind of church that is an association of free and self-interested individuals." Then our mission is to offer an association attractive to self-interested individuals (without consideration of what kind of self they are interested in becoming). Yet another would tell us that we are part of a great country that generously grants freedom of religion as long as religion stays out of politics: "You should be the kind of church that nurtures the inner life of individuals while supporting the national interest of this great country." Then our mission is to pray for military victory over our enemies and to pledge allegiance to the flag while we serve the private spirituality of our members. Our security and our flourishing depend upon "the powers."

The Letter to the Ephesians provides a different narrative, and it answers the question of our identity quite differently. It provides a script for the church, and in that script the church finds its character, its identity, as the church. We are not fundamentally consumers or self-made individuals or Americans; we are fundamentally the beloved children of God, cherished and blessed by God in Christ, and called to serve the cause of God. In Ephesians we are—and are called to be—the kind of church that is called into existence by the will of God who created the world, made covenant promises to Israel, and kept those promises in raising the crucified Jesus from the dead. We are the kind of church that is blessed by God and called to live together to the praise of God's glory. We are the kind of church that already shares in the victory of God over death and sin, over the principalities and powers, and is called to display that victory, to serve God's cause. We are the kind of church that has a script to perform. It is not a narrative we make up as we go along. Performance may require creativity and improvisation, but we know the plot, we know how the story ends, and we are given a role in it. The script has been given to us by a loving God, and others before us have attempted to live out this script, and now it is our moment on stage to respond faithfully to God, who is with us and enables us to live into God's good future.

Ephesians addresses a community, "the saints" (1:1), and concludes with, "Peace be to the whole community" (6:23). We are the kind of church who knows we are not alone on this journey. It is not a solo flight. God has created and has joined us together in the person of Jesus Christ through whom we are adopted as God's children (1:5). We do not live in isolation but as members of the body of Christ. We are "no longer strangers and aliens" but "citizens with the saints" and "members of the household of God" (2:19). Having been brought together by God's reconciling work in Jesus Christ, our task is to show the world how to live in and against the cultures of enmity that threaten to destroy us. There is no greater challenge before the Christian church than to demonstrate that the walls that separate us are not God's design. God continues to be about the difficult work of transforming walled communities into one beloved community, and God entrusts us to join in that work in the world. The church is called to be the demonstration plot for a "new humanity," displaying a politics of peaceable difference.

We are the kind of community called to speak the truth in love (4:15). The difficult work of "speaking truth" begins with an openness to God's truth about us. It begins with the confession that we are often "strangers to the truth," and only by God's grace can we know the truth that sets us free from half-truths, falsehoods, and self-deception. The church is and is called to be a community where words can be trusted, and where people can be trusted to speak the truth in love. It is a community where communication is genuine, where mutual encouragement and discipline happen in the light of Christ, where people are willing to be honest and open in their speech with concern for the others. Barbara Brown Taylor has described the impact of the performance of truth telling in love: "When you speak the truth in love, others get to see what it looks like when the kingdom comes."[2]

We cannot leave Ephesians without the reminder that the church is the kind of community that prays. Prayer is the posture for God's people. In Ephesians we are led in prayer, told that the author of the epistle remembers the community in prayer and encourages the church to pray at all times. This posture grows out of the knowledge that we are not left to our own devices; rather, our lives are in the hands of a gracious God who hears and answers prayers. In prayer we learn to attend to God and to attend to all else in our world as all else is related to God.

Speaking at Duke Chapel during the struggle against apartheid in his home country of South Africa, Bishop Desmond Tutu told the gathered congregation that apartheid would not last even though it had a seemingly invincible grip on his country. He pulled a letter from his pocket from a woman who said she was on her knees early every morning, praying for God's deliverance for those oppressed in South Africa. It was his belief that such prayers were more powerful than the powers and principalities in charge at that time.

The church that seeks to live the script of Ephesians faces the future with confidence because we know

---

In life, in death,
in life beyond death,
    Jesus Christ is Lord.

Over powers and
    principalities,
over all who determine,
    control,
govern or finance the affairs of
    humankind,
    Jesus Christ is Lord.

Of the poor, of the broken,
of the sinned against and the
    sinner,
    Jesus Christ is Lord.

Above the Church,
beyond our most excellent
    theologies
and in the quiet corners of our
    hearts,
    Jesus Christ is Lord.

Thanks be to God.
    Amen!
        —The Iona Community

Prayer from *Stages on the Way: Worship Resources for Lent, Holy Week, and Easter* (Glasgow: Iona Community/Wild Goose Publications, 1998).

---

2. Barbara Brown Taylor, "Who Needs Heaven Now?" Sermon preached at Chautauqua Institution, July 26, 2010.

who is ultimately in charge. So much goes on that shakes our confidence and leads to lives controlled by suspicion, enmity, anxiety, and fear. The church has to contend with the powers and principalities every day and their efforts to define, divide, and dominate us. However, we also know that the Creator of this world by the work of Christ and by the power of his resurrection will "in the fullness of time" gather up and renew "all things" (Eph. 1:10). We know that God has "the power to accomplish abundantly far more than all we can ask or imagine" (3:20). Our confidence in God's good future enables us to be the kind of church that lives in hope. And hope, after all, is what Paul prayed that the church may know and perform (1:17–18).

Selected Bibliography

Barth, Markus. *Ephesians 1–3*. Anchor Bible 34. Garden City, NY: Doubleday, 1974.

Barth, Markus. *Ephesians 4–6*. Anchor Bible 34A. Garden City, NY: Doubleday, 1974.

Beare, Francis W. "The Epistle to the Ephesians: Introduction, Text, Exegesis." In *Interpreter's Bible*, edited by G. A. Buttrick, 10:597–749. Nashville: Abingdon, 1953.

Calvin, John. *The Epistles of Paul the Apostle to the Galatians, Ephesians, Philippians, and Colossians*. Translated by T. H. L. Parker. Edited by David W. Torrance and Thomas F. Torrance. Calvin's Commentaries. Grand Rapids: Eerdmans, 1963.

Cousar, Charles B. *An Introduction to the New Testament: Witnesses to God's New Work*. Louisville: Westminster John Knox Press, 2006.

Guthrie, Shirley C. *Christian Doctrine*, rev. ed. Louisville, KY: Westminster John Knox Press, 1994.

Kirby, John C. *Ephesians, Baptism and Pentecost: An Inquiry into the Structure and Purpose of the Epistle to the Ephesians*. London: SPCK, 1968.

Lincoln, Andrew T. *Ephesians*. Word Biblical Commentary 42. Dallas: Word Books, 1990.

Wink, Walter. *Engaging the Powers: Discernment and Resistance in a World of Domination*. Philadelphia: Fortress Press, 1992.

Wink, Walter. *Naming the Powers: The Language of Power in the New Testament.* Philadelphia: Fortress Press, 1984.

Wink, Walter. *Unmasking the Powers: The Invisible Forces that Determine Human Existence.* Philadelphia: Fortress Press, 1986.

Index of Ancient Sources

Index of Subjects